Economic Growth and the Environment

An Introduction to the Theory

Economic Growth and the Environment

An Introduction to the Theory

Clas Eriksson

OXFORD
UNIVERSITY PRESS

Great Clarendon Street, Oxford, OX2 6DP,
United Kingdom

Oxford University Press is a department of the University of Oxford.
It furthers the University's objective of excellence in research, scholarship,
and education by publishing worldwide. Oxford is a registered trade mark of
Oxford University Press in the UK and in certain other countries

British Library Cataloguing in Publication Data

Data available

ISBN 978-0-19-966389-7

Printed in Great Britain by the
MPG Printgroup, UK

For Marie
and for my parents,
Brith and Thure Eriksson

▪ CONTENTS

■ LIST OF FIGURES

■ PREFACE

This book has developed out of lectures on the course "Economic growth and the environment" at SLU, Uppsala. My first thanks go to the students, who over the years have forced me to clarify the reasonings. Many of them came into the course from a "sustainable development" perspective, fairly skeptical toward mainstream economics. I came in as a traditional growth economist. This "confrontation" has been very influential on the development of the book. It is an important reason for the fairly frequent discussions about cases in which there are severe limits to growth.

The book is inspired by the debate about the possibility of reconciling economic growth with sufficient care for the natural environment, and the closely related discussion on whether an increasing scarcity of natural resources will eventually force economic growth to cease. The debate has had many pessimistic participants, while economists have often tended to be more optimistic, pointing to the possibilities of technological progress and substitution. Nevertheless, economists acknowledge that natural resources and environmental concern do put dampers on economic growth. The difficult question to answer is how strong these are. Modern growth economists have therefore constructed models to examine to what extent the growth pessimism is theoretically warranted, and to what extent it is not. The purpose of this book is to give an introduction to some of these models.

The discussions between growth optimists and growth pessimists have at times been quite hostile. Contributing to this poor discussion climate has probably been a lack of a common theoretical ground, making it difficult for the two sides to understand each other's underlying reasonings. Although it may seem naïve, my ambition during the work with this book has been to present models where both camps can meet, and where both are able to derive their most expected results, by choices of parameter values that they deem appropriate. From there, the discussions can turn to the empirical observations about these parameters. This is of course not an easy matter, but it can be done with open descriptions of what steps should be taken.

This book is intended for the advanced undergraduate level in economics, especially for students who are interested in the feasibility of sustainable development. The prerequisite is a course in advanced undergraduate microeconomics, based on a book like Snyder and Nicholson (2008). Much of the literature that this book builds on emerged after the introduction of optimal control theory and is therefore difficult to follow for undergraduate students. By using rule-of-thumb decisions instead of intertemporal optimization (from which early growth theory benefited a lot) I hope to make the material more accessible for undergraduate students.

The book can be seen as an outgrowth of books such as Jones (2002) *Introduction to Economic Growth* and Romer (2012) *Advanced Macroeconomics*. I expand their sections on natural resources (on a slightly higher technical level) to an entire book. Although they devote little space to these matters, they have given important inspiration in terms of style. The purpose is to stand firmly on received growth theory, and to remain close to it throughout. I am also indebted to Barro and Sala-i-Martin (2004), from which I have taught over the years. In addition, re-reading Dixit (1976) helped a lot in shaping this book. Finally, the arrival of Acemoglu (2009) made it possible to improve the manuscript considerably. For the part on pollution, the surveys by Brock and Taylor (2005) and Xepapadeas (2005) have been very useful.

Ficre Zehaie read the entire manuscript at an early stage. His detailed comments helped me to delete many embarrassing flaws and to take the book a big step forward. In addition, numerous discussions with him have been very valuable. Comments from Rob Hart, Sebastian Hess, and three anonymous reviewers are gratefully acknowledged. I would also like to thank Robert Solow and Yves Surry for their encouraging words.

1 Introduction

It has long been debated whether it is possible to reconcile economic growth with sufficient care for the natural environment. In addition, many people fear that an increasing scarcity of natural resources will eventually force economic growth to cease. A classical representative of such growth pessimism is Thomas Robert Malthus and his major work *An Essay on the Principle of Population*, which was published in 1798. Based on historical observations of the difficulties in supporting a growing population on a limited land area, Malthus' projection was that standards of living would have to decline rapidly if population growth were to remain high.[1] A more recent publication with similar ideas is the book *Limits to Growth*, by Meadows et al. (1972).[2] Here the concern is limited supplies of fossil fuels and other minerals that may retard economic growth, but also increasing pollution, which renders economic growth less desirable.

In response to such growth skepticism modern economists have pointed out that the conclusions of those authors have been too pessimistic, due to inadequate assumptions.[3] Malthus underestimated the potential to increase productivity in agriculture, and therefore came to an incorrect conclusion about the possibility of providing for a growing population. In the modern debate economists have argued that technological progress and the move away from scarce and polluting inputs have much higher potential than the pessimists seem to think. For example, technological progress makes more discoveries of natural resources technically available (and at lower costs) and it leads to a more effective use of, for instance, energy. It can also turn production processes and other economic activities in less polluting directions.[4,5]

---

[1] Another example of an early pessimist is Jevons (1865), who predicted an approaching scarcity of coal.

[2] There are two updated versions of this book: Meadows et al. (1992) and Meadows et al. (2004). As a contemporary publication in a similar spirit, one could mention Jackson (2009).

[3] A representative example is Nordhaus (1992). This was an appraisal of Meadows et al. (1992).

[4] The driving forces toward a cleaner and more resource-conserving economy are both the market mechanism and economic policy. For natural resources that are priced on markets, the market mechanism drives up the market prices of resources that tend to become scarce. This stimulates firms and households to develop technologies that use the resources more effectively, and to develop alternatives that use less scarce resources. When it comes to negative environmental consequences that are not mirrored in market prices, there is a role to play for environmental policy to internalize externalities. Although these issues are important, our discussion of environmental policy will be very limited in this book. One reason is the limited space, but more important is the fact that a proper analysis of optimal environmental policy requires more optimization than we carry out in this book.

[5] For recent examples of this kind of technological progress, see Barrett (2009) and Yergin (2011).

In spite of this technology potential, the drags on economic growth that the pessimists are concerned about do exist, and it cannot *a priori* be excluded that they are sometimes so strong that they dampen growth considerably. Modern growth economists have therefore constructed models to examine the extent to which growth pessimism is theoretically warranted, and to what extent it is not. The purpose of this book is to give an introduction to some of these models.

1.1 The fundamental question: IS SUSTAINABILITY FEASIBLE?

The fundamental question in this book is whether *sustainable development* is *feasible*. To answer this question we need a definition of sustainable development, or more briefly, *sustainability*. Luckily, or sadly, there are more than one.

Probably the most quoted definition of sustainability comes from the so-called Brundtland Report, *Our Common Future* (WCED (1987)), which defines sustainable development as one that

... seeks to meet the needs and aspirations of the present without compromising the ability to meet those of the future (p. 43; quoted from Perman et al. (2011)).

While one can hardly object to this definition, it is not very helpful, since it is not operational. For one thing, the definition does not tell us which indicators of sustainability we should look at. Moreover, even if such variables were pointed out, an ambitious examination of sustainability would involve a huge number of them, and the next difficult question would then be how they should be weighted together.

In this book we will avoid some of these complications by taking an aggregated approach, which means that the number of variables is low. Although this may have the disadvantage of excluding some important aspects of reality, a useful consequence is that the definition of sustainability becomes quite obvious and non-controversial (given that one accepts the chosen approach). It will actually be phrased solely in terms of the long-term trends of one or two variables (namely per capita income and pollution).

To simplify the exposition of the possibility of sustainability, we will follow most of the literature in this area and work along two lines that are separated most of the time. Either limited supplies of natural resources or the desire to keep pollution down will impose dampers on growth, but rarely both simultaneously.

1. In the first case, the constraints imposed by a limited supply of *natural resources*, such as land, energy, and minerals, become a check on growth.

We then say that there is sustainable development if there is non-declining per capita income (and consumption) in the long run, in spite of limited natural resources.[6]

2. In the second case, production generates *pollution*, but is not hampered by limited natural resources. We will then have sustainable development if there is non-declining per capita income (and consumption) along with non-increasing pollution in the long run.

It should be noted that, despite the use of the phrase "sustainable development," there will not be any particular focus on issues raised in the area of development economics, such as how to escape from the poverty trap.

As mentioned above, the feasibility of sustainable development depends a lot on the available production *technology*, and there are two aspects of this that we will highlight. First and foremost, it is important that there is *technological progress*, so that the use of various production factors becomes more effective over time. For instance, such progress can decrease the amount of a natural resource needed to produce a given quantity of a certain good or service, and thereby mitigate scarcity. An example is the decline in the amount of gasoline that is necessary to drive a car (of given weight) 100 kilometers that we have witnessed over the recent decades.

It is also important that there is technological progress towards methods of production releasing lower quantities of toxic substances, by better techniques to clean poisonous emissions, for example catalytic converters in cars and sulfur scrubbers in industries and power plants. These examples can be labeled "end-of-pipe" abatement technologies. It is also possible to have technological progress that makes it possible (and privately beneficial) to substitute clean inputs for polluting inputs (i.e. abatement at the beginning of the production process). Some examples are electricity generated by solar energy instead of coal and cars using biogas instead of gasoline.

One prominent line of research in economics during recent decades has been the introduction of *endogenous technological change* in models of economic growth. An important aspect of this line of work is that technological progress is not exogenous, but produced by some of the economy's scarce productive inputs. This of course means that technological progress has an opportunity cost, because more research means less ordinary production. In this book we will explore the role of allocating some of the economy's labor force to generating various kinds of technological progress, not least of the type that saves resources or makes production "greener." The fundamental question is under what conditions this can ensure sustainability.

The second important aspect of technology concerns how well various production factors can be *substituted* for each other. A long-term issue has been

---

[6] For variation, we will sometimes also use the phrase 'sustained growth' in this case (i.e. when pollution is not involved) interchangeably with sustainability and sustainable development.

the extent to which man-made capital can be substituted for natural resources. The research on this matter has often been concerned with "pure" substitution, that is without the influence of technological progress. It is, however, not always obvious how to make a distinction between these two facets of technology. For instance, technological progress that makes a clean input cheaper leads to a substitution away from a dirtier input. Then both the substitutability and the rate of technological progress influence the final outcome.

1.2 **Why growth?**

In this book we will extensively study the growth of per capita GDP, and it is an underlying assumption that this growth, when looked at in isolation, is desirable. It is therefore appropriate at this point to ask why per capita GDP is an essential indicator of welfare. A simple but important answer is that more income is better than less, because it increases material well-being, which is what a large majority of the world population strongly desires, and not only in developing countries. One could alternatively conduct the analysis on a broader measure of well-being by constructing an index of quality of life, based on such indicators as life expectancy, adult literacy rate, infant mortality, and so on. It has, however, been demonstrated that per capita GDP is often correlated with these variables to a considerable extent.[7] Therefore, it is not unreasonable to use this single variable as an approximate indicator of well-being, but it should be noted that this is (and has long been) (a bit) controversial.[8]

If per capita GDP is accepted as a reasonable indicator of living standards, the next question is why the *growth rate* of this variable should be important. The answer is again simple but forceful: small differences in growth rates between countries give large differences in income *levels* after some decades. To illustrate this fact, we will here look at a simple example which demonstrates the importance of the growth rate for how long it takes for income to double.

To prepare for this example, we start by denoting per capita GDP by y. For now we assume that this variable simply depends on time, t, according to the exponential function

$$y(t) = y_0 e^{gt}, \tag{1.1}$$

where y_0 is the income level at the initial year (i.e. when $t = 0$).[9] Later in this book, the growth of y will depend on capital accumulation, the change of other production factors, and technological progress.

---

[7] See for instance Ray (1998) for a thorough discussion of this.

[8] See for instance the recent so-called happiness literature, for example Layard (2006).

[9] Most variables in this book are functions of time, t. However, t is often suppressed (after the initial indication that a variable is a function of time) if there is no risk that this will cause any confusion.

One way to describe economic growth is by use of the change in income per unit of time. This is given by the derivative

$$\frac{dy}{dt} \equiv \dot{y} = y_0 e^{gt} \cdot g = yg.$$

The "dot" notation is thus a convenient way to signify the time derivative. This expression shows that the change in income per unit of time is the income level multiplied by g. A notable implication is that the higher y is, the larger is the (absolute) change.

It is usually at least as informative to know the *proportional growth rate* of y. This is obtained by simply dividing the change by the absolute value of income:

$$\frac{\dot{y}}{y} = g.$$

The finding is thus that the proportional growth rate is equal to the constant g when the development of the variable is expressed by an exponential function, as in (1.1). If, for example, $g = 0.03$ then income grows by 3% per year (given that the time unit is one year).

We are now prepared to come back to the question: How long does it take for income to double? More specifically, at what time has y doubled from its initial value at $t = 0$, that is, at what time is $y(t) = 2y_0$? Call this point of time t^*. Using (1.1), it is given by the equation

$$y_0 e^{gt^*} = 2y_0,$$

which can be simplified to $e^{gt^*} = 2$. Taking the logarithm of both sides, we have $gt^* = \ln 2$, which can be solved for $t^* = \ln 2/g$. Noting finally that $\ln 2 \approx 0.7$, we have the simple rule that

$$t^* \approx \frac{0.7}{g}. \tag{1.2}$$

The time to double is thus determined by two constants. From this expression it is clear that a higher growth rate implies that income can be doubled in a shorter time.

It may be illuminating to look at some numerical examples in which (1.2) is used. Consider therefore the three growth rates $g = 0.0175$ (1.75%), $g = 0.035$ (3.5%) and $g = 0.07$ (7%). By (1.2) they correspond to the doubling times

$$t^* \approx \frac{0.7}{0.0175} = 40, \quad t^* \approx \frac{0.7}{0.035} = 20 \quad \text{and} \quad t^* \approx \frac{0.7}{0.07} = 10,$$

respectively. This again shows that a higher growth rate means that income is doubled in fewer years.

To take a couple of examples from the real world we know, for example, from Jones (2002) (Table 1.1) that the average growth rate in France was 2.3% during the period 1960–1997, while it was -1.4% in Chad for the same period. If these growth rates were to continue to apply, it would mean that it will take 30 years for France to double its per capita GDP, while the same will shrink to half in 48 years for Chad.

For a related means of seeing how important a difference in growth rates can be, let us compare two countries with the same initial income, y_0, after 40 years. A country with $g = 0.035$ has doubled twice, and therefore has an income equal to $2 \cdot 2 \cdot y_0$. Meanwhile, a country with $g = 0.0175$ has only reached $2 \cdot y_0$. The former country has thus become twice as rich as the latter, due to the higher growth rate.

1.3 **Delimitations**

This book makes a number of simplifying assumptions. The main motivation for this is that it makes the analysis more transparent, and gives the possibility of deriving more definite results. Many of the results carry over to more general settings, so the analysis below should provide a foundation for more advanced analyses. It is nevertheless important to be aware of the limitations that the simplifying assumptions imply, because sometimes the results do not survive the generalizations, as we will see in some examples. I will here mention and briefly comment on four of these simplifications.

First, we work in the tradition of *aggregate* growth models. This means that we will not examine the implications of the specific properties of various production sectors in the economy, because there is just one sector.[10] Moreover, there is only one consumption good, one type of natural resource (at a time), one kind of pollution, and so on. This leaves out many important details of reality, but helps providing rather clear results, which should be a useful background when more detailed models are developed. To appreciate the benefit of this choice of using aggregate models, see Nordhaus (1992), which gives a nice example of how useful a small model can be, compared to a huge non-transparent model.

We also adopt a *long-run perspective*, often focusing on a steady state, in which all variables grow at constant rates. Less emphasis is put on the short-run analysis, that is the transition to the steady state. In reality, the growth process usually goes through various cycles in response to fundamental changes in, for example, the technological paradigm. We have seen many examples of how one energy system is succeeded by another. Such transition processes are here discussed only briefly. This is primarily because our main interest is in sustainability, which is a long-run phenomenon, but another reason is tractability.

---

[10] There will, however, also be a research sector, in addition to the one and only production sector.

Furthermore, there is *not much optimization* in this book. Ideally, we should derive the behavior of agents in the economy from problems that examine whether the growth paths that we describe are optimal. This would involve optimization over time. For example, we would then have to model households' decisions concerning how much to save for the future and how much to consume now. It would also be necessary to analyze the way that entrepreneurs decide how much to invest in research and development, for the prospect of future profits. The optimization techniques that are necessary for such problems are quite advanced, however, and we therefore leave this part of the analysis to the graduate level. There is at least one advantage of doing so, namely that the conditions for feasibility of sustainable development are easier to display than they would have been in more elaborate models with full-fledged optimization.[11]

An additional limitation of this book is that we mostly assume that production is conducted under *constant returns to scale*, implying that a doubling of all inputs will lead to twice as much output. This means that we will not (in detail) examine the potential role of economies of scale. One reason to avoid increasing returns to scale is that the output cannot cover the payments to the production factors if there is perfect competition on the factor markets. It should be mentioned, though, that increasing returns to scale has sometimes been used as a substitute for technological change.[12] However, most economists prefer to model the drivers of growth as results of deliberate allocations of scarce resources to research activities.

1.4 Disposition

Chapters 2 through 4 present some basic tools of economic growth theory, that have been developed over more than half a century. They are then used in the remaining two parts of the book, to analyze the feasibility of sustainable development when natural resources and pollution are taken into account.

1.4.1 PART I: TOOLS

In Chapter 2 we describe the production technology that is typically used in basic growth models. The technology is usually represented by a production function with constant returns to scale. We also show how to express variables

---

[11] We do, however, occasionally describe static profit maximization. This is rather simple, because it just boils down to choosing optimal quantities of inputs at one point in time, without any thought about the future.

[12] As we will see in one example, increasing returns would make it easier to obtain sustainability.

and the production function in intensity forms, such as per capita income. Such transformations are often done in order to get variables that are constant in the long run. It is also demonstrated how the income shares of various production factors can be computed. Finally, the important concept of elasticity of substitution is introduced in this chapter.

Chapter 3 presents the Solow growth model. With the exception of Chapter 9, all models in this book build on this model. Starting from an expression for capital accumulation, a very central dynamic equation is derived. It is demonstrated that the dynamics is stable, meaning that the economy always converges to the steady state (which is unique). Although neither natural resources nor pollution are introduced at this stage, it is nevertheless relevant to ask what is needed to sustain a long-run growth in per capita income. The most preferred solution is unceasing technological progress.

Over the recent three decades there has been impressive progress from the efforts to make technological change endogenous in models of economic growth. Some of this material is presented in Chapter 4. Here technological progress is produced within the model, in the sense that the use of some of the economy's scarce productive resources is necessary for it to take place. We show how sensitive the results (in particular, the long-run growth rates) are to small changes in the values of the parameters of the models. The chapter also introduces the important concept of directed technological change. This provides a possibility for modeling how entrepreneurs decide the degree to which technological change shall be labor-saving, natural resource-saving, environmentally friendly, and so on.

1.4.2 PART II: NATURAL RESOURCES

We first encounter natural resources in Chapter 5, where one of the production factors is land. It is assumed to be available in a quantity that is constant over time. The introduction of land in the production function implies diminishing returns to the variable production factors, capital and labor. A growth in per capita income may then be difficult to sustain in the long run, but if there is sufficient technological change, in the right direction, it will be feasible.

In Chapter 6 the natural resource is non-renewable and exhaustible. This means that the remaining quantity of it declines as it is used up in production, which (at least eventually) leads to a downward trend in the use of this resource. This jeopardizes sustainability further, in addition to the decreasing returns to scale to capital and labor that the introduction of the resource implies. Sustainable development may nevertheless be feasible if the right allocation of research efforts is taken. However, it demands an even higher rate of growth in the technology factor that saves the natural resource than in the case with land as a production factor.

1.4.3 PART III: POLLUTION

The remaining three chapters concern the limits placed on growth by a desire to hold back the emissions of toxic pollutants. Chapter 7 starts by presenting a simple memory (or accounting) rule, which divides the sources of change in pollution into Scale, Composition, and Technology effects. Then follows a discussion about when it may be innocuous to delimit the analysis to flow pollution instead of stock pollution. In the rest of the chapter a growth model is developed, in which it is assumed that a share of gross output is used to abate pollution. It is demonstrated how the model can be reformulated so that pollution can be seen as an input in the production function of net output. Sustainable development is feasible if abatement is sufficiently effective and if there is enough technological progress. However, it seems that the abatement share gets unrealistically high in the long run.

In Chapter 8 there is technological progress in two directions, one of which makes production less polluting. If the speed of "green" technological progress is high enough, and if this technology factor is sufficiently potent in combatting pollution, sustainable development is feasible. The results are quite sensitive to what is assumed about a function that describes how gross pollution and environmental technology are combined to determine net pollution. This chapter also includes a section where the economy is assumed to use two types of energy, of which one is polluting. We analyze how the substitution of clean energy for polluting energy is driven by technological change, and examine whether pollution declines in a growing economy.

The final chapter is quite different from the rest, because it involves consumer optimization. Here we explicitly model the disutility that people experience from pollution. There is no capital accumulation in this chapter, but an exogenously growing capacity to produce and pollute. A representative consumer can decide which technical standard to use and thereby faces a trade-off between high consumption and a clean environment. We follow how the optimal choice changes over time (as productivity grows) and examine if there is any theoretical ground for an environmental Kuznets curve, that is an inverse-U relation between per capita income and pollution.

Part I
Tools

2 Production

In the Solow growth model (the basic model of this book) the character of the growth path depends very much on the properties of the production function. Such a function provides a convenient way to describe how the services of inputs, such as capital and labor, are turned into output, without dwelling too much on practical details of production (leaving that to engineers). This chapter introduces the so-called neo-classical production function, and the assumptions that define it. One of its central features is that there are constant returns to scale in the production factors. This means that, if they are doubled in quantity, then the output is doubled as well. We also present two very common specific functions, namely the Cobb–Douglas and the CES functions.

Most of the variables in the growth models developed in the subsequent chapters will typically be growing over time. It is therefore convenient to transform the variables into ratios that are constant along the long-run growth paths. Moreover, similar transformations of the production function are also useful, not least because they make it possible to reduce the number of variables in it (often to just one).

The feasibility of sustained growth (which can be questioned even before we introduce natural-resource or environmental dampers on growth) depends to some extent on how easy (in a technical sense) it is to substitute one production factor for another. We therefore introduce the concept of elasticity of substitution. The CES production function is suitable for an illustration and explanation of this concept. This elasticity is also important when natural resources and pollution are introduced.

The chapter also defines the income shares of the production factors and examines how they develop over time. The subsequent growth models are often evaluated on whether the implied trends in the income shares correspond well to the empirical observations. The income shares are also important in a useful expression for the proportional rate of growth of output, where they alternatively can be interpreted as output elasticities of the production factors.

2.1 Production function

2.1.1 INPUTS

We assume a closed economy that produces one aggregate output, Y, which is used for consumption and investment. It is produced by use of the production factors capital, K, and labor, L.[1] The production function is

$$Y(t) = F[K(t), A(t)L(t)], \qquad (2.1)$$

where A is a technology factor. By making it multiplicative with labor, we assume that technological progress is *labor-augmenting*, that is directed to increase the productivity of labor.[2] We discuss the reason for this placement of A in Chapter 4. For given values of K, L, and A, the function tells us the maximum quantity of output that it is technically possible to produce. The function is assumed to capture many practical (engineering) details of the production process, which we will not explicitly bother about.

The growth of total output thus depends on the development of the three variables on the right hand side of equation (2.1). We therefore need to specify how they change over time. The first variable in the production function is capital, for example machines and buildings. It will grow endogenously (i.e. it is determined within the model), because some share of the output is set aside for investments. This capital accumulation process is examined in detail in Chapter 3. Note that capital is a *stock* variable, accumulating over the years, whereas investment is a *flow* variable, representing the gross increase of capital during one year.[3]

Turning to the labor force, a first assumption is that it is equal to the population. It would not complicate the analysis much if we were to assume that the labor force is a constant fraction of the population, but we minimize notation by not doing so. At time t the population is equal to

$$L = e^{nt}, \qquad (2.2)$$

which means that the change per unit of time is $\dot{L} = ne^{nt} = nL$. The proportional growth rate of labor is therefore $\dot{L}/L = n$. As opposed to capital, the labor force thus grows at an exogenous rate (determined outside the model). In some contexts, the population size is treated as endogenous, but for simplicity we let it be exogenous here, with the exception of a brief section in Chapter 5.[4] In that chapter we will also examine the consequence of a varying population growth rate.

The third and final variable in the production function is the technology factor, A. For the time being we assume that this factor is exogenous as well, and that it grows with time according to the exponential function

$$A = e^{gt}. \qquad (2.3)$$

---

[1] Because capital and labor are the only inputs, the production function is said to be on the *value added* form.

[2] Alternatively, one could say that the growth in A "saves" labor, in the sense that the same output can be produced with less use of it.

[3] Similarly, the service provided by the capital stock over a year is a flow variable.

[4] Another simplifying assumption is that there will be very little reference to human capital; all labor is assumed to have the same quality.

This of course means that the change per unit of time is $\dot{A} = ge^{gt} = gA$ and that the proportional growth rate is $\dot{A}/A = g$. In modern growth theory technological progress is usually endogenous, requiring the use of some of the economy's scarce resources. In Chapter 4 we extend the model by assuming that a share of the labor force is diverted from production and put into a research sector. The more labor that is put into research activities, the faster A will grow (at the cost of current output).

2.1.2 NEO-CLASSICAL ASSUMPTIONS

After these comments about the variables of the production function, we turn to some properties of the function (2.1) itself. As a benchmark case we assume that it has a set of standard properties, following from what are often called the *neo-classical* assumptions. This allows us to obtain some fairly definite results. We examine the consequences of relaxing these assumptions later.

The following three assumptions define the neo-classical production function:

A1 The first assumption is that there are *constant returns to scale (CRS) in K and L*. This means that, if both K and L are multiplied by the constant $\lambda > 0$, it results in total production being multiplied by that constant as well:

$$F[\lambda K, A\lambda L] = \lambda F[K, AL].$$

If a given quantity of output is produced in a certain way, it is by this assumption possible to replicate this production activity, by doubling the inputs.

A2 The second assumption is that there are *positive but declining marginal products of capital and labor*. Formally, this is expressed by the partial derivatives[5]

$$F_K > 0, \quad F_L > 0, \quad F_{KK} < 0, \quad \text{and} \quad F_{LL} < 0.$$

In words this says that production always increases as the quantity of any factor is raised, but it will do so at a declining rate.

A3 The third central set of assumptions is related to the properties of the production function when an input takes on very small or large values. They are termed the *Inada conditions* and are expressed as follows:

$$\lim_{K \to 0} F_K = \lim_{L \to 0} F_L = \infty \quad \text{and} \quad \lim_{K \to \infty} F_K = \lim_{L \to \infty} F_L = 0.$$

---

[5] These compact expressions for the partial derivatives have their usual more detailed counterparts. For instance:

$$F_K = \frac{\partial F[K, AL]}{\partial K} \quad \text{and} \quad F_{KK} = \frac{\partial^2 F[K, AL]}{\partial K^2}.$$

The first two conditions mean that the marginal product of any factor becomes infinitely large as the use of it approaches zero. At the other end, the marginal products tend to zero as the quantities go to infinity. The first unit adds a lot of output, but additional units contribute very little if the use of a factor is already very large. In Chapter 3 we will see that this implies that the growth model has a unique steady state.

These assumptions have one important implication (which is sometimes, incorrectly, listed as an assumption):

Implication: Both production factors are *essential*. Formally, this is to say that

$$F[0, AL] = 0 \quad \text{and} \quad F[K, A \cdot 0] = 0.$$

This means that no output can be produced if the use of one factor is zero. Clearly, this implication will be particularly relevant when we introduce exhaustible natural resources in Chapter 6.

There are two specific production functions that are frequently used in the theory of economic growth, and which we will use repeatedly in this book. The first is called the Cobb–Douglas function and has the form

$$Y = K^{\alpha}(AL)^{1-\alpha}, \tag{2.4}$$

where $0 \leq \alpha \leq 1$. This means that the two exponents sum to unity, which in turn implies that there are constant returns to scale. It is left as an exercise for the reader to show that this function obeys the neo-classical assumptions.

A somewhat more general example is the so-called CES function (the name of which is explained in Section 2.5). The function is

$$Y = \left(\alpha K^{\varepsilon} + (1 - \alpha)(AL)^{\varepsilon}\right)^{1/\varepsilon}. \tag{2.5}$$

It is assumed that $-\infty < \varepsilon \leq 1$. One can show that this function has the Cobb–Douglas function as a special case when ε approaches zero.[6] It should be emphasized that the CES function does *not* fulfill all the assumptions above. As an indication of this, note that if $\varepsilon > 0$, then none of the production factors is essential in production. We examine the consequences of this further below and thus use this function to show some consequences of deviating from the neo-classical assumptions.

2.2 Variables in intensity form

Since most variables of the model will typically grow over time, it is useful to form ratios of variables such that they are constant in the long run. This is called

---

[6] A proof of this statement, and others that are not proved in this chapter, is found in Barro and Sala-i-Martin (2004), Chapter 1, or Acemoglu (2009), Chapter 2.

transforming variables into intensity forms. Here we will describe two cases, dividing first by just L and then by AL.

2.2.1 PER CAPITA VARIABLES

We use lower-case letters to denote variables in per capita form, that is variables divided by L. Thus, per capita income and capital per capita are[7]

$$y = \frac{Y}{L} \quad \text{and} \quad k = \frac{K}{L},$$

respectively. It is also useful to express the production function on intensity form. To do this, note that L is a constant at any point of time. After dividing (2.1) by L we can therefore use the assumption about constant returns to scale and get

$$\frac{Y}{L} = \frac{1}{L} F[K, AL] = F\left[\frac{K}{L}, \frac{AL}{L}\right] = F[k, A].$$

The constant-returns-to-scale assumption is of course used in the middle equality.

In cases when there is no technological change, which we will assume in the rest of this sub-section, we can put $A = 1$ and write $F[k, 1] = f(k)$. Thus income per capita simply is a function of capital per capita:

$$y = f(k). \tag{2.6}$$

The fact that this is a function of just one variable simplifies the subsequent analysis considerably.

To obtain more information about the properties of this new version of the production function, we note that (2.6) can be rewritten as

$$Y = Lf\left(\frac{K}{L}\right), \tag{2.7}$$

where the definitions of k and y have been used. Equation (2.7) provides a good starting point when we want to express the marginal products of the production factors on intensity form.

In particular the first- and second-order derivatives with respect to capital give useful information about the shape of $f(k)$. The marginal product of capital is

$$\frac{\partial Y}{\partial K} = Lf'\left(\frac{K}{L}\right) \cdot \frac{1}{L} = f'\left(\frac{K}{L}\right) = f'(k).$$

---

[7] Since we assume that everybody works in the economy, we can interchangeably use the phrases "per capita" and "per worker."

It follows that $f'(k) > 0$, because the marginal product of capital is assumed to be positive in Assumption A2 in section 2.1.2. Recall also that $f(k) = F[k, 1]$, that is k is found in the first variable place of the initial function. By the Inada conditions it must therefore hold that $f'(k) \to \infty$ as $k \to 0$ and $f'(k) \to 0$ as $k \to \infty$.

The second-order derivative of the function in (2.7) with respect to capital is

$$\frac{\partial^2 Y}{\partial K^2} = f''\left(\frac{K}{L}\right) \cdot \frac{1}{L} = \frac{f''(k)}{L} < 0.$$

The negative sign follows from the fact that the far left expression is assumed to be negative in Assumption A2. The fact that L is positive then implies that $f''(k) < 0$. These findings allow us to conclude that the general function $f(k)$ has the shape depicted in Figure 2.1, starting very steep and then steadily declining in slope.

To compute the marginal product of labor, we must note that (2.7) has L in two places. The derivative therefore consists of two terms:

$$\frac{\partial Y}{\partial L} = f\left(\frac{K}{L}\right) + Lf'\left(\frac{K}{L}\right) \cdot \left(-\frac{K}{L^2}\right) = f(k) - f'(k)k > 0.$$

This expression is positive, because we have assumed that production always increases when more labor is added.

In Chapter 3, the average product of capital, $f(k)/k$, will be important.[8] The marginal product of labor turns out to be useful when we examine how $f(k)/k$ changes when k grows. The derivative is

$$\frac{d}{dk}\left(\frac{f(k)}{k}\right) = \frac{f'(k)k - f(k)}{k^2} < 0.$$

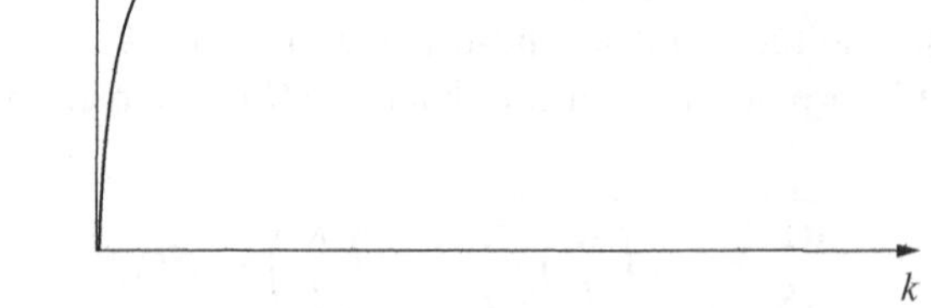

Figure 2.1. Production per capita

---

[8] To see that $f(k)/k$ is the average product of capital, note that $f(k)/k = (F/L)/(K/L) = F/K$.

This expression is negative because the numerator is $-\partial Y/\partial L$, which has been assumed to be negative. The average product of capital is thus everywhere declining in k.

We also need to know how the average product of capital behaves as k approaches very large or small values. It can be demonstrated that a production function that satisfies the neo-classical assumptions has the properties that

$$\lim_{k\to 0}\frac{f(k)}{k} = \infty \quad \text{and} \quad \lim_{k\to\infty}\frac{f(k)}{k} = 0.$$

In words, the average product of capital approaches infinity as k tends to zero, while it approaches zero as k goes to infinity. These properties are illustrated in Figure 2.2.

It is illuminating to look at the intensity form of the Cobb–Douglas production function. Dividing (2.4) (with $A = 1$) by L we have:

$$\frac{Y}{L} = \frac{1}{L}K^\alpha L^{1-\alpha} = \frac{1}{L^\alpha \cdot L^{1-\alpha}}K^\alpha L^{1-\alpha} = \left(\frac{K}{L}\right)^\alpha \left(\frac{L}{L}\right)^{1-\alpha}.$$

Therefore per capita income in the Cobb–Douglas case is given by the simple power function

$$y = k^\alpha.$$

To find the shape of this function we compute the first- and second-order derivatives

$$f'(k) = \alpha k^{\alpha-1} > 0 \quad \text{and} \quad f''(k) = \alpha(\alpha - 1)k^{\alpha-2} < 0.$$

The graph of this function thus shows a positively sloping curve, where the slope declines when k grows, as in Figure 2.1. Moreover, $f'(k)$ approaches

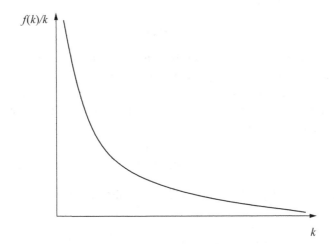

Figure 2.2. Average product of capital

infinity as k goes to 0 and declines toward 0 as k grows large. We finally have that the average product of capital is $f(k)/k = k^{\alpha-1}$. This expression clearly has the properties mentioned for the general function, which are depicted in Figure 2.2.

2.2.2 PER UNIT OF EFFECTIVE LABOR

If there is technological progress, it is often useful to divide output and capital by A and L. We use the symbol ~ ("tilde") to denote variables in per unit of effective labor form. Thus

$$\tilde{y} = \frac{Y}{AL} \quad \text{and} \quad \tilde{k} = \frac{K}{AL}.$$

While variables in per capita form are interesting on economic grounds, variables on per unit of effective labor form are interesting primarily because they make the analysis more tractable when there is technological progress: $\tilde{k}$ is typically constant in the long run under such circumstances. When we have developed knowledge about how $\tilde{k}$ grows, it is a small step towards the understanding of the evolution of k and y.

The production function can be transformed along the same lines as in the previous sub-section. Dividing (2.1) by AL and using the definition of constant returns to scale gives

$$\frac{Y}{AL} = \frac{1}{AL}F[K, AL] = F\left[\frac{K}{AL}, \frac{AL}{AL}\right] = F\left[\tilde{k}, 1\right].$$

Analogously to the previous case, we can here simplify the notation by writing $F\left[\tilde{k}, 1\right] = f(\tilde{k})$, so that

$$\tilde{y} = f(\tilde{k}).$$

Output per unit of effective labor is thus a function of just one variable, the capital stock per unit of effective labor. If the production function is a Cobb–Douglas, we have that $\tilde{y} = \tilde{k}^\alpha$.

To compute the marginal products, we first note that the definitions of $\tilde{y}$ and $\tilde{k}$ mean that total output can be written as

$$Y = ALf\left(\frac{K}{AL}\right).$$

Then the marginal products of capital and labor are given by the partial derivatives

$$\frac{\partial Y}{\partial K} = ALf'\left(\frac{K}{AL}\right) \cdot \frac{1}{AL} = f'(\tilde{k}) > 0$$

and

$$\frac{\partial Y}{\partial L} = Af\left(\frac{K}{AL}\right) + ALf'\left(\frac{K}{AL}\right) \cdot \left(-\frac{K}{AL^2}\right) = A\left[f(\tilde{k}) - f'(\tilde{k})\tilde{k}\right] > 0,$$

respectively. (We can also show that $f''(\tilde{k}) < 0$.) In the Solow model, which we encounter in Chapter 3, $\tilde{k}$ is constant on the long-run growth path, as long as the production function is neo-classical. This means that $\partial Y/\partial K$ is constant in the long run, while $\partial Y/\partial L$ grows at the same rate as A, which is the constant rate g.

Finally, we readily find that the average product of capital, $f(\tilde{k})/\tilde{k}$, is declining in this case as well:

$$\frac{d}{d\tilde{k}}\left(\frac{f(\tilde{k})}{\tilde{k}}\right) = \frac{f'(\tilde{k})\tilde{k} - f(\tilde{k})}{\tilde{k}^2} < 0.$$

It can also be demonstrated that the limit value of $f(\tilde{k})/\tilde{k}$ is infinite as $\tilde{k}$ goes to zero and that it tends to zero as $\tilde{k}$ approaches infinity. All this means that $f(\tilde{k})$ and $f(\tilde{k})/\tilde{k}$ have shapes that are similar to those in Figures 2.1 and 2.2.

2.2.3 THE CAPITAL–OUTPUT RATIO

A final useful normalization comes from dividing the production function (2.1) by capital, K. Because of the CRS property we now get

$$\frac{Y}{K} = F\left[1, \frac{AL}{K}\right]. \tag{2.8}$$

Early growth theorists focused much on this approach, giving a lot of attention to the capital–output ratio, which we will denote by $K/Y \equiv z$ in later chapters. In the models below, it will be clear that K/Y is constant on most long-run growth paths. Therefore, the ratio $(AL)/K = 1/\tilde{k}$ must also be constant.

In cases with more than two inputs, for instance when natural resources are added, division with K and focus on the variable z will turn out to be useful. However, if capital and labor are the only inputs, we shall find the normalizations in the previous two sub-sections preferable.

2.3 The elasticity of substitution

The feasibility of sustained growth depends to some extent on how easily one production factor can be substituted for another. This will become particularly clear when we introduce natural resources in Chapters 5 and 6. It is therefore important to understand what is meant by the *elasticity of substitution*. This concept is entirely internal to the production function, but the idea can be intuitively illustrated in connection to the profit maximization problem of a firm. The elasticity then determines how much the optimal relative demand for the production factors responds to a change in their relative price. At the end of this section we define the concept properly, by replacing factor prices by marginal products.

To formulate a profit-maximization problem, denote the cost of capital[9] by r and the cost of labor by w. The profit function of a representative firm then is

$$\Pi = F(K, AL) - rK - wL.$$

In the first right hand side term the price of the final output is normalized to unity, which means that revenue simply equals the produced and sold quantity. We assume perfect competition on all markets, so that the firm takes all prices as given.

A firm maximizes profits only if the (values of the) marginal products of capital and labor equal the corresponding factor prices.[10] We must therefore have

$$F_K(K, AL) = r \quad \text{and} \quad F_L(K, AL) = w. \tag{2.9}$$

It is useful to combine these conditions by taking the ratios between the left and right hand sides, respectively:

$$TRS \equiv \frac{F_K(K, AL)}{F_L(K, AL)} = \frac{r}{w}. \tag{2.10}$$

Here *TRS* is the technical rate of substitution, which equals minus the slope of an isoquant. In optimum the *TRS* must of course equal the relative factor price.

Since the marginal products are functions of K and L, equation (2.10) ties the optimal factor demands to the factor prices. To get a more explicit description of this relation it is useful to invoke a particular production function, and the CES variety in (2.5) is especially suitable for this. The marginal products in this case are

$$F_K = \left(\alpha K^\varepsilon + (1 - \alpha)(AL)^\varepsilon \right)^{\frac{1}{\varepsilon} - 1} \cdot \alpha K^{\varepsilon - 1}$$

and

$$F_L = \left(\alpha K^\varepsilon + (1 - \alpha)(AL)^\varepsilon \right)^{\frac{1}{\varepsilon} - 1} \cdot (1 - \alpha) A (AL)^{\varepsilon - 1},$$

---

[9] The capital cost r is not equal to the market interest for loans, r_l. Since we will assume that capital depreciates at the rate δ, the correct relation is $r - \delta = r_l$. This gives an investor the same returns from investing a sum of money in capital and renting it to firms and from issuing consumption loans.

[10] The firm takes A as given, and therefore just chooses optimal quantities of K and L.

respectively. Substituting them into (2.10), and noting that the outer derivatives are the same and therefore cancel out, we get

$$\frac{\alpha K^{\varepsilon-1}}{(1-\alpha)A(AL)^{\varepsilon-1}} = \frac{r}{w} \quad \Leftrightarrow \quad \frac{\alpha}{1-\alpha} \cdot \frac{K^{\varepsilon-1}}{A^{\varepsilon}L^{\varepsilon-1}} = \frac{r}{w}.$$

Our aim is to use this equation to write K/L as a function of r/w. Such an expression will tell us how much the optimal relative demand changes in response to a variation in the relative factor price. This in turn says something about how easy it is (in a technical sense) to substitute one production factor for another, given the prevailing production technology.

As a first step toward the solution we move everything except K and L over to the right hand side of the previous equation, and form the ratio between K and L in a parenthesis. This gives

$$\left(\frac{K}{L}\right)^{\varepsilon-1} = \frac{r}{w}\frac{1-\alpha}{\alpha}A^{\varepsilon}.$$

In the final step, both sides are raised to the exponent $1/(\varepsilon - 1)$. The result is

$$\frac{K}{L} = \left(\frac{r}{w}\right)^{\frac{1}{\varepsilon-1}}\left[\frac{1-\alpha}{\alpha}A^{\varepsilon}\right]^{\frac{1}{\varepsilon-1}}.$$

This equation describes how the optimal relative demand for the factors depends on the relative price, the parameters, and the technology factor. Since $\varepsilon \leq 1$, the exponent over r/w is negative. We therefore have a negatively sloping relative demand curve for the production factors: if capital gets relatively more expensive, the relative demand for it becomes lower.

To see how responsive this relative demand is to a change in the relative price, we compute the derivative

$$\frac{\partial(K/L)}{\partial(r/w)} = \frac{1}{\varepsilon-1}\left(\frac{r}{w}\right)^{\frac{1}{\varepsilon-1}-1}\left[\frac{1-\alpha}{\alpha}A^{\varepsilon}\right]^{\frac{1}{\varepsilon-1}}$$

$$= \frac{1}{\varepsilon-1}\left(\frac{r}{w}\right)^{-1}\cdot\left(\frac{r}{w}\right)^{\frac{1}{\varepsilon-1}}\left[\frac{1-\alpha}{\alpha}A^{\varepsilon}\right]^{\frac{1}{\varepsilon-1}}.$$

The result is a bit messy, but if we note that the final part equals the initial expression for K/L, it can be simplified into

$$\frac{\partial(K/L)}{\partial(r/w)} = \frac{1}{\varepsilon-1}\frac{(K/L)}{(r/w)}.$$

This is one way to express how the optimal relative factor demand reacts to a change in the relative price, but the responsiveness becomes more transparent if we transform it into an elasticity. We therefore multiply both sides by $(r/w)/(K/L)$ and obtain

$$\frac{\partial (K/L)}{\partial (r/w)} \frac{(r/w)}{(K/L)} = \frac{1}{\varepsilon - 1} = -\frac{1}{1 - \varepsilon} < 0.$$

The negative sign follows because $\varepsilon \leq 1$, so that the ratio always is positive. This elasticity tells us how many percent K/L falls, due to an increase in r/w by one percent. Since the expression is negative, it is convenient to add a minus sign as we *preliminarily* define the elasticity of substitution as

$$\sigma \equiv -\frac{\partial (K/L)}{\partial (r/w)} \frac{(r/w)}{(K/L)}.$$

The higher this elasticity is, the more the optimal relative demand changes. In the case of the CES function we have just found that

$$\sigma \equiv \frac{1}{1 - \varepsilon} > 0.$$

This explains the name of this particular function: it has a *Constant Elasticity of Substitution* (CES), which means that it is independent of the variables of the production function.

It often turns out that the value $\sigma = 1$ is an important division line between results of the analysis, which are qualitatively very different.[11] It is therefore reasonable to say that the elasticity of substitution is high when $\sigma > 1$ (which is equivalent to $0 < \varepsilon \leq 1$). A given variation in the relative price then leads to a considerable change in relative demand of the factors. On the other hand, if $\varepsilon < 0$ the elasticity of substitution is low: $\sigma < 1$. The relative factor demand then responds moderately to a variation in the factor price ratio.

As mentioned at the beginning of this section, it should be stressed that this presentation of the elasticity of substitution is not exactly the appropriate one (but hopefully the concept is easier to understand in this way). Strictly speaking, the elasticity of substitution is a property that is "internal" to the production function. The proper definition therefore replaces r/w by the ratio of marginal products, $F_K/F_L = TRS$ (cf. (2.10)).[12] The proper *elasticity of substitution* therefore is

$$\sigma \equiv -\frac{\partial (K/L)}{\partial (TRS)} \frac{(TRS)}{(K/L)} = -\left[\frac{\partial (TRS)}{\partial (K/L)} \frac{(K/L)}{(TRS)} \right]^{-1}. \tag{2.11}$$

A high σ therefore means that it is *technically* "easy" to replace one factor by the other. In other words, the isoquants are relatively "flat." Analogously, a low σ corresponds to very "curved" isoquants, indicating that the production factors do not substitute very well for each other.

---

[11] When $\sigma = 1$ we have $\varepsilon = 0$ and the production function is a Cobb–Douglas, as mentioned above.
[12] Or rather, the TRS was replaced by r/w in the exposition above.

2.4 **Income shares (output elasticities)**

This section shows how to compute the income shares of the production factors. One reason for us to be interested in them is that the trends that they follow can be used for a reality check of a growth model. Another reason to be familiar with this concept is that it often shows up in various growth expressions below. In such contexts the income shares can also be called output elasticities.

2.4.1 KALDOR FACTS

A growth model (as well as any economic model) is useful only if it is consistent with empirical observations. Economists therefore often relate growth models to a set of stylized facts, called the *Kaldor facts*, which have appeared to hold reasonably well over long periods of time. Among these facts are:

1. The capital–output ratio, K/Y, shows no trend, upward or downward.
2. The income shares of capital and labor show no trends.
3. The cost of capital, r, shows no trend.

The variables mentioned here are, of course, not absolutely constant over time in reality, but they have only fluctuated within certain limits.

If the Kaldor facts are met by a growth model (along with constant growth rates) we say that the model economy is on a *balanced growth path (BGP)*. In Exercise 2.2 it is demonstrated that a growth path is balanced, for a production function with the neo-classical properties, if $\tilde{k}$ is constant along the growth path. Furthermore, Chapter 3 shows that the Solow model indeed implies that $\tilde{k}$ is constant in the long run, given that the production function fulfills the neo-classical assumptions. The Solow model is thus consistent with the Kaldor facts and implies a balanced growth path.

2.4.2 DEFINING INCOME SHARES

We will now develop expressions for the income shares of capital and labor. It is natural to define them as factor incomes divided by total income, which is equal to total output. The factor incomes are, of course, the prices times the quantities. Using the Greek letter ζ for income shares, the shares thus are

$$\zeta_K = \frac{rK}{Y} \quad \text{and} \quad \zeta_L = \frac{wL}{Y}$$

for capital and labor, respectively. By maintaining the assumption about perfect competition, we can use the equality between marginal products and factor prices in (2.9) to replace r and w. Therefore

$$\zeta_K = \frac{\partial Y}{\partial K}\frac{K}{Y} \quad \text{and} \quad \zeta_L = \frac{\partial Y}{\partial L}\frac{L}{Y}.$$

These expressions can alternatively be defined as *output elasticities*. For instance, ζ_K shows by how many percent output grows if the use of capital increases by one percent.

As an example, we can demonstrate that the income shares are constants when the production technology is represented by a Cobb–Douglas function, that is they are independent of capital and labor quantities. For instance, the marginal product of capital is $\partial Y/\partial K = \alpha K^{\alpha-1}(AL)^{1-\alpha} = \alpha K^{-1}Y$ in this case. Multiplying both sides by K/Y we get $\zeta_K = \alpha$. Along similar lines, one can show that $\zeta_L = 1 - \alpha$. We note that the sum of the income shares is equal to one, which seems quite natural. However, this happens only because the production function exhibits constant returns to scale, which is due to the fact that the exponents of K and L sum to one.

This finding can be generalized: for any production function with constant returns to scale it holds that there is nothing left over after the factors have been paid their competitive market prices. Mathematically, this can be expressed as

$$Y = \frac{\partial Y}{\partial K}K + \frac{\partial Y}{\partial L}L, \tag{2.12}$$

which is an instance of the so-called *Euler Theorem*. In words equation (2.12) says that the factor payments exactly exhaust the total output; neither more, nor less is needed to properly compensate those who provide the inputs to production. Division of both sides in this equation by Y gives

$$1 = \frac{\partial Y}{\partial K}\frac{K}{Y} + \frac{\partial Y}{\partial L}\frac{L}{Y} = \zeta_K + \zeta_L.$$

The property of CRS production functions exposed in (2.12) thus translates into the statement that the income shares sum to unity. An implication is, of course, that $\zeta_L = 1 - \zeta_K$, which will be useful below.

2.4.3 INCOME SHARES AND OUTPUT GROWTH

We now show that the output elasticities (income shares) also appear as we compute the growth rate of total output. This is something that will be done several times in this book, in particular when natural resources are introduced in the production function.

We start these computations by taking the logs of equation (2.1), to obtain $\ln(Y(t)) = \ln(F[K(t), A(t)L(t)])$. An expression for the proportional growth rate of total output is obtained by differentiating this with respect to time. In a first step, we have

$$\frac{1}{Y}\dot{Y} = \frac{1}{Y}F_1\dot{K} + \frac{1}{Y}F_2(\dot{AL}). \tag{2.13}$$

We here have a new notation for the partial derivatives. The numerical sub-indices signify derivatives with respect to variable places, not individual variables. Since there is only one variable (K) in the first variable place of the production function, however, the choice of notation does not matter. We simply have $F_1 = F_K$.

In the second variable place there is, however, a product of two variables, which makes this part a bit more complicated. We first note that

$$F_2 = \frac{\partial F(K, AL)}{\partial(AL)},$$

that is F_2 is the derivative with respect to the composite variable AL. On the other hand, when we differentiate the production function with respect to L we use the chain rule and get

$$F_L = \frac{\partial F(K, AL)}{\partial(AL)} \cdot A.$$

As the outer derivative we have the entire derivative with respect to AL. The inner derivative is then the derivative of AL with respect to L. This means that $F_L = F_2 A$.

Before substituting the derivatives, we expand the expression for the growth rate of output in (2.13), by developing the time derivative of AL, multiplying the first RHS term by K/K and the final term by AL/AL:

$$\frac{\dot{Y}}{Y} = \frac{F_1 K}{Y}\frac{\dot{K}}{K} + \frac{F_2 AL}{Y} \cdot \frac{A\dot{L} + L\dot{A}}{AL}.$$

Now we use the fact that $F_1 = F_K$ and $F_2 A = F_L$ and simplify the final ratio. This yields

$$\frac{\dot{Y}}{Y} = \frac{F_K K}{Y}\frac{\dot{K}}{K} + \frac{F_L L}{Y}\left(\frac{\dot{L}}{L} + \frac{\dot{A}}{A}\right).$$

Recalling finally some earlier definitions and assumptions, the growth rate of total output can be expressed as a weighted average of the growth rates of capital, labor, and the technology factor:

$$\frac{\dot{Y}}{Y} = \zeta_K \frac{\dot{K}}{K} + \zeta_L(n + g). \tag{2.14}$$

The output elasticities (income shares) thus serve as weights in this expression. Extended versions of this expression will appear in Chapters 5 and 6.

2.4.4 SOME IMPLICATIONS

We can develop some implications of (2.14) if we are comfortable with making the assumption that output and capital grow at the same rate. In the chapters below we will often find that they do so in the long run. Thus, supposing $\dot{Y}/Y = \dot{K}/K$ we can rewrite (2.14) as

$$\frac{\dot{Y}}{Y}(1 - \zeta_K) = \zeta_L(n + g).$$

Recalling that $\zeta_L = 1 - \zeta_K$, because the income shares sum to unity when there is constant returns to scale in production, this simplifies to

$$\frac{\dot{Y}}{Y} = n + g.$$

The long-run growth rate of output is thus equal to the sum of the two exogenous growth rates of population and the technology factor. Note that this relation is entirely independent of the production function (except for the CRS assumption).

The growth rate of per capita income is perhaps even more interesting, and it is now readily obtained. The definition $y = Y/L$ implies that $\ln y(t) = \ln Y(t) - \ln L(t)$. By differentiating with respect to time, we directly get that

$$\frac{\dot{y}}{y} = \frac{\dot{Y}}{Y} - n = g.$$

Income per capita thus grows at the exogenous rate g in the long run, given that Y/K is constant.

We finally note that equation (2.14) can be rewritten as something that has proved to be a very useful starting point in empirical work. We simply solve it for the growth rate of the technology factor and get

$$g = \frac{1}{\zeta_L}\left(\frac{\dot{Y}}{Y} - \zeta_K\frac{\dot{K}}{K} - \zeta_L n\right).$$

This expression is called the *Solow residual*, and was developed in Solow (1957). It can be used to compute the rate of technological progress if information is available for everything on the right hand side. Some measures of the growth rates of output, capital, and labor are indeed available, as are measures of the income shares. Therefore g can be "residually" estimated.

2.5 **The CES function**

The CES production function has properties that we will examine the consequences of in many places in this book. One important reason to pay special
attention to this function is that it gives a good possibility for examining how
the results may change when the neo-classical assumptions are not entirely
fulfilled. Moreover, this function provides a convenient way to highlight the
role of the elasticity of substitution in the growth process. We therefore display
some of its special features here. More precisely, we look in turn at the income
shares and at the function in intensity form.

2.5.1 INCOME SHARES

To compute the income shares (output elasticities) of the CES function, we first
need expressions for the marginal products of the inputs in (2.5). Noting that
a part of the outer derivative in each case is Y itself, we conclude that they are

$$\frac{\partial Y}{\partial K} = \frac{1}{\varepsilon}\left(\alpha K^{\varepsilon} + (1-\alpha)(AL)^{\varepsilon}\right)^{\frac{1}{\varepsilon}-1}\alpha\varepsilon K^{\varepsilon-1} = \frac{Y \cdot \alpha K^{\varepsilon-1}}{\alpha K^{\varepsilon} + (1-\alpha)(AL)^{\varepsilon}}$$

and

$$\frac{\partial Y}{\partial L} = \frac{1}{\varepsilon}\left(\alpha K^{\varepsilon} + (1-\alpha)(AL)^{\varepsilon}\right)^{\frac{1}{\varepsilon}-1}(1-\alpha)A^{\varepsilon}\varepsilon L^{\varepsilon-1} = \frac{Y \cdot (1-\alpha)A^{\varepsilon}L^{\varepsilon-1}}{\alpha K^{\varepsilon} + (1-\alpha)(AL)^{\varepsilon}},$$

respectively. The income shares are then obtained after multiplication by the
production factor divided by output. This results in

$$\zeta_K = \frac{Y\alpha K^{\varepsilon-1}}{\alpha K^{\varepsilon} + (1-\alpha)(AL)^{\varepsilon}} \cdot \frac{K}{Y} = \frac{\alpha K^{\varepsilon}}{\alpha K^{\varepsilon} + (1-\alpha)(AL)^{\varepsilon}}$$

$$= \frac{\alpha}{\alpha + (1-\alpha)(AL/K)^{\varepsilon}} = \frac{\alpha}{\alpha + (1-\alpha)\tilde{k}^{-\varepsilon}}$$

and

$$\zeta_L = \frac{Y(1-\alpha)A^{\varepsilon}L^{\varepsilon-1}}{\alpha L^{\varepsilon} + (1-\alpha)(AL)^{\varepsilon}} \cdot \frac{L}{Y} = \frac{(1-\alpha)(AL)^{\varepsilon}}{\alpha K^{\varepsilon} + (1-\alpha)(AL)^{\varepsilon}}$$

$$= \frac{(1-\alpha)}{\alpha(K/(AL))^{\varepsilon} + (1-\alpha)} = \frac{(1-\alpha)}{\alpha\tilde{k}^{\varepsilon} + (1-\alpha)}.$$

These expressions, of course, also hold if there is no technological change, so
that $A = 1$, but then with $\tilde{k}$ replaced by k.

Since Exercise 2.2 shows that the income shares are constant for a general CRS production function, if $\tilde{k}$ is constant, it must also hold for the CES

function. This is indeed obvious from these expressions. However, this function opens for a small possibility that $\tilde{k}$ (or k) is not constant on the long-run growth path, as we will see in Chapter 3. It is therefore interesting to check how the income shares develop if $\tilde{k}$ should happen to grow toward infinity. As could be expected, the results depend much on the elasticity of substitution between the two inputs.

Consider first the case with good substitution possibilities, that is when $\varepsilon > 0$, so that $\sigma > 1$. Then the expressions above imply that $\zeta_K \to 1$ and $\zeta_L \to 0$ as $\tilde{k} \to \infty$. To understand these results, we should first note that two things are happening when $\tilde{k}$ grows large. First, capital comes to dominate labor in terms of quantity, which clearly would imply a growing capital share if factor prices were constant. Second, however, the rising (relative) scarcity of labor makes its marginal product higher and therefore increases the wage. This effect tends to increase the income share of labor, but in the present case it is dominated by the first effect. The reason is that the high elasticity of substitution makes it relatively easy to replace labor by capital, and therefore the wage rate does not rise very much. The moderate growth of the wage rate, together with the declining relative quantity of labor, explains its vanishing income share.

In the opposite case, when $\varepsilon < 0$ and thus $\sigma < 1$, we have the inverse result, namely that $\zeta_K \to 0$ and $\zeta_L \to 1$ as $\tilde{k} \to \infty$. Now the low elasticity of substitution creates a more serious scarcity of labor as its relative size falls. The wage rate therefore rises so much that the income share of labor grows, even though the relative amount of labor declines. Similar results can be obtained for a general production function; see for instance Dixit (1976).

Let us finally return to the claim above that the CES function approaches the Cobb–Douglas function as ε goes to zero. This should imply that the CES income shares tend to the Cobb–Douglas income shares if $\varepsilon \to 0$. It is easy to see from the expressions above that this indeed is true: we have that $\zeta_K = \alpha$ and $\zeta_L = 1 - \alpha$ as $\varepsilon \to 0$.

2.5.2 INTENSITY FORM

In this sub-section we look at the CES function in its intensity form. We consider the case when there is no technological progress, so that $A = 1$, because this will be more useful in Chapter 3. We will compute $f(k), f'(k), f''(k)$, and $f(k)/k$ for this function. It turns out that the average product of capital now has properties that differ significantly from those of neo-classical production functions. This may have important implications for the long-run growth path, as will be demonstrated in Section 3.6.

As a first step toward the intensity form of the function itself, we divide (2.5) by L and get per capita income as

$$\frac{Y}{L} = \frac{1}{L}\left(\alpha K^{\varepsilon} + (1-\alpha)L^{\varepsilon}\right)^{1/\varepsilon} = \left(\alpha\left(\frac{K}{L}\right)^{\varepsilon} + (1-\alpha)\left(\frac{L}{L}\right)^{\varepsilon}\right)^{1/\varepsilon},$$

where we have used the fact that $1/L = (1/L)^{\varepsilon/\varepsilon}$. Recalling the definitions of y and k, this can be reformulated into

$$y = f(k) = \left(\alpha k^{\varepsilon} + (1-\alpha)\right)^{1/\varepsilon}, \tag{2.15}$$

which thus expresses per capita income as a function of capital per capita for this type of function.

Using the expression in (2.15), the marginal product of capital is given by the derivative

$$f'(k) = \frac{1}{\varepsilon}\left(\alpha k^{\varepsilon} + (1-\alpha)\right)^{\frac{1}{\varepsilon}-1}\alpha\varepsilon k^{\varepsilon-1} = \left(\alpha k^{\varepsilon} + (1-\alpha)\right)^{\frac{1-\varepsilon}{\varepsilon}}\alpha k^{\varepsilon-1}.$$

The subsequent analysis will be more convenient if we move the k after the parenthesis inside the parenthesis, in order to get k in just one place. We therefore use the fact that $k^{\varepsilon-1} = k^{\frac{1-\varepsilon}{\varepsilon}\cdot(-\varepsilon)}$ and obtain

$$f'(k) = \alpha\left(\alpha k^{\varepsilon} + (1-\alpha)\right)^{\frac{1-\varepsilon}{\varepsilon}}k^{\frac{1-\varepsilon}{\varepsilon}\cdot(-\varepsilon)} = \alpha\left(\alpha k^{\varepsilon}\cdot k^{-\varepsilon} + (1-\alpha)k^{-\varepsilon}\right)^{\frac{1-\varepsilon}{\varepsilon}}.$$

The final result therefore is

$$f'(k) = \alpha\left(\alpha + (1-\alpha)k^{-\varepsilon}\right)^{\frac{1-\varepsilon}{\varepsilon}}. \tag{2.16}$$

It is clear that the marginal product is positive irrespective of ε being positive or negative. We can see that this function is quite special by examining this marginal product when k goes to extreme values. It turns out, namely, that the function fails to fulfill the Inada conditions, in one way or another, depending on the elasticity of substitution.

If the production factors substitute well, that is when $0 < \varepsilon < 1$, it holds that $f'(k) \to \infty$ as $k \to 0$ but $f'(k) \to \alpha^{1/\varepsilon}$ as $k \to \infty$. This violates the Inada condition because the marginal product of capital does not decline all the way down to zero as k grows large. A possible consequence of this limitation of diminishing returns to capital is that sustained growth may be possible even without technological progress, as we will see in Chapter 3.

By contrast, when the elasticity of substitution is low ($\varepsilon < 0$), it follows from (2.16) that $f'(k) \to \alpha^{1/\varepsilon}$ as $k \to 0$ and $f'(k) \to 0$ as $k \to \infty$. The marginal product of the first unit of capital is then less than infinite, again a violation of an Inada condition. These properties of the CES function are clearly different from those we had for the general function in Section 2.2.

Turning to the second-order derivative, we benefit from using the simplified version of $f'(k)$ in (2.16), and get

$$f''(k) = \alpha\frac{1-\varepsilon}{\varepsilon}\left(\alpha + (1-\alpha)k^{-\varepsilon}\right)^{\frac{1-\varepsilon}{\varepsilon}-1}(1-\alpha)(-\varepsilon)k^{-\varepsilon-1}.$$

Since $-\varepsilon/\varepsilon = -1$, this simplifies to

$$f''(k) = -\alpha(1-\varepsilon)\left(\alpha + (1-\alpha)k^{-\varepsilon}\right)^{\frac{1-2\varepsilon}{\varepsilon}} (1-\alpha)k^{-\varepsilon-1} < 0.$$

The marginal product of capital is thus confirmed to decline as capital per capita grows.

The final expression of interest is the average product of capital, which will be of great importance in subsequent growth models. It follows from dividing (2.15) by k that

$$\frac{f(k)}{k} = k^{-\varepsilon \cdot \frac{1}{\varepsilon}}\left(\alpha k^{\varepsilon} + (1-\alpha)\right)^{1/\varepsilon} = \left(\alpha k^{\varepsilon}k^{-\varepsilon} + (1-\alpha)k^{-\varepsilon}\right)^{1/\varepsilon},$$

where we have again used the fact that $-\varepsilon/\varepsilon = -1$. The average product therefore simply is

$$\frac{f(k)}{k} = \left(\alpha + (1-\alpha)k^{-\varepsilon}\right)^{1/\varepsilon}.$$

This function is declining in k, but it differs from what we see in Figure 2.2, in one way or another, depending on the elasticity of substitution. If $0 < \varepsilon < 1$ it holds that $f(k)/k \to \infty$ as $k \to 0$, but in contrast to the benchmark case $f(k)/k \to \alpha^{1/\varepsilon}$ as $k \to \infty$. That is, the average product has a strictly positive lower bound if the elasticity of substitution is high, as shown in Figure 2.3. When $\varepsilon < 0$, on the other hand, we have that $f(k)/k \to \alpha^{1/\varepsilon}$ as $k \to 0$ and $f(k)/k \to 0$ as $k \to \infty$.[13] In this case, where there are small possibilities for substitution, the average product of capital approaches an upper bound as k

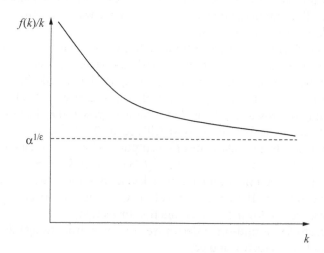

Figure 2.3. Average product of the CES function when $0 < \varepsilon < 1$

[13] Note that $f'(k)$ tends to the same values as $f(k)/k$ at the limiting values of k.

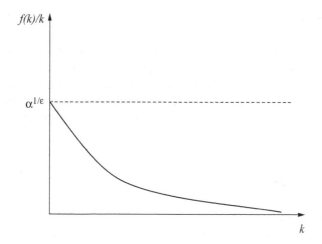

Figure 2.4. Average product of the CES function when $\varepsilon < 0$

goes to zero, whereas the limit value is infinity for the neo-classical production function. This case is illustrated in Figure 2.4.

2.6 **Conclusion**

This chapter introduces the aggregate production function, which is a description of the available production technology. We have looked at some of its most important properties, which will influence the growth paths of later chapters. The reformulations of the production functions into intensity forms will be conveniently substituted into the growth models of later chapters. We devoted much space to the elasticity substitution, because it will be central in many respects to subsequent models.

It should be emphasized that we are assuming constant returns to scale. Increasing returns to scale functions would be more powerful, in that they can generate sustained growth even without technological progress. In other words, with sufficiently strong increasing returns research would not be necessary for a growing per capita GDP in the long run. However, this clashes with empirical evidence about the importance of innovations for economic growth, and therefore we devote little space to increasing returns to scale.

The Cobb–Douglas and CES functional forms are admittedly simple. They are chosen with the purpose of displaying transparent examples. In some empirical work, functions with much more flexible forms are often used. See for instance Snyder and Nicholson (2008) for presentations of the so-called Translog and Generalized Leontief functions.

■ **FURTHER READING**

Careful presentations of the neo-classical production function are found in Barro and Sala-i-Martin (2004) and Acemoglu (2009). In La Grandville (2009), there are two useful chapters on the CES function (written in collaboration with Solow). Most textbooks in microeconomics contain good expositions of production functions. See for instance Snyder and Nicholson (2008).

2.7 **Exercises**

2.1 CES and Inada

The CES function (2.5) does not satisfy the Inada conditions. Show this.

2.2 Balanced growth

Assume a growth path, along which $\tilde{k}$ is constant. Show that the growth path is balanced, that is consistent with the Kaldor facts.

2.3 Dividing Y by K

As mentioned in Section 2.2.3, an alternative way of transforming the production function into efficiency units is to divide the production function by K:

$$\frac{Y}{K} = \frac{1}{K}F[K, AL] = F\left[\frac{K}{K}, \frac{AL}{K}\right].$$

Now define

$$\frac{1}{z} = \frac{Y}{K} \quad \text{and} \quad \tilde{l} = \frac{AL}{K}.$$

Thus

$$\frac{1}{z} = F\left[1, \tilde{l}\right] \equiv g\left(\tilde{l}\right).$$

Show that $g'(\tilde{l}) > 0$ and $g''(\tilde{l}) < 0$.

3 The Solow model

In this chapter we place the production function from the previous chapter in a dynamic context, that is the production function becomes part of an equation describing the accumulation of capital. This law of motion of capital is in turn derived from the macroeconomic identity describing how production output is used either in consumption or investment, in a closed economy without a public sector. The dynamics of such an economy is often best expressed in terms of variables which are constant in the long run. We therefore transform the dynamic equation into efficiency units, using the transformations of the variables and the production function into the intensity form from Chapter 2.

The result of all this is *Solow's fundamental equation*. This equation makes it easy to show that the growth model has a unique steady state, where $\tilde{k}$ is constant. Moreover, this steady state is (globally) stable, which means that the economy will always find its way to the steady state, wherever it starts from. This stability property of the model was a central point of Solow (1956); previous models (see for instance Harrod (1939) and Domar (1946)) had typically been unstable, often leading to implausible patterns of long-run development. For instance, these models could imply monotonously increasing unemployment, if the slightest deviation from the steady state occurred. The main reason for Solow's stability result was his use of a neo-classical production function, as opposed to his predecessors, who used a production function without any substitution possibilities at all.[1]

The stability property of the Solow model means that a typical economy will spend a large share of its time in (or close to) the steady state.[2] This fact makes the steady state interesting, and we will find that an analysis of the implications of this long-run growth path yields important insights. We also examine what determines the steady state, that is how it is affected by exogenous parameters, in quite some detail.

A central question in economic growth theory is whether capital accumulation alone can ensure sustained growth in per capita income. For a strictly neo-classical production function we find that the answer is no, because the average and marginal products of capital fall toward zero as capital grows large.

---

[1] The production function used by these early economists was of the Leontief type: $Y = \min[aK, bL]$, meaning that the output level equals the lowest of the two expressions in the bracket. This implies that a use of the inputs in any other proportion than $K/L = b/a$ would be wasteful.

[2] This is true if unexpected macroeconomic disturbances are disregarded. We choose to do so here, and focus on the long-run development.

Technological change is therefore necessary and sufficient for growth in the long run: as long as the technology factor A grows at the rate g, per capita income will also grow at this rate in the steady state.

If one of the neo-classical assumptions is relaxed, however, there are some forms of the production function for which growth can be sustained, even if technological change is absent. We then have what is sometimes called first-generation models of "endogenous growth." A typical implication of such deviations from the neo-classical assumptions is, however, that the income share of labor vanishes in the long run. The growth paths implied by these modifications of the model are thus not consistent with the data, in particular not with the Kaldor facts.

A well-known implication of the neo-classical growth model is that it has a convergence property, meaning that poor countries tend to catch up on rich countries, in terms of per capita capital and income. In the light of empirical observations, this statement needs some qualifications, though. This leads us to the concept of "conditional convergence," which takes into account the difference between countries in terms of, for example, saving rates and population growth rates. When such differences are controlled for, there may still be an element of convergence in the model.

This chapter finally presents an alternative way to analyze the dynamics of the growth model. It amounts to deriving a differential equation in terms of the capital–output ratio, instead of k or $\tilde{k}$. This approach is useful in models where more production inputs are added, for instance natural resources, which we encounter in Chapters 5 and 6.

3.1 **Capital accumulation**

We start by deriving an equation for capital accumulation from the simplest possible macroeconomic model. It will be assumed throughout that the economy that we study is closed from international trade and that there is no public sector. All output is therefore allocated between consumption, $C(t)$, and investment, $I(t)$. This gives the equation

$$Y = C + I. \tag{3.1}$$

Our goal is to transform this into an equation with just one variable. We therefore start to develop the right hand side, by expressing consumption in terms of output and investment in terms of capital.

For an economist it would be natural to derive the optimal levels of consumption (at different points of time) from a utility maximization problem. This would, however, require the use of some quite advanced optimization technique, which is beyond the scope of this book. We therefore simplify by just assuming that a share s (the *saving rate*) of income is saved at every point of time.[3] The remaining share of the income is consumed, so the consumption function is $C = (1 - s)Y$. Using this in equation (3.1), we get $Y = (1 - s)Y + I$, which can be simplified to

$$sY = I. \tag{3.2}$$

We recognize this from elementary macroeconomics as the requirement that savings always equal investments in a closed economy without a public sector.

Turning to investments, some of them are used to replace worn out capital. The depreciation of capital is here represented by the term δK, where the constant δ is the rate of capital depreciation. Only the rest of the investments raise the stock of capital, and this increase will be represented by the time derivative $\dot{K}$. We thus have $I = \dot{K} + \delta K$. Using this in (3.2) we obtain

$$\dot{K} = sY - \delta K. \tag{3.3}$$

This important equation thus describes how capital accumulation is equal to gross investment minus capital replenishment. Since $Y = F(K, AL)$ contains several variables, we must make further transformations, to obtain a dynamic equation with just one variable ($\tilde{k}$ or k) and the time derivative of this variable. To this end, we now use the intensity forms developed in Chapter 2.

3.2 Solow's fundamental equation

3.2.1 DERIVING THE EQUATION

To transform the dynamic equation (3.3) into intensity units, we start by dividing it by AL and invoking the production function. This yields

$$\frac{\dot{K}}{AL} = s\frac{1}{AL}F[K, AL] - \delta\frac{K}{AL}.$$

By the definitions and computations in Chapter 2 we can directly simplify the right hand side of this equation, so that

$$\frac{\dot{K}}{AL} = sf(\tilde{k}) - \delta\tilde{k}. \tag{3.4}$$

With this step we are done with transforming the right hand side, so that it contains only the variable $\tilde{k}$.

The left hand side of (3.4) can be replaced by something that only contains $\tilde{k}$ (and $\dot{\tilde{k}}$) if we first recall the definition $\tilde{k}(t) = K(t)/(A(t)L(t))$ and take the logarithm of both sides, to get

---

[3] It actually turns out that the saving rate is constant in the long run in more elaborate models too.

$$\ln(\tilde{k}(t)) = \ln(K(t)) - \ln(A(t)) - \ln(L(t)).$$

Differentiating both sides with respect to time yields a relation that must hold between various growth rates, because of the definition of $\tilde{k}$:

$$\frac{\dot{\tilde{k}}}{\tilde{k}} = \frac{\dot{K}}{K} - \frac{\dot{A}}{A} - \frac{\dot{L}}{L}.$$

Now we multiply through by $\tilde{k}$ and use the definition of this variable. We also recall that A and L grow at the constant rates g and n, respectively. The result is

$$\dot{\tilde{k}} = \frac{K}{AL}\frac{\dot{K}}{K} - \tilde{k}g - \tilde{k}n,$$

which is equivalent to

$$\frac{\dot{K}}{AL} = \dot{\tilde{k}} + \tilde{k}g + \tilde{k}n.$$

This is what we were looking for: something useful that can replace the left hand side of equation (3.4).

Performing this substitution, we first obtain the equation $\dot{\tilde{k}} + \tilde{k}g + \tilde{k}n = sf(\tilde{k}) - \delta\tilde{k}$. Rewriting this, we finally have *Solow's fundamental equation*:

$$\dot{\tilde{k}} = sf(\tilde{k}) - (n + g + \delta)\tilde{k}. \tag{3.5}$$

This is *the* equation of the Solow model. It says that, in per unit of effective labor terms, capital accumulation is equal to gross investment minus replacement investments. The latter consists of replacement of worn out capital, furnishing of newborns with capital, and an adjustment due to the continuous upgrading of productivity. Sometimes this negative term on the right hand side is called break-even investment, since $\tilde{k}$ is constant if the gross investment $sf(\tilde{k})$ equals this amount.

On occasions when we want to explore the case with no technological progress, we put $A = 1$ and use k instead of $\tilde{k}$. Since we also have $g = 0$ in this case, equation (3.5) then simplifies to

$$\dot{k} = sf(k) - (n + \delta)k. \tag{3.6}$$

This special version of the Solow equation says that the change in capital per capita equals savings per capita minus break-even investments per capita.

3.2.2 SOME IMPLICATIONS

Equation (3.5) is a *differential equation* in $\tilde{k}$, because it contains this variable as well as its time derivative. It would be desirable to solve this equation for $\tilde{k}$ as a function of t (which would require that we specify the function $f(\tilde{k})$), that is to eliminate $\dot{\tilde{k}}$. Such a solution would explicitly describe how $\tilde{k}$ evolves over time, starting from an initial value, $\tilde{k}_0$, at $t = 0$.

Unfortunately, such solutions are usually difficult to find, but there is one famous exception, namely the Cobb–Douglas case. Solow's equation then becomes $\dot{\tilde{k}} = s\tilde{k}^\alpha - (n + g + \delta)\tilde{k}$. It can be demonstrated that the solution to this differential equation is

$$\tilde{k}(t) = \left[\frac{s}{n + g + \delta} + \left(\tilde{k}_0^{1-\alpha} - \frac{s}{n + g + \delta} \right) e^{-(1-\alpha)(n+g+\delta)t} \right]^{\frac{1}{1-\alpha}}$$

(see Exercise 3.4). The development of $\tilde{k}$ over time here comes out quite clearly. Since the exponential function is declining over time, the second term in the bracket vanishes and $\tilde{k}$ tends to the steady state value

$$\tilde{k}^* = \left[\frac{s}{n + g + \delta} \right]^{\frac{1}{1-\alpha}} \tag{3.7}$$

as $t \to \infty$. Whether $\tilde{k}$ approaches this value from below or above depends on the initial point. If $\tilde{k}_0 < (>)\tilde{k}^*$, then $\tilde{k}$ grows (declines) over time. Since the exponent in (3.7) is positive, $\tilde{k}^*$ is increasing in s and decreasing in n, g, and δ.

When the productions function is not a Cobb–Douglas, it is difficult (or impossible) to solve (3.5) for $\tilde{k}$ as a function of t. Other cases must therefore be studied by alternative methods. For instance, a simple graphic analysis has proved very useful in this respect. It makes it straightforward to get to the important conclusion that the model has a *unique steady state which is globally stable*, that is whatever the initial $\tilde{k}$ is, this variable will always find its way to the unique $\tilde{k}^*$, in a monotonous manner. This can be seen in Figure 3.1.

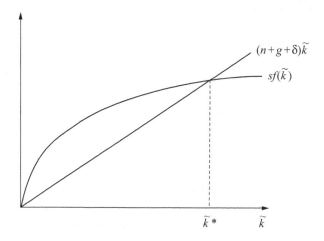

Figure 3.1. Solow's fundamental equation

The two terms of the right hand side of (3.5) are represented by the two curves in this figure. By the assumptions in Chapter 2, in particular the Inada conditions, the $sf(\tilde{k})$ curve is initially very steep and then continuously declines in slope as $\tilde{k}$ grows. It therefore cuts the straight $(n + g + \delta)\tilde{k}$ line once and only once (we ignore the origin). At this crossing point $\tilde{k}$ has its steady state value, $\tilde{k}^*$, because $\dot{\tilde{k}} = 0$ when $sf(\tilde{k}) = (n + g + \delta)\tilde{k}$. Since there is only one crossing point, the steady state is unique.

To see that the model is globally stable, note that the change of the capital stock, $\dot{\tilde{k}}$, equals the vertical distance between the curves. Since $sf(\tilde{k}) > (n + g + \delta)\tilde{k}$ whenever $\tilde{k} < \tilde{k}^*$, we have $\dot{\tilde{k}} > 0$ at all $\tilde{k}$ levels to the left of the steady state. To the contrary, $\tilde{k}$ declines for all $\tilde{k}$ levels above $\tilde{k}^*$, because $sf(\tilde{k}) < (n + g + \delta)\tilde{k}$ there. From this it follows that the Solow model is globally stable: starting from any (strictly positive) initial $\tilde{k}_0$, the economy always approaches the unique steady state, where $\dot{\tilde{k}} = 0$.

The concept of steady state indicates that the variable $\tilde{k}$ is constant at this point. This does not of course imply that everything in the model is at rest. Remember that $\tilde{k}$ is a ratio including three variables, where A and L are steadily growing at constant exogenous rates. Therefore, K must grow at the same rate as the other two variables together in the steady state. Recall also that Exercise 2.2 shows that the Kaldor facts are fulfilled when $\tilde{k}$ is constant. The steady state is therefore also a balanced growth path. We will therefore interchangeably use the phrases steady state and balanced growth path whenever the Kaldor facts are fulfilled.

3.3 **Steady state**

To develop the understanding of the growth process implied by (3.5) or (3.6) further, we first examine the long-run growth path, which is largely characterized by the steady state values of k and $\tilde{k}$, respectively. In the following two sub-sections we examine these two cases in turn. Section 3.4 then analyzes the transition to the steady state.

3.3.1 WITHOUT TECHNOLOGICAL CHANGE

When there is no technological change, equation (3.6) applies. The findings that the interior steady state is unique and globally stable of course carry over to this special case as well. The steady state capital stock per capita is determined by the equation

$$sf(k^*) = (n + \delta)k^*, \tag{3.8}$$

which is obtained by putting $\dot{k} = 0$ in (3.6). Equation (3.8) gives the value of k^* only *implicitly*, in the sense that it is not solved for k^* as a function of everything else. To allow for that, it would be necessary to specify the production function further. However, even if we do so the function may be so complicated that an explicit solution is hard to find. One exception is the Cobb–Douglas function, for which we have the steady state solution in (3.7) (with technological change). Another exception is the CES function, which is demonstrated in Exercise 3.1. In general, however, we have to use other methods to see how k^* changes in response to variations in the exogenous parameters s, n, and δ.

One way to move ahead is to compute the total differential of the steady state condition (3.8).[4] The result is

$$f(k^*)ds + sf'(k^*)dk^* = k^*dn + k^*d\delta + (n + \delta)dk^*.$$

This equation describes (approximately) what relations must hold between changes in k^*, s, n, and δ when the economy makes a small move from one steady state to another.

To find out how k^* responds to variations in the exogenous parameters s, n, and δ, we collect dk^* terms on the right hand side and all other terms on the left hand side. This yields

$$f(k^*)ds - k^*dn - k^*d\delta = \left(n + \delta - sf'(k^*)\right)dk^*.$$

The coefficient in front of dk^* can be defined as $\Delta = n + \delta - sf'(k^*) > 0$. It is positive because the $(n + \delta)k$ line is steeper than the $sf(k)$ curve at the point where they intersect, which can be seen in Figure 3.2.[5]

This definition allows us to rewrite the above equation as

$$dk^* = \frac{1}{\Delta}\left[f(k^*)ds - k^*dn - k^*d\delta\right].$$

We use this equality to examine the effect of one change at a time. If for instance n and δ are constant, so that $dn = d\delta = 0$, the previous equation is reduced to $dk^* = \Delta^{-1} \cdot f(k^*)ds$. We use this to infer that

$$\frac{\partial k^*}{\partial s} = \frac{f(k^*)}{\Delta} > 0.$$

This says that, in the long run, the per capita capital stock is larger in an economy with a high saving rate than in an economy with a low saving rate. While this is a rather expected result, the derivative also provides help to quantify the effect, which would not be possible with an informal analysis. Moving on to the

---

[4] Another possibility is to use implicit differentiation.

[5] Note that $(n + \delta)$ and $sf'(k)$ are the slopes of the curves $(n + \delta)k$ and $sf(k)$, respectively. The steady state would be unstable if $\Delta \leq 0$.

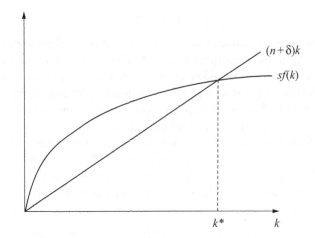

Figure 3.2. Solow's fundamental equation with $A = 1$

effects of changes in the other two parameters, we find by similar reasoning that the steady state capital stock is affected as follows:

$$\frac{\partial k^*}{\partial n} = -\frac{k^*}{\Delta} < 0, \quad \text{and} \quad \frac{\partial k^*}{\partial \delta} = -\frac{k^*}{\Delta} < 0.$$

An economy with low rates of population growth and capital depreciation will thus have a comparatively large per capita capital stock along the balanced growth path.

Since the per capita capital stock is constant on the long-run growth path, so are income and consumption per capita, taking the values $y^* = f(k^*)$ and $c^* = (1 - s)f(k^*)$, respectively. An important lesson is therefore that per capita income and consumption cannot grow in the long run, in the absence of technological change (and given that the production function satisfies the neo-classical assumptions). Thus we have already found a possible *limit to growth*, even though natural resources or environment-related dampers on growth have not yet been introduced. As can be seen in Figure 3.2, this is due to the decline in $f'(k)$, which leads to crossing of the curves and the halt in the growth of k. The diminishing returns to capital is thus a reason for the limit to growth.

An implication of the constancy of k^* is, of course, that the long-run growth *rate* is not affected by the saving rate. In other words, it is not possible to raise the long-run growth rate by an economic policy that promotes saving (such as lower taxes on capital income). However, the *level* of growth is also important, in the sense that a higher per capita capital stock in steady state raises income and consumption per capita in steady state. This is obvious if we for instance write the steady state income as $y(s)^* = f(k(s)^*)$. We know that a higher s

leads to an increased k^*, which in turn means that $f(k^*)$ will be larger. There can thus be some benefit to gain from providing good incentives to save. It should be stressed, however, that a higher saving rate does not always lead to an improvement for the households; there could be excessive savings, as we will see in Section 3.3.3.

Although k, y, and c are constant in the steady state, there is an underlying growth in the variables that make up these ratios. Since the lower-case variables are obtained by division of K, Y, and C by L, the non-transformed variables all grow at the exogenous population growth rate n. For example, $Y = Lf(k^*)$ in the long run, which implies that Y and L grow at the same rate, because k^* is constant. Finally, the investment relation $I = \dot{K} + \delta K$ implies that $I/K = \dot{K}/K + \delta$. This means that I must grow at the same rate as K, since $\dot{K}/K$ is constant in steady state.

3.3.2 WITH TECHNOLOGICAL CHANGE

We now go back to the general case, when there is technological progress, that is when equation (3.5) describes the dynamics of $\tilde{k}$. It was demonstrated above that the economy will converge to a unique steady state value, $\tilde{k}^*$, regardless of which point it starts from. The value of $\tilde{k}^*$ is implicitly given by putting $\dot{\tilde{k}} = 0$ in equation (3.5) and rewriting the result as

$$sf(\tilde{k}^*) = (n + g + \delta)\tilde{k}^*. \tag{3.9}$$

As mentioned in the previous sub-section, an explicit solution may be out of reach in most cases. We must then use total differentiation (or implicit differentiation) to investigate how the steady state value is affected by changes in the exogenous parameters. A good thing about doing this is that we obtain the results for a *general* production function, for which only a small number of assumptions have been made. This means the results are not driven by some more specific assumptions about the production function.

Following the same procedure as in the previous section, we start by computing the total differential of the steady state condition. The result now is

$$f(\tilde{k}^*)ds + sf'(\tilde{k}^*)d\tilde{k}^* = \tilde{k}^*dn + \tilde{k}^*dg + \tilde{k}^*d\delta + (n + g + \delta)d\tilde{k}^*.$$

Collecting $d\tilde{k}^*$ terms on the right hand side gives

$$f(\tilde{k}^*)ds - \tilde{k}^*dn - \tilde{k}^*dg - \tilde{k}^*d\delta = \left[(n + g + \delta) - sf'(\tilde{k}^*)\right]d\tilde{k}^*.$$

In this case, the coefficient on the right hand side is defined as $\Theta = n + g + \delta - sf'(\tilde{k}^*) > 0$. It is positive because of the relation between the slopes of the curves at the intersection in Figure 3.1. The differential can then be rewritten as

$$d\tilde{k}^* = \frac{1}{\Theta}\left(f(\tilde{k}^*)ds - \tilde{k}^* dn - \tilde{k}^* dg - \tilde{k}^* d\delta\right),$$

and the partial derivatives of $\tilde{k}^*$ are obtained by assuming that only one exogenous parameter changes at a time. The results are

$$\frac{\partial \tilde{k}^*}{\partial s} = \frac{f(\tilde{k}^*)}{\Theta} > 0, \qquad \frac{\partial \tilde{k}^*}{\partial n} = -\frac{\tilde{k}^*}{\Theta} < 0, \qquad \frac{\partial \tilde{k}^*}{\partial g} = -\frac{\tilde{k}^*}{\Theta} < 0$$

$$\text{and} \quad \frac{\partial \tilde{k}^*}{\partial \delta} = -\frac{\tilde{k}^*}{\Theta} < 0.$$

We thus have the quite expected result that $\tilde{k}^*$ increases with the saving rate, but declines if any of the other parameters increases. In other words, the capital stock is larger, compared to the other inputs in production, if the economy has a high propensity to save. To the contrary, a more demanding break-even investment implies a downward press on $\tilde{k}^*$.

Given the knowledge about how $\tilde{k}^*$ is determined, we go on to note that $\tilde{y}^* = f(\tilde{k}^*)$ and $\tilde{c}^* = (1-s)f(\tilde{k}^*)$, which are also constant in the steady state. The corresponding per capita variables are obtained after multiplication of both sides of these equations by A. This gives $y^* = Af(\tilde{k}^*)$ and $c^* = A(1-s)f(\tilde{k}^*)$. Since all things on the right hand sides of these equations are constant, except A, per capita income and consumption grow in step with A, that is at the rate g. In remarkable contrast to the previous case, there is now no limit to growth, due to the exogenous growth in the technology factor.

As in the previous sub-section, however, there is no way for the economy to influence the growth rate; it is simply exogenously given. This is a shortcoming if we want to give a theoretical explanation of economic growth, and we will therefore make technological change endogenous in Chapter 4. It should be emphasized, though, that it is a great merit of the Solow model that it shows the role (and effect) of technological progress with such clarity.

While the growth *rate* is given here, the *level* of growth is affected by the propensity to save, which we can expect to be responsive to the incentives to save (e.g. the tax policy). A higher s makes per capita income, $y^* = Af(\tilde{k}^*)$, larger at every point of time along the balanced growth path, because $\tilde{k}^*$ gets larger. This is to say that the growth path lies at a higher level.

3.3.3 THE GOLDEN RULE

We cannot say what saving rate is the "best," because we leave out consumer optimization. It is, however, straightforward to show which saving rate maximizes per capita consumption in steady state. To do this, note that

$$c^* = A(1-s)f(\tilde{k}^*) = A\left[f(\tilde{k}^*) - (n+g+\delta)\tilde{k}^*\right],$$

if we use the steady state condition (3.9). Since $\tilde{k}^*$ (and therefore c^*) is a function of s, the derivative of the steady state consumption with respect to the saving rate is

$$\frac{\partial c^*}{\partial s} = A\left[f'(\tilde{k}^*) - (n+g+\delta)\right]\frac{\partial \tilde{k}^*}{\partial s}.$$

Because the final derivative is always strictly positive, the necessary condition for maximization of per capita consumption along the long-run growth path is that $\tilde{k}^*$ must be chosen so that the bracket equals zero. Denoting this value by $\tilde{k}_G$, the condition reads

$$f'(\tilde{k}_G) = n + g + \delta.$$

By choosing a saving rate such that $\tilde{k}^* = \tilde{k}_G$ the economy would obey the so-called *Golden Rule*. The saving rate that leads to this solution, s_G, satisfies the steady state condition

$$s_G f(\tilde{k}_G) = (n+g+\delta)\tilde{k}_G.$$

Note that this equation defines s_G after the previous equation has pinned down $\tilde{k}_G$.

Although we have not formulated any optimization problem, it is clear that an economy would be *dynamically inefficient* if it had a saving rate higher than s_G. To see why, note first that a reduction of the saving rate, from such a high level down to s_G, would mean a higher consumption in the long run, Moreover, consumption would be higher also in the short run, because of the lower saving rate (see Figure 3.3). An economy in steady state with $s > s_G$

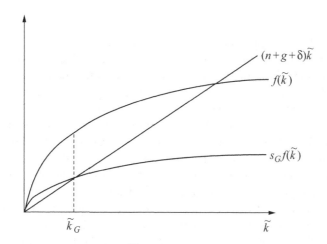

Figure 3.3. The Golden Rule

would thus definitely be better off (in terms of per capita consumption) if it were to lower the saving rate to s_G.

If initially $s < s_G$, an increased saving rate would mean more consumption in the long run but less consumption in the short run. The well-being of consumers is thus affected in two opposite directions. It takes formulation of a full-fledged optimization problem to answer the question of whether the costs of such a change are worth the benefits. We leave this question to graduate studies.

3.4 Transition to steady state

Even if we disregard short-term business cycle fluctuations, an economy can be expected to experience shocks that push it away from steady state. They can take the form of sudden changes in productivity (growth) or the saving rate, if not war or social unrest. It is therefore important to understand the transition to a steady state. We will again examine the cases without and with technological change separately.

3.4.1 WITHOUT TECHNOLOGICAL CHANGE

To study the growth rate of k outside the steady state, it is useful to divide equation (3.6) by k, so that we obtain the proportional growth rate of capital per capita

$$\frac{\dot{k}}{k} = s\frac{f(k)}{k} - (n + \delta). \tag{3.10}$$

In Figure 3.4 each right hand side term is represented by a curve. The final term is constant, giving a horizontal line in the figure. From Chapter 2 we know that the assumptions about the neo-classical production function imply the shape of the $sf(k)/k$ curve shown in this figure. As in Figure 3.1, it is here obvious that the economy finds it way to a unique steady state, wherever it starts from.

Another, and much discussed, phenomenon that is apparent from this figure is that the closer k is to k^*, the lower the growth rate is. That is, an economy with a low k_0 has a higher initial growth rate than one that starts off with a larger capital stock per capita. This means that poor countries "catch up" on rich countries. The phenomenon is also called *absolute convergence*.

To see that the convergence property also applies to per capita income, consider the Cobb–Douglas case, where $y(t) = (k(t))^\alpha$. The logarithmic version of this equation is $\ln y(t) = \alpha \ln k(t)$. Differentiating both sides with respect to time yields

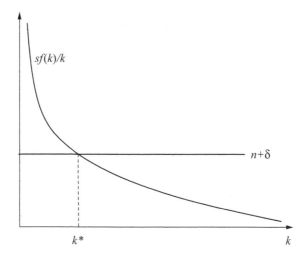

Figure 3.4. Transition without technological change

$$\frac{\dot{y}}{y} = \alpha \frac{\dot{k}}{k}.$$

Since $\dot{k}/k$ declines as k grows towards k^*, so does $\dot{y}/y$. In other words, the per capita income grows faster in an initially poor country than in a country that starts with a higher income. A similar result holds for the general function $y = f(k)$ (see Barro and Sala-i-Martin (2004), ch. 1).

The concept of absolute convergence builds on the assumption that countries are identical in every respect, except for the initial per capita capital stock. This is, of course, far from realistic, and it is thus not surprising that a simple inspection of the data does not confirm the convergence hypothesis. In Figure 3.5 the initial per capita incomes for all countries in the world are plotted against their respective average growth rates over the period 1960–2000.[6] If there were absolute convergence, we would see a clear pattern in which countries with low initial incomes would show the highest average growth rates over the period. We clearly do not see such a downward-sloping pattern.

It thus becomes evident that it is essential to take differences between countries into account. In the model this means differences in s, n, and δ, which immediately implies that the countries will have different steady states. Therefore the concept of *conditional convergence* has been suggested. It means that the further away a country is from *its own* steady state, the faster it grows. As an example, Figure 3.6 assumes that two countries differ in one (and just

[6] The data for Figures 3.5 and 3.7 were retrieved from David Weil's "Dataplotter," at http://wps. aw.com/aw_weil_econgrowth_3/230/58938/15088217.cw/index.html. It builds on the so-called Penn World Table.

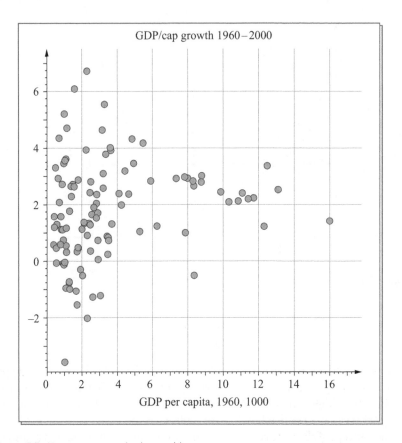

Figure 3.5. No convergence in the world

one) respect, namely that they have different saving rates, where the country with the higher saving rate has a higher k^*. As seen in Figure 3.6, it is now possible that the richer country grows faster than the poor country. This is because here the richer country starts further away from its own steady state than the poor country does.

There is some empirical support for the theory of conditional convergence.[7] For example, consider a relatively homogeneous group of countries, like the OECD. There are hardly any dramatic variations in s, n, or δ between these countries. We can therefore expect the differences in steady states to be small, and that countries that start at low per capita income levels grow faster than countries with higher initial incomes. This is also what we see in Figure 3.7, where only OECD countries from Figure 3.5 are plotted. (It shows that initially poor countries grow faster than those that are initially rich.)

---

[7] For further discussions about conditional convergence, see Barro and Sala-i-Martin (2004). Note, however, that their methods have been questioned; see Acemoglu (2009), Chapter 3.

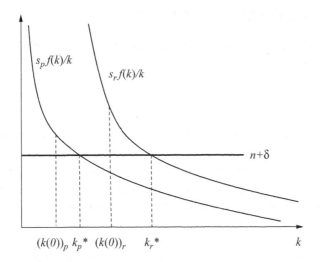

Figure 3.6. Conditional convergence

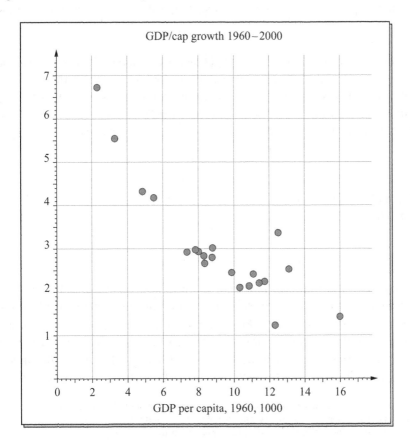

Figure 3.7. Convergence in the OECD

3.4.2 WITH TECHNOLOGICAL CHANGE

Coming to the general case, with technological progress, we divide (3.5) by $\tilde{k}$ and get the proportional grow rate

$$\frac{\dot{\tilde{k}}}{\tilde{k}} = s\frac{f(\tilde{k})}{\tilde{k}} - (n + g + \delta). \tag{3.11}$$

Given the previous analysis, the implications of this equation are not surprising and they can be summarized quickly. The equation is globally stable, that is $\tilde{k}$ approaches the unique steady state value $\tilde{k}^*$ from every possible starting point. Moreover, the rate of change is higher the further $\tilde{k}$ is below $\tilde{k}^*$, which means that we have a convergence property also in terms of capital per unit of effective labor.

As the determinants of $\tilde{k}^*$, and its dynamics around the steady state, are now well understood, we could go on to an analysis of $\tilde{y} = f(\tilde{k})$. However, an examination of the per capita income is probably more interesting from an economic point of view.[8] Therefore, recalling that $y = A\tilde{y}$, we investigate how

$$y(t) = A(t)f(\tilde{k}(t))$$

changes over time. Since we know that $\tilde{k}$ approaches its steady state value in the long run, with a declining rate of change, the path of y is also rather obvious, even when the economy has not yet reached the steady state. This is seen by taking the logarithm of both sides, to get $\ln y(t) = \ln A(t) + \ln f(\tilde{k}(t))$, and then differentiating through with respect to time. The result is

$$\frac{1}{y} \cdot \dot{y} = \frac{1}{A} \cdot \dot{A} + \frac{1}{f} \cdot f' \cdot \dot{\tilde{k}}.$$

We multiply the final term by $\tilde{k}/\tilde{k}$ and recall that the growth rate of A is g. Therefore

$$g_y \equiv \frac{\dot{y}}{y} = g + \zeta_K \cdot \frac{\dot{\tilde{k}}}{\tilde{k}},$$

where $\zeta_K = f'\tilde{k}/f$ and we introduce the condensed expression for the proportional growth rate, g_y, for subsequent convenience. Assume now that the economy starts at some $\tilde{k}_0 < \tilde{k}^*$. Then both terms on the right hand side are positive, so the growth rate of per capita income is initially higher than g. As the growth rate of $\tilde{k}$ gradually declines toward zero, g_y falls towards the underlying growth rate g.[9] This is seen in Figure 3.8. It has been shown already in

---

[8] The differential equation in terms of $\tilde{k}$ is constructed mostly for technical reasons: it is easier to understand the dynamics of a variable that becomes constant in steady state.

[9] Exercise 3.5 shows that $\dot{y}/y$ actually falls monotonically toward g as $\tilde{k}$ grows.

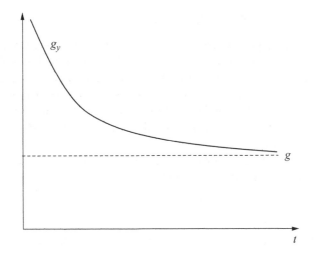

Figure 3.8. Time path of per capita income

Section 3.3.2 that the exogenous technological progress provides the economy with a sustained growth in per capita income (and consumption) in the long run. Here we see that the growth rate is even higher than g during the transitory phase, due to the growth of $\tilde{k}$, but it is clear that this addition to the growth rate eventually peters out.

3.5 **Endogenous growth**

From the discussion so far it seems like the growth in per capita variables will vanish unless there is growth in the technology factor A. This is indeed true as long as the production function fulfills the neo-classical assumptions. But if they are relaxed in a certain way economic growth can be sustained even if there is no technological progress. What is needed is that the average product of capital does not decline below a critical value. More precisely, and referring to (3.10), it is required that

$$s\frac{f(k)}{k} > (n + \delta)$$

for all values of k from k_0 to infinity. That is, the average product of capital cannot fall below $(n + \delta)/s$. If this inequality holds, the capital stock per capita will grow at all points of time. We will look closer at this, in order to give an example of what the neo-classical assumptions can rule out.

A famous example of a production function for which the requirement above can be true is

$$Y = F(K, L) = \Lambda K^\alpha L^{1-\alpha} + \Omega K, \tag{3.12}$$

where Λ and Ω are positive constants. This function exhibits constant returns to scale in K and L, as well as positive and declining marginal products. However, it violates one of the Inada conditions: the marginal product of capital, $F_K = \Lambda \alpha K^{\alpha-1} L^{1-\alpha} + \Omega$, does not approach zero as K goes to infinity. Instead it is bounded from below by the positive constant Ω. This beneficial property of the returns to capital is the reason for the possibility of unlimited growth in k that we find below.

The function in (3.12) implies that output per capita is $f(k) = \Lambda k^\alpha + \Omega k$ and that the average product of capital is

$$\frac{f(k)}{k} = \Lambda k^{\alpha-1} + \Omega.$$

The growth rate in capital per capita is obtained by substituting this into equation (3.10), which now becomes

$$\frac{\dot{k}}{k} = s\left(\Lambda k^{\alpha-1} + \Omega\right) - (n + \delta). \tag{3.13}$$

From this expression we can infer that the growth rate of k can be maintained as positive if Ω is not too small. More precisely, if $s\Omega > n + \delta$ the saving term will never come down to a value as low as the "depreciation" term. Then

$$\frac{\dot{k}}{k} \to s\Omega - (n + \delta) \quad (> 0) \quad \text{as} \quad k \to \infty.$$

The growth path of capital per capita implied by (3.13) in this case is illustrated in Figure 3.9.[10]

A particularly illuminating special case of (3.13) is obtained if we assume that the production function simply is linear in capital, that is, we put $\Lambda = 0$, so that $Y = \Omega K$. This gives

$$\frac{\dot{k}}{k} = s\Omega - (n + \delta). \tag{3.14}$$

The growth rate is then equal to one and the same constant at every point of time.[11] Equation (3.14) has one very striking implication (which applies to other endogenous growth models as well) that has been given a considerable amount of attention: *a country with a higher saving rate has a higher long-run growth rate.* This contrasts sharply with the strictly neo-classical growth model, in which a higher saving rate induces a higher level of growth but not a higher

---

[10] In contrast, the two curves of this figure would intersect if $s\Omega < n + \delta$. Then the growth of k would stop when the steady state level $k^* = \left[\frac{s\Lambda}{n+\delta-s\Omega}\right]^{1/(1-\alpha)}$ is reached.

[11] A drawback is that this rules out convergence, which we seem to see in the real world, but let us leave that aside for now.

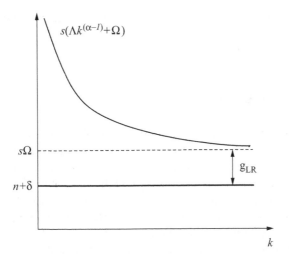

Figure 3.9. Endogenous growth

growth rate (in the long run). According to the endogenous growth model, an economy where the attitudes to saving are very positive (an economy with thrifty inhabitants) or where savings are encouraged by political means, for example by low taxes on capital income, can be expected to have a high growth rate. This implication is very appealing to economists, who tend to think that incentives matter for economic performance.[12]

Although the model of this section seems to provide a convenient way around the non-appealing assumption about exogenous technological progress, it becomes questionable when we examine the income shares in the long run. To compute the share of capital (going back to the case when $\Lambda > 0$), we first note that $f'(k) = \Lambda \alpha k^{\alpha-1} + \Omega$. Since $f(k) = (\Lambda k^{\alpha-1} + \Omega)k$, we have

$$\zeta_K = \frac{(\Lambda \alpha k^{\alpha-1} + \Omega) \cdot k}{(\Lambda k^{\alpha-1} + \Omega)k} = \frac{(\Lambda \alpha k^{\alpha-1} + \Omega)}{(\Lambda k^{\alpha-1} + \Omega)}.$$

As $k \to \infty$, $\zeta_K \to \Omega/\Omega = 1$, that is the capital share of income tends to unity in the long run. This contradicts empirical observations.

An additional shortcoming of the model discussed here, with regard to the label "endogenous growth model," is that there is no distinction between capital accumulation and technological progress in it. In newer endogenous growth models there is a separate innovation sector that produces technological progress by use of some of the economy's scarce production factors. We will discuss this in detail in Chapter 4 and we will build on that type of endogenous growth in the chapters that follow. To avoid confusion it is

---

[12] Recall, however, that we do not model the decision to save here.

useful to call the models presented here "first-generation endogenous growth models."

3.6 The CES case

Although we have just expressed some doubts about the type of endogenous growth models that just build on modifications of the production function (away from the neo-classical assumptions), we will now use the CES production function to provide another example of the possibility of sustained growth without technological progress. The reason for doing so is that we will have reason to use the CES function in subsequent chapters and the results here help us to better understand the findings there.

Consider now the slightly modified version of the CES production function in (2.5)

$$Y = \Gamma \left(\alpha K^{\varepsilon} + (1 - \alpha) L^{\varepsilon} \right)^{1/\varepsilon}, \tag{3.15}$$

where $-\infty < \varepsilon \leq 1$ and Γ is a positive constant, which can be interpreted as a productivity shift parameter. We maintain the assumption from the previous section that the technology factor is constant and normalized to unity, while the labor force grows at the rate n.

To examine the possibility of sustained growth we recall from Section 2.5.2 that the average product of capital for this function can be written as $f(k)/k = \Gamma \left(\alpha + (1 - \alpha) k^{-\varepsilon} \right)^{1/\varepsilon}$. (The only difference is that we here multiply by Γ.) Using this in equation (3.10) we get the growth rate

$$\frac{\dot{k}}{k} = s\Gamma \left(\alpha + (1 - \alpha) k^{-\varepsilon} \right)^{1/\varepsilon} - (n + \delta).$$

The results now depend a great deal on the elasticity of substitution. If it is high, that is $\varepsilon > 0$, the average product of capital tends to $\Gamma \alpha^{1/\varepsilon}$ as k gets large. If in addition $s\Gamma \alpha^{1/\varepsilon} > (n + \delta)$, then the growth rate of capital per capita is strictly positive in the long run, and approaches

$$\frac{\dot{k}}{k} = s\Gamma \alpha^{1/\varepsilon} - (n + \delta)$$

as k goes to infinity. The reason for this is that the high elasticity of substitution makes capital substitute well for labor. Capital accumulation then has a large effect on growth in output and can therefore ensure that income per capita grows forever.

As a reality check, we examine how the income share of capital develops over time in this case as well. Recall from Section 2.5.1 that the income share of capital for the CES function is

$$\zeta_K = \frac{\alpha}{\alpha + (1 - \alpha)k^{-\varepsilon}}.$$

Given that $\varepsilon > 0$, this share approaches 1 as k goes to infinity, implying that the income share of labor tends to zero. The low degree of complementarity between capital and labor keeps the returns to capital high, even though labor declines in relative terms. The bounded decline in the returns to capital, along with a steady growth in its relative quantity, accounts for the strong growth in its income share. Since we do not see the income share of labor vanishing in reality, we should be skeptical about the description of a growth path coming out of this particular model. Thus, neither model makes it plausible that capital accumulation can fully replace technological change.

For completeness, we finally note that the CES function can imply a degenerate case, in which the growth is always negative. This can happen if $\varepsilon < 0$, and the elasticity of substitution consequently is low. Then $f(k)/k \to \Gamma\alpha^{1/\varepsilon}$ as $k \to 0$ and $f(k)/k \to 0$ as $k \to \infty$. Therefore, it may be that

$$\frac{\dot{k}}{k} = s\Gamma \left(\alpha + (1 - \alpha)k^{-\varepsilon}\right)^{1/\varepsilon} - (n + \delta) < 0$$

for all levels of k, that is, the capital stock per capita is always declining, and eventually reaches zero. For this it is required that $s\Gamma\alpha^{1/\varepsilon} < n + \delta$. We will, however, not discuss this case further, but similar cases will be enlightening in the more elaborate models of later chapters.

3.7 **An alternative solution method**

This section demonstrates an alternative way to analyze the dynamics of the Solow model. The approach is to study the dynamics of $z = K/Y$ instead of k or $\tilde{k}$. It will turn out to be useful when more than two production factors are included in the production function, for instance when natural resources are accounted for. We explore this method here, even though labor and capital remain the only inputs, to be better prepared when we come to the extended models in later chapters.[13]

The logarithmic version of the definition of the capital–output ratio z is $\ln z = \ln K - \ln Y$, and the time derivative is

$$\frac{\dot{z}}{z} = \frac{\dot{K}}{K} - \frac{\dot{Y}}{Y}. \tag{3.16}$$

---

[13] The approach displayed so far will be used in Chapter 8, whereas the method that we encounter here is applied extensively in Chapters 5 through 7. The reason for devoting so much space to the approach that will be less used is that it is more well known, and that some implications are easier to show in this way. Moreover, the analysis that we turn to now tends to leave some loose ends (when it comes to the issue about stability) in the general case with more than two production factors.

Since our goal now is to formulate a differential equation in terms of the variable z, we must find expressions to replace the right hand side terms, preferably with z as the only variable in them.

To substitute for the growth rate of capital, we simply divide the capital accumulation equation (3.3) by K and get

$$\frac{\dot{K}}{K} = s\frac{1}{z} - \delta. \tag{3.17}$$

The right hand side of this equation clearly contains just constants and the variable z, so it already fits well into (3.16).

For the growth rate of output we already have an expression in equation (2.14), which is restated here for convenience:

$$\frac{\dot{Y}}{Y} = \zeta_K \frac{\dot{K}}{K} + \zeta_L(n + g). \tag{3.18}$$

Recall that this equation was obtained by time differentiation of the (general) production function (2.1). (It implies that the growth rate of output is equal to the growth rates of inputs, weighted by their output elasticities.) We eliminate the growth rate of capital in (3.18) by use of (3.17). The result is

$$\frac{\dot{Y}}{Y} = \zeta_K s\frac{1}{z} - \zeta_K\delta + \zeta_L(n + g). \tag{3.19}$$

Unfortunately, the income shares are functions of other variables than z. However, by separating them out in this way, it is easier to keep track of them; the remaining parts of the right hand side are just constants and z.

The final step to get the desired differential equation in z, is taken by using (3.17) and (3.19) on the right hand side of (3.16). This gives

$$\frac{\dot{z}}{z} = (1 - \zeta_K)s\frac{1}{z} - (1 - \zeta_K)\delta - \zeta_L(n + g).$$

The equation is easier to analyze if we multiply both sides by z. We then have

$$\dot{z} = (1 - \zeta_K)s - z\big[(1 - \zeta_K)\delta + \zeta_L(n + g)\big].$$

We can simplify this further, by using the fact that the sum of income shares is unity, that is $1 - \zeta_K = \zeta_L$. The equation then becomes

$$\dot{z} = \zeta_L\big(s - z[\delta + n + g]\big). \tag{3.20}$$

This differential equation is illustrated in Figure 3.10, with each right hand side term represented by a straight line.

Because the income share is variable (outside steady state), the curves are likely to move as z changes. Since ζ_L is always positive, however, the difference in the parenthesis of (3.20) will be monotonously closing. For instance, if $s > z[\delta + n + g]$, z will grow and the model eventually reaches the point at which $s = z[\delta + n + g]$, and thus $\dot{z} = 0$. This implies that the steady state value of z is

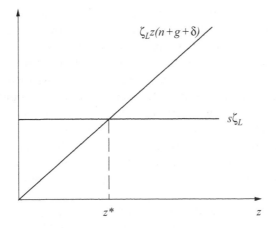

Figure 3.10. Dynamics of the capital–output ratio

$$z^* = \frac{s}{\delta + n + g}.$$

It is, of course, not surprising to find that the model is stable when we analyze it in the way we do in this section, given that equation (3.5) was demonstrated to be stable in Section 3.2.

The finding that the model has enough stability to converge to a constant z means that we were right to use $\dot{Y}/Y = \dot{K}/K$ in the growth rate for Y given in Section 2.4.4 (reproduced in (3.18)), to give a simplified long-run expression. Recall that we also used $1 - \zeta_K = \zeta_L$, which allowed us to conclude that

$$\frac{\dot{Y}}{Y} = n + g \quad \text{and} \quad \frac{\dot{y}}{y} = g \tag{3.21}$$

are the long-run growth rates of total output and per capita income, respectively. Although this solution method does not seem to add much in the present case, it will prove very useful when the production function is expanded to more than two inputs, which is the case from Chapter 5 onward.

3.8 Conclusion

In the basic Solow model, the only use of production is for consumption or investment. There are thus no public expenditures, nor any affairs with the rest of the world. By introducing depreciation and a simple behavioral rule for the division between consumption and saving, an equation describing the dynamics of capital was readily obtained. It was quite a complicated equation, because there were many variables in it. Here the preparations from Chapter 2 came in handy; by transformations to intensity forms, the Solow equation emerged, which is a differential equation with just one variable.

The Solow model provides a number of very clear-cut results. First, if the neo-classical assumptions are fulfilled, the model always follows a path to a steady state. Second, this steady state is unique. Third, the growth rates of all variables in the steady state are easy to find, and it is straightforward to see how the steady state changes if some exogenous parameter is altered. Unfortunately, the transitional dynamics is more complicated to analyze than the steady state. Sometimes it is useful to approximate the transition path in the vicinity of the steady state by a straight line, but we leave such extensions for graduate studies.

The (first-generation) endogenous growth models that were presented here are appealing because they are often easy to handle, and because they have the close link between the saving rate and the growth rate. However, one could also call that last property deceiving: it strongly confirms the priors of many economists, but this effect may sometimes be unrealistically strong. Moreover, these models can make you forget about entrepreneurs and innovations, which are central for long-run growth, and therefore highlighted in the models of Chapter 4.

■ FURTHER READING

There are now a large number of textbooks on economic growth where the Solow model is presented. At the simplest level, there are Jones (2002) and Weil (2008). Romer (2012) (Chapters 1–4) is a bit more advanced. Acemoglu (2009), Barro and Sala-i-Martin (2004), and Aghion and Howitt (2009) are mainly for the graduate level, but the sections on the Solow model are quite accessible.

It is not a bad idea to go back to some "vintage" references. Solow (1956) is still very pleasant reading, as is his book Solow (2000) (first edition 1970). You can also get a useful flavor of early growth theory by looking at Jones (1975) and Dixit (1976).

3.9 **Exercises**

3.1 CES steady state
Compute k^* in the CES case, assuming that the steady state defined by (3.8) exists.

3.2 CES income shares
Start from the production function on intensity form, $f(k) = \Gamma(\alpha k^\varepsilon + (1 - \alpha))^{1/\varepsilon}$. Compute the income share of capital.

3.3 Dividing Y by K

In exercise 2.3 you showed that division of the production function by K yields the function

$$\frac{1}{z} = g\left(\tilde{l}\right),$$

where $g'\left(\tilde{l}\right) > 0, g''\left(\tilde{l}\right) < 0$ and $\tilde{l} = (AL)/K$. Using this in (3.17), we have

$$\frac{\dot{K}}{K} = sg\left(\tilde{l}\right) - \delta.$$

Use this to derive a differential equation in $\tilde{l}$. Analyze the dynamics of $\tilde{l}$ graphically.

3.4 The Cobb–Douglas case

In Section 3.2 we claimed that the Solow equation in the Cobb–Douglas case, $\dot{\tilde{k}} = s\tilde{k}^{\alpha} - (n + g + \delta)\tilde{k}$, has the solution

$$\tilde{k}(t) = \left[\frac{s}{n+g+\delta} + \left(\tilde{k}_0^{1-\alpha} - \frac{s}{n+g+\delta}\right)e^{-(1-\alpha)(n+g+\delta)t}\right]^{\frac{1}{1-\alpha}}.$$

While it is a bit difficult to show that the latter expression is the solution for the former, it is straightforward to show that the latter implies the former, by differentiation. Do this!

3.5 Convergence in y

Given that $\tilde{k} < \tilde{k}^*$ and

$$\frac{\dot{\tilde{k}}}{\tilde{k}} = s\frac{f(\tilde{k})}{\tilde{k}} - (n+g+\delta), \quad \text{show that} \quad \frac{\partial}{\partial \tilde{k}}\left(\frac{\dot{y}}{y}\right) < 0.$$

4 Endogenous technological change

It is clear from Chapter 3 that technological progress is necessary for a long-run growth in per capita income, unless some questionable assumption is made about the production function. It is also obvious that there was no attempt to explain the growth of A in Chapter 3. Technological progress was simply assumed to be fed into the economy at no cost. While neo-classical growth theory has been praised for showing the role and importance of technological progress, its lack of explanation of the growth of A (the engine of growth) has also been pointed out.

This chapter shows, however, how a rather small extension of the Solow growth model can fill this gap.[1] Here new technology is *endogenously* produced, by use of some of the economy's scarce resources.[2] We will choose labor for this role, although other possibilities have been explored in the literature.[3] This of course means that less labor is available for production of the "ordinary" output, which is used for consumption or capital investments. Technological change thus has an *opportunity cost* in terms of lost current output, but the benefit of reallocation of some of this labor is increased future output.

The fact that decisions about research involve trade-offs between the present and the future makes the problems intertemporal. We should therefore preferably formulate an intertemporal optimization problem, which finds a desired balance between present and future production levels, given the constraints of the economy. However, we continue to relegate the explicit modeling of dynamic optimization to graduate studies, because of the advanced techniques that this requires. Instead, it will be assumed that the allocation of labor between production and research is decided by a simple rule-of-thumb, analogous to the exogenous saving rate in the Solow model. It is simply posited that a constant share of the labor force spend their working time in the research sector.

A striking feature of the model presented below is that small changes in the parameter values can have quite dramatic consequences for long-run growth paths. This holds in particular for a parameter that influences the usefulness

---

[1] In a fully fledged model, with intertemporal optimization, the extension is not that simple, though. This is obvious from Romer (1990), which is the seminal article in this area.

[2] Therefore, the model presented in this chapter can be regarded as a truly endogenous growth model, as opposed to the one in Section 3.5.

[3] For instance, it is rather common to assume that some of the final output is used in the research sector.

of knowledge from old discoveries in the process of making new discoveries. This sensitivity of the model generates debate, because a model that "balances on a knife-edge" may not feel reliable as a description of reality. On the other hand, this means that the model is sufficiently rich to allow for many different scenarios.

This chapter also introduces the concept of *directed technological change*, which takes into account the fact that research can be conducted with the purpose of saving any production factor, not just labor. In this book this becomes relevant when we introduce natural resources into the production function: some research may be devoted to making labor more productive while other research efforts have the purpose of saving, for instance, energy. Moreover, the direction of technological change can be chosen with a special emphasis on reducing the amount of polluting emissions generated by production. This expansion of technological progress to more than one dimension is accomplished by the introduction of more technology factors.

When the idea of directed technological change is introduced, we can suggest why technological change must be labor-augmenting in the steady state of the Solow growth model. Thereby we also develop a procedure for deciding the necessary steady state direction of technological change in models with natural resources in later chapters.

4.1 Some properties of technology

A technology factor, like A in the previous chapters, is quite different from other inputs in the production function. The reason for this is that improved technology to a large extent builds on new *ideas*, whereas capital, labor, natural resources, and so on can be classified as *objects*. An example of a new idea may be a chemical recipe for a new alloy that is harder than previous ones, and therefore can make turning work more effective, for example. This recipe can be easily replicated, on paper or in electronic form, at virtually no cost. The important implication is therefore that ideas are *non-rival*: one firm's use of a chemical formula does not preclude the use by another firm. By contrast, capital, labor, and natural resources are *rival* production factors, because they cannot be used simultaneously by different firms. For example, if one farmer grows corn on a plot of land, it cannot be rented to another farmer for grazing cows during the same period.[4]

The non-rival element of technology may lead one to suggest that the use of it should be free. This would, however, seriously weaken the incentives to develop new ideas, which is often extremely costly. To provide incentives

---

[4] Insightful discussions about this are found in Romer (1990) and Romer (1993).

to develop new technology, most countries have set up patent systems, with the purpose of giving innovators property rights to what they create. Although these systems do not always provide a perfect protection, they typically lead to monopoly situations, where entrepreneurs can extract profit flows from their successful research.[5] In a microeconomic jargon, the patents make the innovations (more or less) *excludable.*

Unfortunately, the existence of such monopolies implies social costs, because the owners of patents find it optimal to charge prices that are higher than the marginal costs. However, some element of monopoly seems to be unavoidable if a society wants there to be research on a significant scale. In other words, there is a trade-off between the positive and negative effects of patents. An important issue is therefore how strong the protection on innovations should be, for instance how long the optimal length of a patent period is. As explained above, however, it is quite difficult to answer such questions, so we will refrain from doing this here.

Before going into formal modeling, the reader should be alerted to the fact that the seeming simplicity of the model below stems from our choice to overlook some important aspects of the original Romer (1990) model. Among these are: (1) the entrepreneurs balance the present values of the profits that the innovations generate (stemming from their monopoly power) against the development costs; (2) the results of the innovations are carried by some (excludable) objects/machines, sold at prices higher than the marginal costs; (3) in the production function $F(K, AL)$, A now becomes a *decision* variable, the size of which is determined by profit considerations. Since the function is CRS in capital and labor, it exhibits increasing returns to scale in all three inputs. (The monopoly property and the non-rivalry of ideas take care of the complications that arise because of this.) The benefit of the simplifications that follow from not addressing these issues explicitly is that it is much easier to display the conditions for the feasibility of sustainable development, which is our main concern. This should provide a good background for subsequent studies of optimal economic growth.[6]

4.2 **The extended model**

4.2.1 THE RESEARCH SECTOR

The fact that research is costly can quite easily be incorporated by adding a research sector to the Solow model, where the number of new ideas produced at time t is $\dot{A}(t)$. Thereby we will also be able to examine the extent to which

---

[5] The innovator can exploit his discovery himself, or sell the user right to another firm.

[6] As a first step, see Chapter 5 in Jones (2002) for more about this.

the intensity of research influences the growth rate of the technology factor A (and other technology factors that will be introduced later in this book). It is then a short distance to the *incentives* to do research, but, as mentioned above, we will not go into this in detail. Nevertheless, there are many places in the text below where it will be very clear how important such incentives are.

As mentioned in the introduction to this chapter, technological progress will from now on be costly because research requires the use of some of the economy's labor force, which is therefore withdrawn from ordinary production. Denote by L_Y the quantity of labor used in ordinary production and let the number of researchers be L_A. The labor constraint then, of course, is

$$L = L_Y + L_A$$

and the production function becomes $Y = F[K, AL_Y]$. From this it is obvious that technological progress has an opportunity cost, in terms of lost ordinary output, because a higher L_A requires that L_Y decreases (at given L).

In formulating the production function for improved technology, it is reasonable to assume that more new and useful ideas will be produced the more researchers there are, that is, the development of better technology is an increasing function of the research intensity, captured by L_A. In addition, the productivity in this sector is related to the number of previously discovered useful ideas, which is captured by the current stock of technology, A. (We will discuss some reasons for this below.) Based on these considerations, it seems natural to let the production function for new technology take the form

$$\dot{A} = \eta L_A^\lambda A^\phi, \tag{4.1}$$

where η captures the productivity of the research sector. We assume that $\phi \leq 1$, and $0 < \lambda \leq 1$.

One potential objection to the formulation in (4.1) is that it does not allow for any uncertainty in the research process; if we know what the values of the variables and parameters on the right hand side are, we know *for sure* what $\dot{A}$ will be. In reality, on the other hand, the outcomes of research activities are notoriously uncertain, which could be expressed by some stochastic term in the research production function. The reason that we leave this out is that (4.1) is considered to describe the aggregate research output. Investors are assumed to diversify their investments over many research projects, and a fairly safe fraction of them are successful.

The values of the parameters in (4.1) will have a large influence on the growth path of our model economy. For one thing, it is important whether the exponent of A is positive or negative. If $\phi > 0$, then the productivity of research increases with the number of ideas already developed. New research thus makes use of the insights generated by old research. In the words of Isaac Newton, researchers are "standing on the shoulders of giants," benefiting from the achievements of previous talents. Another possibility is, however, that $\phi < 0$, implying that the productivity of research declines as the knowledge stock grows. This can be understood as there being a "fishing out" phenomenon, meaning that the most obvious ideas are discovered first, while the remaining ones are more difficult to extract.

From here on, the analysis will be limited to the case when $\phi > 0$, thereby taking the optimistic viewpoint that the net benefit for current research of old research is always positive. Finally, it is very important whether ϕ is exactly equal to, or smaller than 1, and how this is combined with the assumption about the population growth rate. This will be examined in detail in Section 4.3.

Concerning the exponent of labor in the research output function, it seems reasonable to assume that $\lambda < 1$. The implication would then be that the research output is less than doubled if the number of researchers is doubled (at given A). This would express the phenomenon that several research teams work on the same problems simultaneously, leading to some duplication of discoveries. However, although the case with $\lambda < 1$ is well motivated, it is less important for the qualitative results than the value of ϕ. We will therefore frequently put $\lambda = 1$ in the analysis below, to simplify the notation.

4.2.2 THE FULL MODEL

To incorporate (4.1) into the model, we start by considering the allocation of labor between research and ordinary production. It will be assumed that a constant fraction, s_A, of labor is used in the innovating sector, that is $L_A/L = s_A$. This implies that

$$L_A = s_A L \quad \text{and} \quad L_Y = (1 - s_A)L. \tag{4.2}$$

Given that s_A is constant, the quantities of labor in research and production will grow at the same rate as L, that is, n.

For a full description of the economic growth implied by the extended model, we substitute the labor quantities from (4.2) into the research and production functions, respectively. First, after dividing (4.1) by A, we have

$$g_A(t) = \eta s_A^\lambda (L(t))^\lambda (A(t))^{\phi-1}, \tag{4.3}$$

where we use the notation $g_X \equiv \dot{X}/X$ for the growth rate of any variable X; here $g_A \equiv \dot{A}/A$. As opposed to g in the previous chapters, this growth rate is clearly not an exogenous constant.

Next, with the second part of (4.2) in the production function, the capital accumulation equation becomes

$$\dot{K} = sF[K, A(1 - s_A)L] - \delta K. \tag{4.4}$$

In Chapter 3 the dynamics of the economy was represented by just one differential equation, namely (3.5). Here we have a system of two equations, (4.3) and (4.4), in the two endogenous variables A and K. The analysis is, however, simplified by the fact that (4.3) contains only one of them, A. This means that we can study the dynamics of A first, and then use the result of this in (4.4) to see how K develops (or rather, how $\tilde{k}$ develops in a modified version of (4.4)).

Concerning the development of A, several possibilities are examined in the next section. For our present discussion it is sufficient to note that in principle just three possibilities arise: (1) either g_A is a positive constant from time 0 and for ever on; or (2) g_A approaches a positive constant in the long run, but takes varying values during the transition; or (3) g_A falls toward zero in the long run. The various outcomes are, of course, results of different assumptions about equation (4.3). This is about all we need to know when we go on to an examination of the dynamics of capital.

The growth of the capital stock is again best understood if we develop (4.4) into a differential equation in $\tilde{k}$. Analogously to (3.5) it reads

$$\dot{\tilde{k}} = sf(\tilde{k}) - (n + g_A + \delta)\tilde{k}. \tag{4.5}$$

There are two important differences to note between (4.5) and (3.5). First, we now define $\tilde{k} = K/(AL_Y)$, which means that we take into account that only a share of labor works in ordinary production. Second, g is here replaced by g_A. Because the latter is an endogenous variable, possibly varying during a transition period, the dynamics now becomes somewhat more complicated. This is seen in Figure 4.1, where the break-even investment line now rotates a bit, as g_A approaches its long-run value, g_A^*.[7] In this example, it rotates down

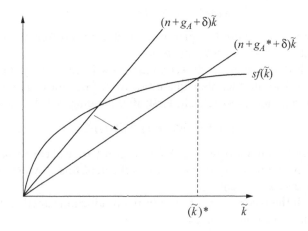

Figure 4.1. Dynamics of $\tilde{k}$

---

[7] In the case when g_A is constant at all times, the break-even line does, of course, not rotate.

right, because g_A is assumed to be declining during the transition. As g_A comes close to g_A^*, the curve almost stays put and $\tilde{k}$ finally approaches the steady state value, which is implicitly given by $sf(\tilde{k}^*) = (n + g_A^* + \delta)\tilde{k}^*$.

The long-run implications of this model show considerable, but not full, similarities with the neo-classical model. To see this, we now define $\tilde{y} = Y/(AL_Y)$. The production function $\tilde{y} = f(\tilde{k})$ can then be rewritten as $Y = AL_Y f(\tilde{k}) = A(1 - s_A)L f(\tilde{k})$. As $\tilde{k}$ reaches the constant $\tilde{k}^*$, Y will grow at the same rate as AL_Y. Perhaps more interestingly, the per capita income (obtained upon division by L) in steady state is given by $y = A(1 - s_A)f(\tilde{k}^*)$. Since s_A is constant, y grows at the rate g_A on the balanced growth path. A novelty, compared to the neo-classical model in Chapter 3, is that the growth rate of A here can be determined by decisions within the model (namely by the choice of s_A), at least for one version of (4.3). It is therefore important to examine the endogenous growth in A more closely, which we will do next.

4.3 **Four cases**

As mentioned above, the long-run growth rate of A can change greatly if the assumptions about the parameter values in (4.3) are altered. The growth rate is also influenced by the assumption about n. It is therefore useful to distinguish between the four different cases presented below.

4.3.1 ENDOGENOUS GROWTH (ROMER)

The seminal paper by Romer (1990) initiated enormous research activity among growth economists. An indication of the importance of this paper is the fact that there has been written a popular book about this scientific breakthrough and the economic profession's way to it (Warsh, 2006).

In the Romer case it is assumed that there is no population growth and that the research production function is exactly linear in A. Moreover, the duplication-in-research aspect is disregarded. This means that the choices of parameter values are $\lambda = \phi = 1$ and $n = 0$, so that equation (4.3) boils down to

$$g_A = \eta s_A L. \tag{4.6}$$

Because the right hand side is constant, the technology factor A grows at a constant exponential rate at all points of time. This expression has two important implications.

First, the growth rate depends on the choice of s_A, the share of (costly) labor that is allocated to research. Many economists find this property very appealing, because an economy in which much effort is taken to develop the technology now is rewarded in the form of a higher growth rate. Although it is not explicitly modeled here, the research intensity depends on the thriftiness of the inhabitants of the economy, and can also be influenced by economic policy, for example patent length, taxes, and research subsidies. In other words, the incentives to do research are very important for growth according to this version of the model.

A problematic feature of (4.6) is, however, that the growth rate is proportional to the size of the population. A larger economy would thus have a higher growth rate, if everything else were equal. This is obviously not consistent with empirical observations: in the real world we do not see that large countries (in terms of population) systematically grow faster than small ones.

To see another potential problem with this special case, note that (4.6) is equivalent to $\dot{A} = \eta s_A L A^1$, that is the exponent of A is exactly equal to unity. This means that the growth path "balances on a knife-edge": if the exponent were to fall the slightest below unity, the growth rate of A would decline monotonously toward zero (as will be seen in Section 4.3.3). Similarly, if the exponent of A were just slightly higher than unity, growth would be accelerating (meaning a steadily increasing growth rate in the long run), which of course is too good to be true.

Despite these flaws of this special case it is often considered as the default example in the modern growth literature. The main reason for this is probably the close connection between the growth rate and the research intensity (and the incentives driving this intensity). The Romer version will also be the basic case in this book. Other possibilities must be considered, however, and the next section presents an attempt to get around the two "anomalies" mentioned in the previous two paragraphs.

4.3.2 SEMI-ENDOGENOUS GROWTH (JONES)

In the semi-endogenous growth model, developed by Jones (1995), it is assumed that $\phi < 1$. This means that there are diminishing returns to the accumulable factor A in the knowledge production function, which is expressed by the fact that the term $A^{\phi-1}$ on the right hand side of (4.3) declines as A grows, creating a tendency of g_A to decline. This is, however, counteracted by a growth in the number of researchers, because we now have population growth.

In this case g_A varies during the transition phase, but it will approach a constant in the long run. To see this, we take logs of both sides of (4.3), which gives

$$\ln g_A(t) = \ln \eta + \lambda \ln s_A + \lambda \ln L(t) + (\phi - 1) \ln A(t),$$

where we now have $\lambda \leq 1$. Recalling that s_A is constant, differentiation of both sides of this equation with respect to time gives

$$\frac{1}{g_A} \cdot \dot{g}_A = \lambda \frac{1}{L} \cdot \dot{L} + (\phi - 1)\frac{1}{A} \cdot \dot{A} = \lambda n + (\phi - 1)g_A.$$

Multiplying through by g_A, we finally have an equation for the dynamics of the growth rate:

$$\dot{g}_A = \lambda n g_A + (\phi - 1)g_A^2. \tag{4.7}$$

This equation is illustrated in Figure 4.2. The curve starts at the origin, because the right hand side is equal to zero when the growth rate is zero. Since the first-order term is positive, while the quadratic term has a negative coefficient, the curve grows initially but eventually turns down and has a unique intersection with the horizontal axis at g_A^*. It is clear from the figure that, whatever the initial g_A is,[8] the dynamics of equation (4.7) implies a convergence to the steady state at g_A^*, where $\dot{g}_A/g_A = 0$ and thus $\lambda n + (\phi - 1)g_A = 0$. The long-run growth rate of A therefore is

$$g_A^* = \frac{\lambda}{1 - \phi}n, \tag{4.8}$$

which is constant, because the right hand side consists merely of constant exogenous parameters.

From this expression for the long-run growth rate we note several important implications. First, sustained technological progress requires population growth; if $n = 0$ then $g_A^* = 0$, because of diminishing returns to A in

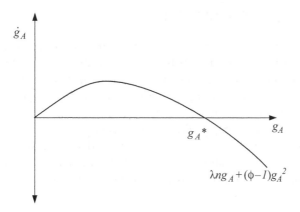

Figure 4.2. Semi-endogenous growth

[8] The initial g_A is $g_A(0) = \eta s_A^\lambda (L(0))^\lambda (A(0))^{\phi-1}$.

research.[9] Moreover, a faster population growth rate leads to a higher g_A^*. The explanation is that, with the population growing at a higher pace, the economy can afford to let the number of researchers grow faster, which leads to a higher rate of development of new ideas. Note also that (4.8) applies for a wide range of values of ϕ; the model provides long-run growth without requiring a specific exponent over A. The knife-edge property of the Romer model is thus not to be found here. Furthermore, the growth rate is not a function of L, so the semi-endogenous growth model does not have a scale effect that we encountered in the previous sub-section.

Equation (4.8) also reveals one less appealing implication of this model, namely that g_A^* is independent of s_A. This means that the long-run growth rate is not influenced by the research effort. The possibilities for promoting growth by stimulating research are therefore limited to the transitional period (and to the level). Many economists, who often think that incentives are important, find this implication a bit hard to accept.

Finally, there are some natural but interesting relations between the parameters and the growth rate. For instance, a larger ϕ leads to a higher growth rate in A. The insights from old research results are then more useful in the production of new innovations. In the special case when $\phi \to 1$ it is clear that $g_A \to \infty$. This unrealistic implication is of course too good to be true, and we therefore rule out the case when $\phi = 1$ and $n > 0$, and the accelerating growth that it implies. The growth rate of A is also positively related to λ. This follows because the aggregate output of the research sector is enhanced if there are fewer duplications of research results.

4.3.3 WEAK LIMITS TO GROWTH

The previous two cases have a considerable amount of optimism built into them, since they imply strictly positive long-run growth rates in the technology factor. We now turn to two less optimistic cases. In the first example, the growth of A is still unbounded, but the growth rate is less than exponential. In the next sub-section there is an upper bound on A.

For the first case, we simply take away the helping hand of the growing population from the semi-endogenous growth model, that is, we assume that $n = 0$ and maintain the assumption that $\phi < 1$. Since the issue about duplications of successful research is not important for the results here, we also put $\lambda = 1$. Equation (4.3) then becomes

$$\frac{\dot{A}}{A} = \eta s_A L (A(t))^{\phi-1}, \tag{4.9}$$

---

[9] This explains the name "semi-endogenous growth." The growth in A cannot be sustained without the help of the exogenous population growth.

where L is constant. As A increases, the right hand side falls, so the proportional growth rate of A declines and eventually approaches zero. The reason is that there are decreasing returns to existing knowledge. Thus, a weak potential for technological progress would here constitute a kind of *limit to growth*, since the long-run growth of per capita income tracks the growth of A (as was seen in Section 4.2).

To see more precisely how strong this limit to growth actually is, it is informative to examine how A develops over time. One can show that the solution to the differential equation in (4.9) is

$$A(t) = \left[A(0)^{1-\phi} + \eta s_A L (1 - \phi) t\right]^{\frac{1}{1-\phi}},$$

where $A(0)$ is the starting value of A at time $t = 0$. For confirmation, Exercise 4.1 shows that the derivative of this expression gives the differential equation in (4.9).

The implication of this solution is rather interesting, because the prospects of a society with the technology production function in (4.9) are not as bleak as one might guess. It is clear that the proportional growth rate declines to zero, but the absolute magnitude of A is nevertheless continuously growing, in fact tending to infinity.[10] There is thus not an absolute limit to economic growth; it is just that the proportional rate of growth is less than exponential.

4.3.4 ABSOLUTE LIMITS TO GROWTH

Finally, as an example of an *absolute limit to the growth* in A (and thereby to y), let us extend the Romer knowledge production function in (4.6) by a factor that declines as A grows:

$$\frac{\dot{A}}{A} = \eta s_A L \left(1 - \frac{A}{v}\right). \tag{4.10}$$

Recall that the factor in front of the parenthesis on the right hand side is constant. Equation (4.10) is a so-called logistic growth function. It is often used by natural scientists to describe simple biological growth processes.[11]

Since everything except A is constant on the right hand side of (4.10), the growth rate is high (and close to exponential) when A is small. As A increases,

---

[10] The absolute change in A is actually getting larger as time runs and A grows. This is seen from rewriting (4.9) to $\dot{A} = \eta s_A L A^{\phi}$.

[11] This special case could have been included in (4.3), such that

$$g_A(t) = \eta s_A^{\lambda} (L(t))^{\lambda} (A(t))^{\phi-1} \left(1 - \frac{A}{v}\right).$$

For the cases in Sections 4.3.1–4.3.3 we would then have to assume that $v \to \infty$.

its growth rate declines, because the value of the parenthesis falls. When time goes to infinity, A approaches the upper bound v, and its growth rate goes to zero. The interpretation of this case could be that research is bounded by a "pond" of potential ideas, which tends to be totally "fished out" when A approaches v. The total amount of potential ideas is thus v.

It is again helpful to look at the solution to the differential equation, describing the development of A over time. In this case the solution to equation (4.10) is

$$A(t) = \frac{v}{1 + \mu e^{-\eta s_A L t}},$$

which is shown in Exercise 4.2.[12] As time runs, the denominator declines and approaches 1. The limit value of A as time goes to infinity is therefore v. If this would be an accurate description of the possibilities for technological development, the economy would have to be content with a limited technological progress, settling at the level $A = v$ in the long run. This would in turn mean that the growth in per capita income ceases, given that the neo-classical assumptions hold. If v were very large, this would not be too bad, but nevertheless the idea that mankind comes to a point from where it cannot in any way improve its conditions contradicts many people's view of the world.

4.4 Directed technological change

Up to this point, our analysis has included just one technology factor. It has primarily been included to increase the productivity of labor. However, research efforts may have purposes other than to save on that particular production factor. It may, for instance, also be interesting to improve the productivity of the other production factor of the present model, capital. Moreover, in subsequent chapters we will, for example, find it important to consider the desirability of enhancing the technological efficiency in the use of energy or making production less polluting.

A framework for such *directed technological change* has recently been developed by growth economists, notably by Acemoglu (1998) and Acemoglu (2002). We introduce this concept in the present section, by adding a capital-augmenting technology factor in the production function. There will also be a separate research sector for that factor in which some share of the labor force spends its working time.

---

[12] The constant μ is determined by putting $t = 0$. This gives $A(0) = \frac{v}{1+\mu}$, which means that $\mu = \frac{v - A(0)}{A(0)}$.

We also address the question of which direction technological progress must take, to ensure a balanced growth path, and thereby motivate the choice to include only labor-augmenting technological progress, which was made above. This is first done heuristically, but Section 4.5 gives a rigorous proof of this assertion. This prepares us for analyses of what directions of technological change are necessary to ensure balanced growth paths in models with natural resources and pollution.

We denote the additional productivity factor by B and assume that it enters the production function in such a way that it increases the productivity of capital (or saves capital). The aggregate production function then is

$$Y(t) = F[B(t)K(t), A(t)L_Y(t)].$$

An alternative placement of the new technology factor could have been in front of the production function, but the choice made here will suit our present purposes best.[13]

Since labor can now be used in a third activity, namely to do research intended to enhance the technology factor B, the labor constraint is modified to

$$L = L_Y + L_A + L_B, \tag{4.11}$$

where $L_B = s_B L$ is the quantity of labor that is devoted to increase B and s_B is a constant. Assume also that the two kinds of research are based on the same type of technology, similar to (4.1), but that the parameters may differ between the two. For instance, we have η_A and η_B instead of η, and so on. The endogenous growth rates of the two technology factors are thus described by

$$g_A = \eta_A s_A^{\lambda_A} L^{\lambda_A} A^{\phi_A - 1} \quad \text{and} \quad g_B = \eta_B s_B^{\lambda_B} L^{\lambda_B} B^{\phi_B - 1}. \tag{4.12}$$

Both these growth functions include several possible special cases, in particular the Romer, Jones, and "weak-limits-to-growth" varieties.[14]

Due to the modification of the production function, the dynamics of the capital stock is changed to

$$\dot{K} = sF[BK, A(1 - s_A - s_B)L] - \delta K, \tag{4.13}$$

where $(1 - s_A - s_B)L = L_Y$. Equation (4.13) and the two in (4.12) together describe how K, A, and B grow, and the developments of Y and C are then implicitly given. The growth path is obviously determined by the choices of the allocation parameters s, s_A, and s_B. Before commenting on the growth path, however, we need to address the issue of the direction of technological change.

---

[13] There is a special taxonomy associated with various placements of the technology factor (if there is only one of them): labor-augmenting technological change is called Harrod neutral; if the technology factor is placed to be multiplicative with the production function, technological progress is Hicks neutral; finally, it is Solow neutral if there is a technology factor just in front of capital.

[14] To save some space, we leave out the "absolute-limits-to-growth" variety here, but it can easily be invoked whenever it seems useful.

The claim from Chapter 2, that a balanced growth path exists only if technological progress is labor-augmenting, means that B must be constant in the long run. We now argue that this result is likely, without strictly proving it. The proof is given in the next section.

As a first step, the production function is divided by BK. Using the assumption about constant returns to scale in capital and labor, the average product of capital can be written as

$$\frac{Y}{K} = BF[1, \kappa], \qquad \text{where} \qquad \kappa \equiv \frac{AL_Y}{BK}. \tag{4.14}$$

Substitution of this into (4.13), after it has been divided through by K, gives

$$g_K = sBF[1, \kappa] - \delta. \tag{4.15}$$

On a long-run growth path, where capital grows at a constant rate, the first term on the right hand side must be constant. This would hold if B and κ were constant, implying that technological change were purely labor-augmenting.[15] A natural *conjecture* is therefore that this is a requirement for the existence of a steady state.[16] It will be confirmed in the next section. This means that

$$g_B = 0 \quad \text{and} \quad g_A + n = g_K = g_Y,$$

which in turn implies that labor must be allocated such that $s_B = 0$ in the long run. Moreover, income per capita grows at the rate g_A, as in the basic Solow model.

To see that such a growth path is also a balanced growth path, we examine the income shares. According to Exercise 4.3, the share of capital is

$$\zeta_K = \frac{F[1, \kappa] - F_2[1, \kappa] \kappa}{F[1, \kappa]}$$

in this case. From this expression it is clear that a constant κ ensures a constant income share of capital. This should not be surprising, since we are back to a model that is very similar to the one in Chapter 3, with the exception that the growth of A here is endogenous.

The growth path implied by these findings is very similar to that described in Section 4.2, but we can now add some details, by using the research production functions of Section 4.3. We first note that the growth rate of A now is $g_A = \eta_A s_A L$ for the Romer case. As in the model with just one productivity factor, the growth rate is proportional to the share of labor allocated to labor-related research, so that an economy which is more willing to postpone consumption will have a higher growth rate. For the semi-endogenous case

---

[15] Another possibility seems to be that both B and κ change in such a way that the middle term is still constant. The proof in the next section rules out this case.

[16] The Cobb–Douglas production function is an exception, which is demonstrated in Chapter 5.

we apply the same logic as in Sub-section 4.3.2, and come to the conclusion that $g_A = \frac{\lambda_A}{1-\phi_A} n$ in the long run. As in the simpler model, the growth rate is determined by the knowledge production function in this case; it cannot be influenced by labor allocation in the long run.

The capital growth rate must in the steady state adapt to these growth rates, so that $g_A + n = g_K$. This means that the steady state growth rate of capital is $g_K^* = \eta_A s_A L$ in the first case, which implies that the long-run growth rate of capital in the Romer model is determined by the choice of s_A. In the second case $g_K^* = \frac{\lambda_A}{1-\phi_A} n + n = \frac{\lambda_A + 1 - \phi_A}{1-\phi_A} n$, which means that it is entirely ruled by the magnitudes of exogenous parameters.

The solution for g_K^* can in turn be substituted back into (4.15), to pin down the steady state output–capital ratio:

$$g_K^* + \delta = s\left(\frac{Y}{K}\right)^*.$$

With the left hand side determined, the output–capital ratio can be influenced by the saving rate. Not surprisingly, a higher s implies more capital per unit of output. Finally, as the solution for $(Y/K)^*$ is substituted into (4.14), a value for κ^* is implicitly obtained as

$$\frac{g_K^* + \delta}{sB} = F[1, \kappa^*].$$

To be more specific about the value of κ^*, more information is needed about the function F.

The introduction of directed technological change does not seem to add much in this case. However, the apparatus presented here is going to be indispensable in later chapters, where richer production functions are used.

4.5 Steady state direction (optional)

In this section a proof is provided for the assertion that a balanced growth path exists only if technological progress is labor-augmenting.[17] We start from the general production function

$$Y(t) = \tilde{F}\left[K(t), L(t), \tilde{\mathbf{A}}(t)\right], \tag{4.16}$$

where $\tilde{\mathbf{A}}(t)$ represents the technology at time t, and $L = e^{nt}$ as before. The reason that $\tilde{\mathbf{A}}(t)$ is written in bold face is that it may be a *vector*, that is it may consist of more than one technology factor. The function in (4.16) exhibits constant returns to scale in K and L. By putting $\tilde{\mathbf{A}}(t)$ in a separate variable place,

---

[17] This proof builds on Schlicht (2006). The analysis is further developed in Acemoglu (2009).

we avoid imposing an assumption that technological progress is, for instance, labor- or capital-augmenting; the placement of the technology factor(s) will be a *result* of the analysis.

It is now useful to write consumption explicitly in the capital accumulation equation. Since $sY = I = Y - C$, (3.3) is modified to

$$\dot{K}(t) = Y(t) - C(t) - \delta K(t). \tag{4.17}$$

It will be helpful to rewrite this equation slightly, using the definition $g_K = \dot{K}(t)/K(t)$. The result is

$$(g_K(t) + \delta)K(t) = Y(t) - C(t). \tag{4.18}$$

It is assumed that investments are strictly positive at all points of time, that is $Y(t) - C(t) > 0$ for $t \in [0, \infty)$. This is of course totally reasonable, because there are always some investments in all (functioning) economies.

The analysis builds on the presumption that there exists an asymptotic growth path (i.e. a growth path as $t \to \infty$) where output, capital, and consumption grow at constant rates, that is $\dot{Y}(t)/Y(t) = g_Y$, $\dot{K}(t)/K(t) = g_K$ and $\dot{C}(t)/C(t) = g_C$ are all constant. More formally, as $t \to \infty$, there is some point of time, $\tau < \infty$, from which output, capital, and consumption grow at constant rates. This means that

$$Y(t) = Y(\tau)e^{g_Y(t-\tau)}, \quad K(t) = K(\tau)e^{g_K(t-\tau)}, \quad \text{and} \quad C(t) = C(\tau)e^{g_C(t-\tau)} \tag{4.19}$$

for $t \geq \tau$. We can also write $L(t) = L(\tau)e^{n(t-\tau)}$ and $L_Y(t) = L_Y(\tau)e^{n(t-\tau)}$.[18]

To prove that technological progress must be labor-augmenting along this asymptotic growth path, we now proceed in two steps.

4.5.1 STEP 1

The first step is to prove that Y, K, and C all grow at the same rate along the asymptotic growth path, that is that $g_Y = g_K = g_C$. We start by using the exponential expressions in (4.19) to replace $Y(t)$, $K(t)$, and $C(t)$ in (4.18):

$$(g_K + \delta)K(\tau)e^{g_K(t-\tau)} = Y(\tau)e^{g_Y(t-\tau)} - C(\tau)e^{g_C(t-\tau)},$$

for all $t \geq \tau$. After division of both sides by $e^{g_K(t-\tau)}$, this equation becomes

$$(g_K + \delta)K(\tau) = Y(\tau)e^{(g_Y-g_K)(t-\tau)} - C(\tau)e^{(g_C-g_K)(t-\tau)}.$$

Note that the left hand side is a constant, because $K(\tau)$ is the capital stock at a specific point of time. Differentiating both sides with respect to t gives the equality

---

[18] To see that this is true, note that $L(\tau) = e^{n\tau}$. Thus $L(t) = e^{n\tau}e^{n(t-\tau)} = e^{nt}$. Of course, we also have $L_Y(t) = (1 - s_A)L(\tau)e^{n(t-\tau)}$.

$$0 = (g_Y - g_K)Y(\tau)e^{(g_Y-g_K)(t-\tau)} - (g_C - g_K)C(\tau)e^{(g_C-g_K)(t-\tau)},$$

which can be rewritten as

$$(g_Y - g_K)Y(\tau)e^{(g_Y-g_K)(t-\tau)} = (g_C - g_K)C(\tau)e^{(g_C-g_K)(t-\tau)}.$$

There are two possibilities that this equation can hold.[19] One is that $g_Y = g_K = g_C$, which makes both sides equal to zero. The other possibility is that $g_Y = g_C$ and $Y(\tau) = C(\tau)$. The latter equality would, however, contradict the assumption that $Y(\tau) - C(\tau) > 0$; there can be no investment at time τ if production and consumption are equal at that date. We therefore rule out this second possibility, and conclude that our assumptions imply that

$$g_Y = g_K = g_C, \tag{4.20}$$

that is all three growth rates must be equal on the long-run growth path. The most important part, for our purposes here, is the necessity of an equal growth rate for Y and K. Note that this result is independent of the production function. We can therefore rely on it when we introduce natural resources in Chapters 5 and 6, using production functions that are different from (4.16).

4.5.2 STEP 2

We now examine the consequences of this equality in growth rates, when the properties of the production function are taken into account. The production function in (4.16) applies for all points of time, including $t = \tau$. We are thus allowed to write

$$Y(\tau) = \tilde{F}\big[K(\tau), L_Y(\tau), \tilde{A}(\tau)\big]. \tag{4.21}$$

The next step is to replace variables dated at τ by alternative expressions. Therefore, note that the exponential expressions for Y, and K in (4.19), can be rewritten as

$$Y(\tau) = Y(t)e^{-g_Y(t-\tau)} \quad \text{and} \quad K(\tau) = K(t)e^{-g_K(t-\tau)}.$$

Likewise, $L_Y(\tau) = L_Y(t)e^{-n(t-\tau)}$. These expressions are substituted into (4.21) and the result is

$$Y(t)e^{-g_Y(t-\tau)} = \tilde{F}\Big[K(t)e^{-g_K(t-\tau)}, L_Y(t)e^{-n(t-\tau)}, \tilde{A}(\tau)\Big].$$

To simplify this equation, we divide both sides by $e^{-g_Y(t-\tau)}$, and use the assumptions that the production function is CRS in the first two arguments. This renders

---

[19] There are actually two more, but uninteresting, possibilities: $g_Y = g_K$ and $C(\tau) = 0$; or $g_C = g_K$ and $Y(\tau) = 0$.

$$Y(t) = \tilde{F}\Big[K(t)e^{(g_Y-g_K)(t-\tau)}, L_Y(t)e^{(g_Y-n)(t-\tau)}, \tilde{A}(\tau)\Big].$$

In the first variable place of the function we can use the finding that $g_Y = g_K$, from the first step of the proof, so that

$$Y(t) = \tilde{F}\Big[K(t), L_Y(t)e^{(g_Y-n)(t-\tau)}, \tilde{A}(\tau)\Big].$$

In this version of the production function, most variables are dated at time t. The exception is $\tilde{A}(\tau)$, but this is a constant, so it can be embedded in the function. The production function can thus be represented by

$$Y(t) = F[K(t), A(t)L_Y(t)],$$

where

$$\frac{\dot{A}}{A} = g_A = g_Y - n.$$

This proves that technological progress must be labor-augmenting on the asymptotic growth path (or at least it should be possible to represent it in this way).

4.6 Conclusion

We saw in Chapter 3 that technological progress is important for long-run growth, even if natural resources and pollution are not taken into account. When the latter aspects are included, technological change is even more important. This is good to know, but it is even better if we can account for the growth of the technology factors. Therefore this chapter presents models in which technological progress requires that the economy gives up some of the use of labor in ordinary production and diverts it to research.

It was emphasized that the long-run growth rates of the technology factors are sensitive to small changes in some of the parameters of the functions that determine the growth paths of these factors. The model is thus often a small step from a poor growth outcome, which would mean great difficulties in maintaining a constant percentage increase of per capita income. The reader is advised to keep this in mind, even though we choose the Romer case as default.

Technological change has many dimensions. Thus, research decisions can be made with the intention to save on labor, capital, or energy, or to reduce emissions. We have demonstrated how this can be modeled by a multiple of technology factors, which serve at different places of the model, and which may grow at different rates. The reader should be aware that the modeling of this gets quite complicated if (intertemporal) optimization is added.

■ **FURTHER READING**

The properties of technology and their implications for research are discussed in Romer (1990), Jones (2002), and Jones (2005), in particular with respect to non-rivalry and excludability. Romer (2012) (Chapter 3) gives a good overview of the structures of various growth models. Chapter 12 in Acemoglu (2009) provides an accessible discussion about how to model technological change. Endogenous growth theory was the topic of a symposium that was published in the *Journal of Economic Perspectives* 1994. See for instance the articles by Romer (1994), Grossman and Helpman (1994), and Solow (1994). An important paper is also Aghion and Howitt (1992), which formalizes the schumpeterian idea of creative destruction. However, since this article is quite difficult to read, the reader is recommended to look into Aghion and Howitt (2009) instead.

4.7 **Exercises**

4.1 Growth in A 1
Show that

$$A(t) = \left[A(0)^{1-\phi} + \delta s_A L(1-\phi)t\right]^{\frac{1}{1-\phi}} \quad \text{implies} \quad \frac{\dot{A}}{A} = \delta s_A L (A(t))^{\phi-1}$$

when L is constant.

4.2 Growth in A 2
Show that

$$A(t) = \frac{v}{1 + \mu e^{-\delta s_A Lt}} \quad \text{implies} \quad \frac{\dot{A}}{A} = \delta s_A L\left(1 - \frac{A}{v}\right).$$

4.3 Income share
Given the production function $Y(t) = F[B(t)K(t), A(t)L_Y(t)]$, show that the income share of capital is

$$\zeta_K = \frac{(F[1,\kappa] - F_2[1,\kappa]\kappa)}{F[1,\kappa]}.$$

4.4 Directed technological change with a CES production function
Consider the special case when the production function of this model takes the CES form

$$Y = \left(\alpha(BK)^\varepsilon + (1-\alpha)(A(1 - s_A - s_B)L)^\varepsilon\right)^{1/\varepsilon}$$

and the equations in (4.12) still apply. Follow the same steps as in Section 4.4 to make it likely that s_B must equal zero in the long run.

Part II
Natural Resources

5 Land

The previous three chapters presented some basic tools of modern economic growth theory. We now start using these tools to study the possibilities of sustained growth (which is equivalent to sustainable development in all of Part II) when the use of limited natural resources in production is taken into account. The relation between growth and pollution is the topic of Part III.

In this chapter we introduce the natural resource land, T, as a production factor. It is used together with capital and labor to produce the aggregate output.[1] The amount of land is here assumed to be constant over time. In reality there is some loss of land, due to erosion, when for instance some soil is flushed away by heavy rain. While this tends to reduce T, there is (and has historically been) a tendency in the other direction, in the form of conversion of idle land to productive land. A constant T may thus be a reasonable compromise, at least for the parts of the world where soil erosion is not a serious problem, and where there are insignificant opportunities for the breaking of new land today.[2]

We maintain the assumption that the production function exhibits constant returns to scale in all inputs. Since there are now three of them, there will be *decreasing* returns to scale in the two growing production factors, capital and labor. This makes it more difficult to sustain growth in per capita income. The constancy of the service *flow* of land is thus *the* potential obstacle to sustainable development in this chapter.[3]

Not surprisingly, however, we will see that sustainability is feasible if there is sufficient technological progress, and in the right direction. We use the logic from Chapter 4 and examine what relations are required between the growth rates of two technology factors to sustain long-run growth in the case of a general production function. It turns out that there is a rather tough requirement on the growth rate of the productivity factor of land: it must equal the growth rate of the productivity factor of labor, plus the population growth rate. Nevertheless this is fully feasible (at least in the Romer type of model) and just calls for a particularly strong effort to increase the productivity of land.

[1] While the classical economists regarded land as an important production factor, it has rarely appeared in modern growth theories. This is probably in part due to the rapid decline in the employment share of the agricultural sector. An interesting exception is Meade (1961), which in a way stands between the two eras. A modern exception is the literature on the take-off of industrialization, surveyed by Galor (2005), where the productivity of the agricultural sector may have had a major role. There is also a literature on two-sector growth models, of which one is the agricultural sector.

[2] "At the global level, soil loss and degradation are not likely to represent a serious constraint on agricultural production over the next half-century" (Ruttan, 2002, p. 171).

[3] In Chapter 5, an initially given *stock* of the natural resource will imply a declining service flow from the resource. This will make it even more difficult to sustain economic growth.

A case with a CES production function is used to show that long-run growth in per capita income may still be feasible, even if land-augmenting technological progress is falling short of the requirement that arises from the analysis of the general case. This result is obtainable if there are good possibilities to substitute the services of capital and labor for land in the aggregate production function. A consequence will be, however, that the income share of land vanishes in the long run, which is not observed in the data.

If the production technology is represented by a Cobb–Douglas function, the long-run growth rate of per capita income can be neatly expressed in terms of a race between technological progress and a drag on growth. The latter is due to the population growth and the scarcity of land that it generates. The direction of technological change is not important here. Actually, one technology factor is enough, since it can be split into several parts and distributed to all production factors.

We also briefly examine a model in which the population growth is variable and even "endogenous" (along with a simplifying assumption that there is no capital accumulation). This gives an opportunity to analyze the growth in per capita income outside the steady state and touch on Malthusian themes about the two-way interaction between population and income growth, with the importance of land at the center of the analysis.

5.1 The production factor land

Modern man may tend to forget it, but land is absolutely essential for our existence. We are totally dependent on the food that grows in the soil and rely quite a lot on the basic fibers that it delivers for clothing. Land is also necessary to grow timber, which can be used to build shelter (houses) and infrastructure (bridges). Finally, the service of soil is essential for the production of biomass that can be used as a source of energy (for instance, ethanol from sugar cane or corn).

This production factor cannot, however, be taken for granted. There are numerous historical examples of rapid and serious soil erosion, due to intensive use, that have made civilizations collapse. Some of the most famous were on Easter Island and on Greenland, which has been described vividly by Diamond (2005). It has also been suggested that a major reason for the fall of the Roman Empire was extensive tree cutting and the soil erosion that followed it (see e.g. Bradford, 2006).

History has, however, also produced vast and proud examples of the expansion of productive land, upon which civilizations have been built and maintained. This has taken place by clearing vegetation, moving stones aside, and drainage to lead water away. In Europe the breaking of new land often went in a northern direction; in North America the movement went westward.

The breaking of new land has its limits, however. For one thing, there comes a point where the marginal land is not productive enough to motivate the costs of taking it into use (at least for the time being). Moreover, global warming issues make it questionable to cut down trees because this reduces the carbon sinks. A much discussed case is the conversion of rain forests in the Amazon, for the purpose of growing soy beans to feed cattle, and so on.

In some parts of the world, land erosion is not a big issue, for instance in parts of continental Europe, Scandinavia, and North America. The increasingly popular practice of reducing to plowing in agriculture also helps the soil to stay where it is. This, and the balance between the two opposing forces mentioned above, will be our support for the assumption that the quantity of land is constant throughout this chapter. In Chapter 6, the use of natural resource declines over time.

5.2 **The general model**

5.2.1 DIRECTION OF TECHNOLOGICAL CHANGE

With T representing a constant amount of land, a qualified guess about what is a suitable representation of the aggregate production technology would be

$$Y(t) = F[K(t), A(t)L_Y(t), B(t)T]. \tag{5.1}$$

We immediately add the assumption that there are constant returns to scale in K, L_Y, and T together, and therefore decreasing returns to scale in K and L_Y jointly. Based on the findings in Chapter 4, we include no capital-augmenting technology factor in this function; technological progress is solely labor and land saving (with the land-augmenting technology factor denoted by B). Appendix 5.9.1 shows that this is a requirement for the existence of a balanced growth path. It also demonstrates what the relations between the different growth rates must be on such a path.

Here we will obtain the same results heuristically. Remember from Chapter 4 that a central feature of a balanced growth path is that capital and output grow at the same rate. To use this result, we first divide (5.1) by K, using the CRS property, and get

$$\frac{Y}{K} = F\left[1, \frac{AL_Y}{K}, \frac{BT}{K}\right]. \tag{5.2}$$

Since the left hand side is constant, so must the right hand side also be. It is natural to assume that this is accomplished by having constant expressions in all variable places. This would mean that AL_Y/K and BT/K do not change, so that the implied relations between the growth rates are

$$g_A + n = g_K \quad \text{and} \quad g_B = g_K,$$

respectively. In the latter equation, we use the assumption that $g_T = 0$. It thus appears (and is proved in the appendix) that technological progress must be labor- and land-augmenting in the steady state, whereas there can be no growing capital-augmenting factor.

Since $g_Y = g_K$ on the balanced growth path, the two previous equations imply that a necessary relation between the growth rates is

$$g_Y = g_K = n + g_A = g_B. \tag{5.3}$$

We first note that $g_Y = n + g_A$, which implies that $g_y = g_A$, that is per capita income grows at the same rate as A. Although this is similar to the result in the basic model, there is an important difference in that the necessity to keep B growing here tends to reduce g_A. We return to this below.

From the last equality in (5.3) we have the central result that the growth of the productivity factor of land must be faster than the growth of the productivity factor of labor, by a magnitude equal to the population growth rate. If the population grows at a high rate, this means that B must grow much faster than A.

One might think that this is too strong a requirement to meet in the long run, but it should be noted that the technological progress in agriculture has been impressive during the twentieth century, as has been described in, for instance, Ruttan (2002) and Mundlak (2005). Actually, Mundlak (2005) notes that the average productivity of labor has been increasing faster in the agricultural sector than in the rest of the economy for a large number of countries.

However, Ruttan is rather pessimistic about the possibilities of future technological progress in the agricultural sector, because diminishing returns seem to be arising in most branches of agricultural research, according to his view.[4] Moreover, Mundlak (2005) provides another observation that seems to violate the final equality in (5.3). It comes from a detailed examination of the technological progress in the agricultural sector in the United States in a multisectoral analysis (as opposed to the aggregate approach that we follow in this book). The result is that the technology factor that can be associated to land has quite a poor record, as opposed to the labor technology factor. It is not evident, however, which of these facts are the most relevant for our model. The last result is found on a disaggregated level, whereas our approach is placed at the aggregate level. The findings reported in the previous paragraph may therefore apply better. If so, this would allow for the possibility that (5.3) can hold, in particular if we account for the fact that population growth rates are falling in many countries.

---

[4] However, he notes that he started his career arguing (correctly as it turned out) that some of his older colleagues were too pessimistic. He does not seem to totally exclude the possibility that the same pattern could repeat itself.

5.2.2 IMPLICATIONS

What are the theoretical possibilities to fulfill the final equality in (5.3)? We maintain the view that the rate and direction of technological progress is best regarded as endogenous and depending on economic decisions, as described in Chapter 4. Thus, the labor force could be allocated such that equation (5.3) holds exactly, at least if there is endogenous technological change à la Romer.[5] To see this, consider equations (4.12) with the Romer-type assumption that $\lambda_A = \phi_A = \lambda_B = \phi_B = 1$. This gives

$$g_A = \eta_A s_A L \quad \text{and} \quad g_B = \eta_B s_B L.$$

Recall also that we need to have $n = 0$ in the Romer version of the endogenous growth model, to avoid accelerating growth. The requirement in (5.3) therefore translates to $\eta_A s_A L = \eta_B s_B L$. This implies that the following relation must hold between the labor allocation variables:

$$s_B = \frac{\eta_A}{\eta_B} s_A. \tag{5.4}$$

For many choices of s_A it is clearly possible to find a value of s_B that keeps the growth in balance.

We thus find that the introduction of land does not force economic growth to cease, as long as efforts are taken to make A and B grow at the required rates. Recalling the labor constraint $L = L_Y + L_A + L_B$, however, the allocation of some labor to enhance B means that L_Y and L_A have to be lower than if there were no land in the production function. Thus, both the level of growth and the growth rate g_A will be lower because of the introduction of land in the model. As an example, suppose that the share of labor in ordinary production has been decided, so that the remaining share for research is s_R. This means that $s_B = s_R - s_A$. Substituting this into equation (5.4) gives

$$s_R - s_A = \frac{\eta_A}{\eta_B} s_A \quad \Leftrightarrow \quad s_A = \frac{\eta_B}{\eta_A + \eta_B} s_R.$$

A low productivity in agricultural research (η_B) reduces the labor that can be allotted to raise A, and thereby implies an impediment to growth in per capita income. The conclusion is that the necessity of land in production certainly does put a limit to economic growth, but it does not stop growth (at least not in the Romer version of the model).

In a semi-endogenous (Jones) growth model the situation is more problematic, because the growth rates of the technology factors are then in the long run entirely determined by the parameters of the technology production functions. It is therefore very unlikely that the last equality in (5.3) can be fulfilled.

---

[5] In more elaborate models, with intertemporal optimization, such an outcome can also be a natural equilibrium solution. See for example Acemoglu (2003).

To see this, we follow the procedure in Section 4.3.2, to analyze the transitional dynamics of both equations in (4.12). We then find that $g_A = \frac{\lambda_A}{1-\phi_A}n$ and $g_B = \frac{\lambda_B}{1-\phi_B}n$ in the long run. The requirement that $n + g_A = g_B$ then translates into

$$\frac{\lambda_A + 1 - \phi_A}{1 - \phi_A} = \frac{\lambda_B}{1 - \phi_B}. \tag{5.5}$$

Since there is no decision variable in this equation, but instead only exogenously given parameters, there is of course no reason to assume that this equality should hold. A semi-endogenous growth model therefore seems very unlikely to deliver a balanced growth path when the natural resource is provided in a constant quantity.[6] In Chapter 6, we will see that this knot can be untied when the use of the natural resource changes over time, at a rate that is endogenous.

Let us finally consider the less optimistic cases with weak or absolute limits to growth in the technology factors. Recall from Section 4.3 that the long-run growth rate(s) of the technology factor(s) then tend to zero. Assume also that the population growth rate declines to zero in the long run. This is not an unlikely scenario according to UN forecasts. We summarize this as $n = g_A = g_B = 0$. Then (5.3) can be used to infer that Y, K, and y are all constant in steady state.[7] The presence of a natural resource like land does not therefore preclude a constant per capita income if population is constant. In this case, the tendency to increased scarcity of land is not in effect, simply because the labor force does not grow. In conclusion, even in the absence of technological change, a stationary state is feasible in this model, as in the original Solow model. Of course, the size of the land resource has an important effect on the per capita income.

We have established the relations that must hold between the various growth rates in the long run, and developed some implications of this. It is now necessary to examine whether the dynamics of the model is such that it eventually reaches the steady state.

5.3 Transitional dynamics

Since the production function is now expanded to three production factors, it is not suitable to examine whether the model is likely to reach a steady state by transforming the variables into per (effective) capita form. Instead, the method in Section 3.7 is useful. From there, we restate equations (3.16) and (3.17) for convenience:

---

[6] We examine some consequences of this in Section 5.4.
[7] In the production function (5.1), all variables are constant.

$$\frac{\dot{z}}{z} = \frac{\dot{K}}{K} - \frac{\dot{Y}}{Y} \qquad (5.6)$$

$$\frac{\dot{K}}{K} = s\frac{1}{z} - \delta. \qquad (5.7)$$

Recall that the latter was obtained by dividing the capital accumulation expression (3.3) by K, and that the former is the time derivative of the capital–output ratio $z = K/Y$. Equation (5.7) can be used directly to eliminate $\dot{K}/K$ from (5.6). There remains to obtain an alternative expression for $\dot{Y}/Y$. This is done in Appendix 5.9.2 and the result is[8]

$$\frac{\dot{Y}}{Y} = \zeta_K \left(s\frac{1}{z} - \delta \right) + \zeta_L(n + g_A) + \zeta_T g_B, \qquad (5.8)$$

where we have used equation (5.7) to eliminate the growth rate of capital in the first right hand side term. Following the earlier notation, the income share (or output elasticity) of land is represented by ζ_T.

Our aim is to obtain a differential equation in z. We therefore substitute (5.8) and (5.7) into (5.6), which gives

$$\frac{\dot{z}}{z} = s\frac{1}{z} - \delta - \zeta_K \left(s\frac{1}{z} - \delta \right) - \zeta_L(n + g_A) - \zeta_T g_B.$$

After multiplying both sides of this equation by z and collecting terms, it becomes

$$\dot{z} = (1 - \zeta_K)s - z\left[(1 - \zeta_K)\delta + \zeta_L(n + g_A) + \zeta_T g_B \right]. \qquad (5.9)$$

The change in z is thus determined by a difference between two terms, one of which is proportional to z. This is similar to the differential equation for z in (3.20), but here we have one more term on the right hand side because of the inclusion of land in the production function.

In Figure 5.1 the two expressions of the right hand side of equation (5.9) are represented by two straight lines. If the lines stay put, the capital–output ratio will surely converge to the steady state value, wherever it starts from. Whenever z is smaller (larger) than z^*, z will increase (decrease) and thus approach z^*. This will, of course, happen if the production function is of the Cobb–Douglas form, because the income shares are constant in that case.

But since the income shares cannot generally be assumed to be constant, the lines are likely to move as z and other variables change. On the other hand, there is nothing indicating that the typical case is that the lines move so much that the model never reaches z^*. On the contrary, the income shares

---

[8] It should be noted that this analysis accounts only for the shares of income in the production of ordinary output. Since a part of labor is used in research, some labor income accrues there as well. This is not accounted for here. The reader is referred to the graduate textbooks for a full analysis of payments in the research sector.

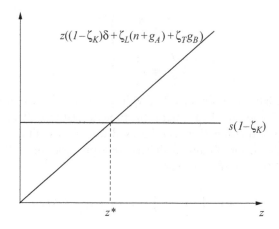

Figure 5.1. Transitional dynamics

may contribute to the stability, through the fact that they are constant along the the long-run growth path, as you will show in Exercise 5.1. It is therefore not unlikely that the income shares are almost constant in the neighborhood of the steady state. The lines should therefore be quite still, allowing z to fairly safely reach z^*. An analysis of the steady state should therefore be interesting enough.

Stability is actually ensured if it is reasonable to assume that $n + g_A = g_B$ also outside the steady state. This assumption implies that (5.9) becomes

$$\dot{z} = (1 - \zeta_K)s - z\left[(1 - \zeta_K)\delta + (\zeta_L + \zeta_T)(n + g_A)\right].$$

We simplify this by using the implication of constant returns to scale that the income shares sum to one. This means that we can use $1 - \zeta_K = \zeta_L + \zeta_T$ in the previous equation and get

$$\dot{z} = (\zeta_L + \zeta_T)\left(s - z\left[\delta + n + g_A\right]\right).$$

Irrespective of the developments of ζ_L and ζ_T, the final parenthesis on the right hand side will always approach zero. For example, if $s > z\left[\delta + n + g_A\right]$, then $\dot{z} > 0$ and the difference between s and $z\left[\delta + n + g_A\right]$ decreases and eventually vanishes. This means that $\dot{z}$ approaches zero and z reaches its steady state value.

The long-run value of z is obtained by putting $\dot{z} = 0$, so that $0 = (\zeta_L + \zeta_T)\left(s - z\left[\delta + n + g_A\right]\right)$. This gives

$$z^* = \frac{s}{\delta + n + g_A}. \tag{5.10}$$

As in Chapter 3, this value is independent of the production function.[9] The only difference from there is that the growth rate of A is now endogenous.

---

[9] This is quite natural if we look at equation (5.7): when the steady state growth rate of capital is determined to be $n + g_A$ this equation immediately gives (5.10). There is no need to know what the production function is, because equation (5.7) only uses the variable $z = K/Y$.

Finally, using (5.2) and the steady state capital–output ratio found in (5.10) we have

$$\frac{\delta + n + g_A}{s} = F\left(1, \frac{AL_Y}{K}, \frac{BT}{K}\right). \tag{5.11}$$

Suppose that choices are taken about saving and the allocation of labor. This means that the left hand side is a given constant. Moreover the time paths of A, B, and L_Y are pinned down. Consequently, the only unknown variable in this equation is K. With more information about the production function, the steady state path of this variable could be determined in principle, although the expression may be complicated.

5.4 The CES case

Further details about the long-run growth path can be displayed if we are more specific about the production function. This section therefore assumes that it has a CES form, which will be particularly useful for an analysis of growth paths that are not of the balanced type that we have discussed so far.

It has been found that it is useful to first formulate the production function as if it had just two inputs, say F and BT. Thus

$$Y = \left(\beta F^\varrho + (1 - \beta)(BT)^\varrho\right)^{1/\varrho},$$

where it is assumed that $-\infty < \varrho \le 1$. Following the same procedure as in Chapter 2, it is readily found that the elasticity of substitution between F and T is $1/(1 - \varrho)$.

A production function should arguably include labor and capital, and therefore the input F is the familiar function $F = (\alpha K^\varepsilon + (1 - \alpha)(AL_Y)^\varepsilon)^{1/\varepsilon}$, where the assumption that $-\infty < \varepsilon \le 1$ is maintained. If this expression is substituted for F in the function above, the complete production function becomes

$$Y = \left(\beta \left(\alpha K^\varepsilon + (1 - \alpha)(AL_Y)^\varepsilon\right)^{\varrho/\varepsilon} + (1 - \beta)(BT)^\varrho\right)^{1/\varrho}. \tag{5.12}$$

This means that $1/(1 - \varrho)$ can be interpreted as the elasticity of substitution between land on the one hand and the input service provided jointly by capital and labor on the other. One reason for this formulation, which in a way "separates" land from the other two factors, is that it becomes very challenging to analyze the elasticity of substitution if there are more than two inputs (see, for instance, Solow (1967)). Here we avoid such complications, by using a two-level production function, with no more than two inputs at each level.[10]

---

[10] See also Meade (1961) for more on this.

The output–capital ratio will be important for the analysis below. We therefore divide (5.12) by K, to obtain it for this special case:[11]

$$\frac{Y}{K} = \left(\beta \left(\alpha + (1-\alpha) \left(\frac{AL_Y}{K} \right)^{\varepsilon} \right)^{\varrho/\varepsilon} + (1-\beta) \left(\frac{BT}{K} \right)^{\varrho} \right)^{1/\varrho}. \tag{5.13}$$

As in the general case, a long-run growth path with a constant capital–output ratio is feasible if the ratios AL_Y/K and BT/K are constant.

The income shares of the three production factors are computed in Exercise 5.2. They are:

$$\zeta_K = \frac{\beta \left(\alpha + (1-\alpha)(AL_Y/K)^{\varepsilon} \right)^{\varrho/\varepsilon}}{\beta \left(\alpha + (1-\alpha)(AL_Y/K)^{\varepsilon} \right)^{\varrho/\varepsilon} + (1-\beta)(BT/K)^{\varrho}} \cdot$$

$$\cdot \frac{\alpha}{\alpha + (1-\alpha)(AL_Y/K)^{\varepsilon}},$$

$$\zeta_L = \frac{\beta \left(\alpha + (1-\alpha)(AL_Y/K)^{\varepsilon} \right)^{\varrho/\varepsilon}}{\beta \left(\alpha + (1-\alpha)(AL_Y/K)^{\varepsilon} \right)^{\varrho/\varepsilon} + (1-\beta)(BT/K)^{\varrho}} \cdot$$

$$\cdot \frac{(1-\alpha)(AL_Y/K)^{\varepsilon}}{\alpha + (1-\alpha)(AL_Y/K)^{\varepsilon}}$$

and

$$\zeta_T = \frac{(1-\beta)\varrho(BT/K)^{\varrho}}{\beta \left(\alpha + (1-\alpha)(AL_Y/K)^{\varepsilon} \right)^{\varrho/\varepsilon} + (1-\beta)(BT/K)^{\varrho}}.$$

Not surprisingly, it immediately follows that they are all constant in a steady state where AL_Y/K and BT/K are constant.

As mentioned in the introduction to this section, the CES function is suitable for examinations of non-balanced growth paths. In particular, this function makes it convenient to show the importance of the substitution possibilities for the properties of such a path. Thus, we now consider the case in which the technological change related to the use of land cannot match the requirement in the last equality in (5.3), that is, we assume that $g_B < g_A + n$. A direct consequence of this assumption is that BT/K approaches zero as capital grows. The question now is whether it nevertheless is possible that Y/K converges to a positive constant in the long run, with both K and Y growing at the rate $g_A + n$. The answer depends very much on the sign of ϱ.

---

[11] We first get

$$\frac{Y}{K} = \frac{1}{K} \left(\beta \left(\alpha K^{\varepsilon} + (1-\alpha)(AL_Y)^{\varepsilon} \right)^{\varrho/\varepsilon} + (1-\beta)(BT)^{\varrho} \right)^{1/\varrho}.$$

Noting that $1/K = \left(K^{-\varrho} \right)^{1/\varrho}$ and that $K^{-\varrho} = \left(K^{-\varepsilon} \right)^{\varrho/\varepsilon}$, this can be modified to (5.13).

We examine first the implications of assuming that $\varrho > 0$. The output–capital ratio in (5.13) approaches the positive constant

$$\frac{Y}{K} = \left(\beta \left(\alpha + (1 - \alpha) \left(\frac{AL_Y}{K} \right)^\varepsilon \right)^{\varrho/\varepsilon} + (1 - \beta) \cdot 0 \right)^{1/\varrho}$$

$$= \beta^{1/\varrho} \left(\alpha + (1 - \alpha) \left(\frac{AL_Y}{K} \right)^\varepsilon \right)^{1/\varepsilon}$$

in the long run. Because of the high elasticity of substitution between land on the one hand, and capital and labor on the other, it is possible to maintain a long-run growth of output (equal to $n + g_A$), in spite of the lack of sufficient land-related innovations to match the labor-augmenting technological progress. This result can also be understood by the fact that land is not essential in production when $\varrho > 0$. In fact, production is in the long run mostly carried by capital and labor.

However, this scenario implies that the income shares approach quite implausible values in the long run. This is immediately seen if we evaluate the income shares above for $BT/K = 0$:

$$\zeta_T = 0, \qquad \zeta_L = \frac{(1 - \alpha)(AL_Y/K)^\varepsilon}{\alpha + (1 - \alpha)(AL_Y/K)^\varepsilon}$$

and

$$\zeta_K = \frac{\alpha}{\alpha + (1 - \alpha)(AL_Y/K)^\varepsilon}.$$

In this case the model thus implies that the share of income going to land vanishes, leaving all to the remaining two factors (the shares of which are constant in the long run). The model-based explanation for this scenario is that land can be replaced quite easily, and its productivity does not increase over time. However, this pattern for the income shares is not seen in reality. To be sure, the income shares to land have been declining for a long time, but they do not seem to go all the way to zero.

The opposite case is when $\varrho < 0$, which means that the productive services of land cannot easily be substituted by capital and labor. It is then useful to rewrite the production function by pulling BT out of the parenthesis:

$$Y = \left(\beta \left(\alpha \left(\frac{K}{BT} \right)^\varepsilon + (1 - \alpha) \left(\frac{AL_Y}{BT} \right)^\varepsilon \right)^{\varrho/\varepsilon} + (1 - \beta) \right)^{1/\varrho} BT.$$

Since $\varrho < 0$, we have that

$$Y \to (1 - \beta)^{1/\varrho} BT$$

as $K/(BT) \to \infty$ and $AL_Y/(BT) \to \infty$. Total income is thus essentially bounded by B, the technology factor of land. In the long run, per capita income therefore is proportional to B/L. If $g_B > n$, then y can keep growing. A low degree of substitutability between land and the combined service of capital and labor, combined with some limit to growth in B, will thus not necessarily impose a strict limit to growth in per capita income. On the other hand, if there are serious limitations to enhance the productivity of land, that is $g_B < n$, per capita income is bound to fall.

We finally note that the income share of land tends to unity in this case. As in the previous case, this is an implausible implication. Both these examples are therefore questionable, but they provide elements of what could happen if we leave the balanced growth paradigm.

5.5 A Cobb–Douglas case

To get an even more detailed (albeit more special) description of a balanced growth path when land is a production factor, we finally turn to an example where the production technology is represented by a Cobb–Douglas function. It then takes the form

$$Y = K^\alpha T^\beta (AL_Y)^{1-\alpha-\beta}. \tag{5.14}$$

The sum of the exponents over K and L is $\alpha + 1 - \alpha - \beta = 1 - \beta < 1$, which illustrates that this function exhibits decreasing returns to the variable factors capital and labor together. Recall also that the Cobb–Douglas function means that the elasticity of substitution is unity. This means that we are now analyzing the limiting case between the good and bad substitution possibilities that were encountered in the previous section.

At first glance, technological progress seems to be directed toward labor only in (5.14). But upon closer examination it becomes clear that A is "neutral" between the inputs, because it can be arbitrarily divided into several factors, each of which can be moved in front of a particular production factor. For example, if we make the factorization $A = A_1 \cdot A_2 \cdot A_3$, the production function can be written as follows:

$$Y = K^\alpha T^\beta (A_1 \cdot A_2 \cdot A_3 \cdot L_Y)^{1-\alpha-\beta} = A_1^{1-\alpha-\beta} K^\alpha A_2^{1-\alpha-\beta} T^\beta (A_3 \cdot L_Y)^{1-\alpha-\beta}.$$

Putting production and productivity factors together, we get

$$Y = \left(A_1^{\frac{1-\alpha-\beta}{\alpha}} K \right)^\alpha \left(A_2^{\frac{1-\alpha-\beta}{\beta}} T \right)^\beta (A_3 L_Y)^{1-\alpha-\beta}$$

$$\equiv (A_K K)^\alpha (A_T T)^\beta (A_L L_Y)^{1-\alpha-\beta},$$

where the definitions of A_K and so on should be obvious. There is thus no need for technological progress to be explicitly directed toward land. In addition, we can allow for capital-augmenting technological progress, without ruling out a balanced growth path (as will be clear below). These are typical properties of the Cobb–Douglas production function.

The analysis of the dynamics in Section 5.3 still applies. In particular the differential equation (5.9) is valid (with $g_B = 0$), and since the income shares are now constant (with $\zeta_K = \alpha$, $\zeta_T = \beta$ and $\zeta_L = 1 - \alpha - \beta$) the curves in Figure 5.1 stay put during the transition. We can therefore be absolutely sure that the model is stable, converging to the unique constant z^*, so that output and capital grow at the same rate in the long run. We will now use this stability property to derive an expression for the long-run growth rate of income per capita.

First, the production function is used to compute the proportional growth rate of total output. Taking the logarithm of equation (5.14) gives

$$\ln Y(t) = \alpha \ln K(t) + \beta \ln T +$$

$$+ (1 - \alpha - \beta) \ln A(t) + (1 - \alpha - \beta) \ln L_Y(t).$$

Noting that T is the only production factor that is not a function of time, differentiation of both sides with respect to time renders the following relation between the growth rates:

$$\frac{\dot{Y}}{Y} = \alpha \frac{\dot{K}}{K} + (1 - \alpha - \beta)g_A + (1 - \alpha - \beta)n. \tag{5.15}$$

This equation applies in steady state as well as on the way to it. Focusing from here on the former, we can use the conclusion that $\dot{K}/K = \dot{Y}/Y$ in the long run to eliminate $\dot{K}/K$ from equation (5.15), and get

$$\frac{\dot{Y}}{Y} - \alpha \frac{\dot{Y}}{Y} = (1 - \alpha - \beta)(g_A + n).$$

After division of both sides by $1 - \alpha$, the growth rate of total output can be written as

$$\frac{\dot{Y}}{Y} = \frac{1 - \alpha - \beta}{1 - \alpha}(g_A + n). \tag{5.16}$$

In contrast to the original Solow model, the growth rate is now somewhat lower than the sum of the growth rates of labor and the productivity factor. Only if $\beta = 0$, so that land is inessential and the diminishing returns to capital and labor are suspended, will the growth rate be as high as $g_A + n$.

The final step, which will enable us to see whether this economy can sustain growth in per capita income, consists of transforming (5.16) into an equation in y. Recall that the definition of per capita income, $y = Y/L$, implies that $\dot{y}/y = \dot{Y}/Y - n$. We use this in (5.16):

$$\frac{\dot{y}}{y} = \frac{1 - \alpha - \beta}{1 - \alpha}(g_A + n) - n.$$

By multiplying the final term by $(1 - \alpha)/(1 - \alpha)$ and collecting the n terms, we have

$$\frac{\dot{y}}{y} = \frac{1}{1 - \alpha}\left[(1 - \alpha - \beta)g_A + (1 - \alpha - \beta - 1 + \alpha)n\right].$$

The final term can be simplified. This gives us the important expression for the growth rate of per capita income

$$\frac{\dot{y}}{y} \equiv g_y = \frac{1}{1 - \alpha}\left[(1 - \alpha - \beta)g_A - \beta n\right]. \tag{5.17}$$

In this equation, the damper that a natural resource imposes on economic growth is very obvious. The bracket describes a "race" between two opposing forces. The positive part comes from technological progress, which of course promotes growth. The negative term is due to the diminishing returns to scale, caused by the fact that the quantity of land is fixed.

The underlying conflict basically arises because the population growth makes land increasingly scarce, continuously pushing down the area available per individual. The faster the population grows, the larger is the "drag" on growth. This effect is more prominent the higher β is, because land then is more important in production; β is the output elasticity of land. The higher β also makes the decreasing returns to K and L more severe.[12]

Albeit extremely pessimistic, the case when there is no technological progress at all is illuminating. If $g_A = 0$, then per capita income declines at the rate

$$g_y = -\frac{\beta n}{1 - \alpha} < 0. \tag{5.18}$$

This means that y approaches 0 asymptotically. The population pressure on the fixed resource leads to an ever-declining marginal product of labor, an effect which capital accumulation cannot (fully) offset. This is an example of what Nordhaus (1992) calls a "Lethal condition." It could perhaps also be called an "extreme Malthusian case," but it should be emphasized that Malthus had an endogenous population development in mind, with population growth declining as per capita income fell. We return briefly to this in Section 5.6.

This negative tendency in (5.17) is counteracted by technological progress, the "spur" to growth. If this occurs at a sufficient speed, growth in per capita income turns positive. It happens if

$$(1 - \alpha - \beta)g_A > \beta n, \tag{5.19}$$

so that the technology effect wins the race against the drag. This is thus the condition for sustained growth in per capita income in the present context.

[12] On the other hand, if $\beta = 0$ then $g_y = g_A$, as in the basic Solow model.

Note that g_A is weighted by the output elasticity of A; it is not only the growth rate of A that matters, but also the effect that it has on output.

For an alternative interpretation of (5.19), write $A = e^{g_A \cdot t}$ and reformulate the production function (5.14) so that the productivity factor seems to augment the input land:

$$Y = K^\alpha T^\beta e^{(1-\alpha-\beta)g_A t} L_Y^{1-\alpha-\beta} = K^\alpha (T e^{(1-\alpha-\beta)g_A t/\beta})^\beta L_Y^{1-\alpha-\beta}.$$

The condition in (5.19) can thus be understood to mean that the productivity factor associated with land must grow faster than the population $((1 - \alpha - \beta) g_A/\beta > n)$. This would suspend the tendency of (effective) land to become scarce as population grows.

From Chapter 4 we know that the long-run rate of growth of productivity rises if more of the economy's scarce labor is allocated for this purpose, for the default (Romer) version of the model. If the incentives for entrepreneurs in the research sector are good enough, it is fully possible to fulfill the condition in (5.19), and thus have sustained growth.

5.6 **Variable population growth**

It has often been pointed out that exponential population growth forever is impossible. Mother Earth has some maximum carrying capacity, and although it may be pushed further away by the ingenuity of mankind, there may be some limit to how far it can be advanced, for space reasons if no other. The actual population growth may not seem to take these limitations into account, but according to some UN forecasts world population will stabilize around the middle of the twenty-first century (and in many industrialized countries the population growth is already close to zero). In this section we therefore allow population growth to vary over time and possibly go to zero asymptotically, and then analyze how this influences income growth.

Another interesting issue is why the world population started to increase considerably about 200 years ago. We will examine one possible explanation for this take-off, by looking at a model in which the population is endogenous and proportional to per capita income in Section 5.6.2, thus exploring some Malthusian ideas.

This analysis will mainly concern the dynamics outside the steady state, which in general tends to be complicated. It is therefore convenient to assume that there is no capital in the model (and we still obtain some interesting insights). We thus assume that $\alpha = 0$ in (5.14), so that it simplifies to $Y = T^\beta (AL_Y)^{1-\beta}$, and furthermore assume that the amount of land can be normalized to $T = 1$. The production function of this section is thus

$$Y = (AL_Y)^{1-\beta}. \tag{5.20}$$

Note that the property of diminishing returns to labor remains in the function, since $\beta > 0$.

By familiar differentiation with respect to time we have $g_Y = (1 - \beta) (g_A + g_L)$, where g_L is used instead of n since population growth can vary. In this setting $y = Y/L$ implies that $g_y = g_Y - g_L$, so

$$g_y = (1 - \beta)g_A - \beta g_L. \tag{5.21}$$

This equation corresponds to (5.17), with the difference that $\alpha = 0$, g_A and g_L may be non-constant, and that they both may be endogenous. Just like in (5.17) there is a race between the output effect of technological progress and a drag on growth. As before, a higher β makes the growth rate lower; the more important land is in production, the larger is the drag on growth. In the absence of capital accumulation, all output is consumed, so the growth rate of per capita income is also the growth rate of per capita consumption.

5.6.1 EXOGENOUS POPULATION GROWTH

In this section L remains exogenous, but now it follows a logistic path, that is the population size at time t is

$$L(t) = \frac{\bar{L}}{1 + \chi e^{-nt}},$$

where χ, n, and $\bar{L}$ are positive constants. As time runs, the nominator goes to unity and the population size approaches its upper level, $\bar{L}$. It is left as an exercise for the reader to show that the time derivative of this expression is

$$g_L = \frac{\dot{L}}{L} = n\left(1 - \frac{L}{\bar{L}}\right).$$

The population growth rate is high (and almost exponential) at low levels of population, but declines as L grows. Concerning A, we assume here for simplicity that it grows exponentially at the constant rate g_A.

One might conjecture that the initially rapid population growth presses per capita income down during the early phase of the economic development, but that this will be followed by an era of increasing per capita income as g_L declines. To examine this possibility more closely, we substitute the expression for g_L above into equation (5.21). The growth rate of per capita income (and consumption) then is

$$g_y = (1 - \beta)g_A - \beta n\left(1 - \frac{L}{\bar{L}}\right).$$

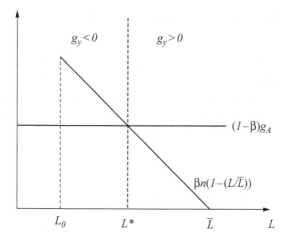

Figure 5.2. Population dynamics

In Figure 5.2, the two right hand side terms of this equation are represented by two curves.

The first term is a constant, and is thus represented by a horizontal line. The final term is monotonously declining in L, falling towards 0 as $L \to \bar{L}$. Its starting point depends on the initial population level, L_0. If L_0 is sufficiently low,[13] the curves intersect once (and only once), at a point where $g_y = 0$ and the population size is

$$L^* = \bar{L} \frac{\beta n - (1 - \beta)g_A}{\beta n}.$$

When the population level is below L^*, per capita income is declining. As L rises above L^*, y starts growing. Even if technological progress is unable to provide growth in per capita income during an early period, population growth eventually comes down enough to bring the economy away from the regime of declining y. By curbing population growth and going into the second phase of the demographic transition, the economy can go from a stagnation regime to a growth regime where the drag on growth ultimately vanishes. The stagnant phase could be shortened if the economy were able to provide better incentives to make innovations, so that g_A rises. Alternatively, a slowdown in g_L (perhaps captured by a lower n) could be induced by public intervention in the form of education and provision of contraceptives.

---

[13] It is required that $(1 - \beta)g_A < \beta n \left(1 - \frac{L_0}{\bar{L}}\right)$, which implies that $L_0 < \frac{\bar{L}(\beta n - (1-\beta)g_A)}{\beta n}$.

5.6.2 ENDOGENOUS POPULATION GROWTH

We now introduce a Malthusian element in the model, by allowing the population size to depend on income. The higher the income is, the larger the population that can be maintained. More precisely, we follow Kremer (1993) and simply assume that the population is always (instantly) adjusted to a level such that an income exactly equal to the subsistence level $\bar{y}$ can be delivered to each citizen. This means that the population size is

$$L = Y \cdot \frac{1}{\bar{y}}. \tag{5.22}$$

From the production function (5.20) we can now eliminate Y and get $\bar{y}L = (A(1 - s_A)L)^{1-\beta}$. Because A is endogenous, we have used the assumption that $L_Y = (1 - s_A)L$. We solve the previous equation for the population size as a function of the technology level:

$$L = \frac{1}{\bar{y}}A^{1-\beta}(1 - s_A)^{1-\beta}L^{1-\beta} \quad \Leftrightarrow \quad L^\beta = \frac{(1 - s_A)^{1-\beta}}{\bar{y}} \cdot A^{1-\beta}.$$

Thus

$$L = \left(\frac{(1 - s_A)^{1-\beta}}{\bar{y}}\right)^{\frac{1}{\beta}} \cdot A^{\frac{1-\beta}{\beta}} \equiv \xi_1 A^{\frac{1-\beta}{\beta}}. \tag{5.23}$$

Naturally, the population size is higher the more developed the technology is, the larger the fraction of the population that is used in production, and the lower the subsistence level of income is. Note also that the population size is more responsive to growth in A if β is low. That is, if the importance of land in production is small, technological progress can easily induce the population to grow. This will in turn feed back on the growth of A, because it makes more researchers available.

We assume that technological change is ruled by (4.1), with $\lambda = 1$ for simplicity. It can therefore be formulated as

$$g_A = \eta s_A L A^{\phi-1}.$$

At this point, we just assume that $\phi \leq 1$. Using equation (5.23) to eliminate L, we get

$$g_A = \eta s_A \xi_1 A^{\frac{1-\beta}{\beta}} A^{\phi-1}.$$

Before going further, we note that the final factor on the right hand side (with a non-positive exponent) tends to reduce the growth rate of A, whereas the first A factor (with a positive exponent) tends to make the growth in A accelerate. Simplifying now the previous equality, by collecting the A terms, we have

$$g_A = \eta s_A \xi_1 A^{\frac{1-\beta(2-\phi)}{\beta}}. \tag{5.24}$$

The development of the technology factor depends a good deal on the sign of the exponent, because this decides whether the A term on the right hand side of (5.24) grows or falls as A increases. This in turn determines whether the growth rate of A (the left hand side) accelerates or decelerates.

We note that the exponent,

$$\frac{1 - \beta(2 - \phi)}{\beta},$$

is high if ϕ is high or β is low. A high ϕ, of course, means that the conditions for research are good, because previous discoveries are very useful in the development of new innovations. In the special case when $\phi = 1$, the exponent clearly is positive. Thus, in contrast to the Romer model, we here have accelerating growth, which is due to the fact that population is growing. That, on the other hand is driven by the growth of A, as described by (5.23), because it makes income higher. There is thus a two-way interaction between these two variables.

The reason that a high β will hold back the acceleration in A, or even revert it to deceleration, is that it reinforces the decreasing returns to labor (and A) and thereby impedes the growth of total income. This lowers population growth, which has a negative effect on innovation.

The condition for accelerating growth (i.e. a positive exponent on the right hand side of (5.24)) is $\beta(2 - \phi) < 1$. If $\phi = 1$, it is sufficient that $\beta < 1$, which is clearly plausible. Even if ϕ equals a modest $1/2$, growth accelerates if $\beta < 2/3$, which is where the realistic income share of land is found in most places of the world. The model thus seems inclined to predict an accelerating growth in A.

The development of A is described more precisely by the solution to the differential equation in (5.24), which is[14]

$$A(t) = \left[A(0)^{\frac{\beta(2-\phi)-1}{\beta}} + \left(\frac{\beta(2 - \phi) - 1}{\beta} \right) \eta s_A \xi_1 \cdot t \right]^{\frac{\beta}{\beta(2-\phi)-1}}. \quad (5.25)$$

This can be confirmed along the same lines as in Chapter 4: differentiate (5.25) and check that the derivative can be rewritten as (5.24). In the previous discussion it was concluded that $\beta(2 - \phi) < 1$ is the more reasonable parameter constellation. If this inequality holds, the exponent and the coefficient of t are both negative in (5.25). The expression within brackets therefore approaches zero from above. Because of the negative exponent, the growth starts slowly and then accelerates. Actually, A goes to infinity in finite time.

This gives a rudimentary description of the "take-off" in population growth that took place around two centuries ago, and which is discussed thoroughly

[14] Once we have the solution for A, the values of Y and L are easily obtained by use of equations (5.22) and (5.23).

in Kremer (1993). The ever-increasing growth rate is, however, unrealistic. We therefore need an additional mechanism to create a declining growth in population as per capita income surpasses some level. The model would then describe the so-called demographic transition. However, we will not go deeper into this, but refer the interested reader to Kremer (1993) and Galor (2005) for more details.

5.7 **Conclusion**

In this chapter the natural resource is not depletable; a constant quantity remains year after year. Nevertheless, it imposes a drag on economic growth, by causing decreasing returns to scale in the growing production factors, capital and labor. However, if the conditions for research are sufficiently generous, sustained growth is clearly within reach, although the rate and level of growth are reduced compared to the benchmark case in Chapter 3. If the conditions for research are less generous, sustainability may still be feasible if there are good substitution possibilities in the production function. Remember, however, that the long-run income shares approach questionable values in this case.

Although we tend to take the service of land for granted, it is advisable to bear the risk of soil erosion in mind. Moreover, some land areas have become poisoned because of dumping or leaking of toxic substances. It is also important to be aware of the increasing competition among the uses of land. Food and fiber production is rivaled by energy production, both for the traditional use of wood, but also for the presently high production of biofuels such as ethanol from corn and sugar cane. Finally, forests are useful as sinks of CO_2, so leaving them standing is yet another rival for food an fiber production.[15]

▓ FURTHER READING

The book by Meade (1961) is an accessible exposition of a growth model that includes land as a production factor. The book by Mundlak (2000) is also useful, but the emphasis is less on economic growth (and more on trade) than the title suggests. Further guidance to this strand of literature is found in Irz and Roe (2005), although the analysis uses inter-temporal optimization techniques. See also Chapter 10 in Aghion and Howitt (2009) for more on the topic "From Malthus to Solow."

---

[15] It should also be emphasized that agricultural activities can be polluting. For instance, there are considerable run-offs of nitrogen into the Baltic sea. The channels in the Netherlands are also heavily loaded with agricultural wastes.

5.8 **Exercises**

5.1 Income shares
Show that the income shares are constant in the general case, if AL/K and BT/K are constant.

5.2 CES income shares
Show that the income shares in the CES case are those that are given in Section 5.4.

5.3 Increasing returns to scale
Consider a growth model with the following production function:

$$Y = K^\alpha T^\beta (AL_Y)^\mu.$$

Here we do not impose any assumptions about the magnitudes of the exponents; their sum may be smaller than, equal to, or larger than unity. As in the previous models the capital–output ratio is constant in the long run, so

$$\frac{Y}{K} = K^{\alpha-1} T^\beta (AL_Y)^\mu$$

is constant. Use this to derive expressions for the long-run growth rates of Y and y. Explain how increasing returns may be a "substitute" for technological progress.

5.9 **Appendix**

5.9.1 BALANCED DIRECTION

With T denoting a constant amount of land, and following the approach in Section 4.5, it is natural to start by expanding the aggregate production function to

$$Y = \tilde{F}(K, L_Y, T, \tilde{\mathbf{A}}). \tag{5.26}$$

The motivation for writing $\tilde{\mathbf{A}}$ in boldface is again that it allows for the possibility that it is a vector, that is it may consist of more than one technology factor. This production function exhibits constant returns to scale in K, L_Y, and T together.

To see what is required in terms of technological progress along a balanced growth path, we follow the same steps as in Section 4.5. The assumptions are thus that net investment is always strictly positive, and that there is a point of time, $\tau < \infty$, after which output, capital, and consumption grow at constant rates:

$$Y(t) = Y(\tau)e^{g_Y(t-\tau)}, \quad K(t) = K(\tau)e^{g_K(t-\tau)}, \quad \text{and} \quad C(t) = C(\tau)e^{g_C(t-\tau)}.$$

The first part of the proof, giving the conclusion in (4.20) that it is necessary to have equality in the growth rates, $g_Y = g_K = g_C$, applies here as well. This holds because the first step of the proof in Section 4.5 was independent of the properties of the production function.

The second part of the proof is also similar to that in Chapter 4, starting by writing the production function at time τ as

$$Y(\tau) = \tilde{F}\Big[K(\tau), L_Y(\tau), T, \tilde{A}(\tau)\Big].$$

We note once again that the exponential expressions above are equivalent to $Y(\tau) = Y(t)e^{-g_Y(t-\tau)}$ and $K(\tau) = K(t)e^{-g_K(t-\tau)}$, respectively. In addition, $L_Y(\tau) = L_Y(t)e^{-n(t-\tau)}$. The aggregate production function at time τ can therefore be written as

$$Y(t)e^{-g_Y(t-\tau)} = \tilde{F}\Big[K(t)e^{-g_K(t-\tau)}, L_Y(t)e^{-n(t-\tau)}, T, \tilde{A}(\tau)\Big].$$

Dividing both sides by $e^{-g_Y(t-\tau)}$, using the constant returns to scale property, and the finding that $g_Y = g_K$ from the first part of the proof, we have

$$Y(t) = \tilde{F}\Big[K(t), L_Y(t)e^{(g_Y-n)(t-\tau)}, e^{g_Y(t-\tau)}T, \tilde{A}(\tau)\Big].$$

Since $\tilde{A}(\tau)$ is constant, it can be subsumed under the production function. This function can therefore be written as

$$Y(t) = F[K(t), A(t)L_Y(t), B(t)T],$$

where

$$\frac{\dot{A}}{A} = g_A = g_Y - n \quad \text{and} \quad \frac{\dot{B}}{B} = g_B = g_Y.$$

This concludes the proof.

5.9.2 OUTPUT GROWTH

The logarithmic version of the production function in (5.1) is $\ln Y(t) = \ln[F(K(t), A(t)L_Y(t), B(t)T)]$. This has the time derivative

$$\frac{\dot{Y}}{Y} = \frac{F_1}{F} \cdot \dot{K} + \frac{F_2}{F} \cdot (A\dot{L_Y}) + \frac{F_3}{F} \cdot (B\dot{T}),$$

where, for example, F_2 is the partial derivative with respect to the second variable place, or the composite variable AL_Y.

We now multiply the first right hand side term by K/K, the second by $(AL_Y)/(AL_Y)$, and the third by $(BT)/(BT)$. Computing also the time derivatives of the products AL_Y and BT, we have

$$\frac{\dot{Y}}{Y} = \frac{F_1 K}{F} \cdot \frac{\dot{K}}{K} + \frac{F_2 A L_Y}{F} \cdot \left(\frac{\dot{A}}{A} + \frac{\dot{L}_Y}{L_Y}\right) + \frac{F_3 BT}{Y} \cdot \frac{\dot{B}}{B}.$$

Noting now that $F_K = F_1$, $F_{L_Y} = F_2 A$, and $F_T = F_3 B$, this equation is modified to[16]

$$\frac{\dot{Y}}{Y} = \frac{F_K K}{F} \cdot \frac{\dot{K}}{K} + \frac{F_{L_Y} L_Y}{F} \cdot \left(\frac{\dot{A}}{A} + \frac{\dot{L}_Y}{L_Y}\right) + \frac{F_T T}{Y} \cdot \frac{\dot{B}}{B}.$$

Using our definitions of factor income shares (or output elasticities), this equation can be simplified to

$$\frac{\dot{Y}}{Y} = \zeta_K \left(s\frac{1}{z} - \delta\right) + \zeta_L(n + g_A) + \zeta_T g_B,$$

where we have used equation (5.7) to eliminate the growth rate of capital in the first right hand side term.

---

[16] For example:

$$F_T = \frac{\partial F(K(t), A(t)L_Y(t), B(t)T)}{\partial(BT)} \cdot B = F_3 B,$$

where the first part of the middle expression is the outer derivative with respect to the function BT. The next part is the inner derivative: the derivative of the function BT with respect to T.

6 Exhaustible resources

In this chapter we analyze the feasibility of sustained growth when an *exhaustible* and *non-renewable* resource is used in production. The definition of such a resource is that the remaining stock declines at the rate of its use. The use is thus "destructive" (although recycling is sometimes possible), and there is no biological process that restores the resource. Typical examples of exhaustible resources are fossil fuels such as oil, coal, and natural gas. Another important category is minerals such as iron, copper, and aluminium.

To some extent, it is not correct to say that the remaining stocks of these resources decline at the same rate as they are used. For instance, the available quantity of oil has been increasing for long periods of time. This has been made possible by new discoveries and because discoveries that were previously considered too costly (or technically impossible) to extract, have now become available due to improved technologies.[1] Nevertheless, these resources are not infinite, which has become especially clear after the so-called Peak Oil debate, and once they are used they cannot be used again. For simplicity, we will therefore describe the resource as a finite quantity in this chapter (with the exception of Section 6.5), and for concreteness we will call it (non-renewable) "energy."

As in Chapter 5 we here ignore pollution. The main question is therefore again whether it is possible to maintain a non-declining per capita income when a natural resource is an important factor in production. The natural resource here causes diminishing returns to capital and labor, as the factor land did in Chapter 5, but in addition the use of the resource will *decline* over time. This, of course, puts another damper on economic growth.

Also in analogy with Chapter 5, we will here show that technological progress and substitution provide two important possibilities to suspend the limits to growth. The steps are similar to those in Chapter 5, but are modified in some important respects. In the general case, the new challenge is that the technological progress connected to energy must be stronger than the technological progress associated with land in Chapter 5, to compensate for the decline in the use of the resource. This necessitates further diversion of labor away from production and from labor-augmenting research.

---

[1] For instance, Darmstadter (1999) gives some interesting examples of technological improvements in oil extraction, notably horizontal (kinked) drilling, off-shore drilling, and computer intensive acoustic methods for screening the earth crust for oil deposits. See also Smil (2003).

The elasticity of substitution was at the center of the analysis when exhaustible resources were first introduced into economic growth models in the 1970s.[2] We therefore devote considerable attention to it here. If we assume poor possibilities for technological progress that augment energy, growth can still be sustained if it is easy to substitute manmade capital for the resource. An implication is, however, that the income share of energy will tend to zero in the long run, which is a phenomenon that we do not see in the data.

As in Chapter 5, the Cobb–Douglas case gives an illuminating description of per capita income growth as depending on a race between technological progress and dampers on growth. The latter are now stronger than in Chapter 5, because the economy will have to cope with less and less energy over time. We also look at an example where it is possible to sustain a constant consumption level forever even if there is no technological progress, in spite of the fact that energy is essential in a Cobb–Douglas production function. In such a growth process, the growth of the capital stock can exactly cover up for the decline in the use of energy, if the output elasticity is larger for capital than for energy. A (questionable) requirement is, however, that capital depreciation can be modeled as negligible.

An alternative possibility for achieving sustainable development, which has been given much attention in the recent public debate, is to (gradually) replace the exhaustible energy by renewable energy. We describe such a process in Section 6.5. The analysis shows how the speed of this transition depends on the evolution of the relative prices of the two types of energy, and on how easily they are substituted for each other. Technological change can here help in achieving sustainability, by lowering the cost of renewable energy. In this section the scarcity of non-renewable energy is less important than in the earlier parts of this chapter, since renewable energy is available in an infinite quantity. This weakens the drag on growth drastically. Instead, this section provides a link to the next part of the book, where we focus on pollution: in Section 8.4 we assume that the non-renewable energy (fossil fuels) in the model of Section 6.5 is polluting, and study the process of phasing it out.

This book assumes that all institutions that are essential for good economic performance work well. There is, however, a wealth of examples where this is not so, particularly in developing countries. Moreover, there has been much discussion on whether the combination of natural resources and bad institutions are responsible for resource "curses," which are manifested in low (or even negative) growth rates. We give a brief overview of this literature in Section 6.6.

---

[2] There was a famous special issue of the *Review of Economic Studies* in 1974, where classic articles such as those by Dasgupta and Heal (1974), Solow (1974) and Stiglitz (1974) were published.

6.1 **The energy constraint**

We now introduce the variable E for the exhaustible resource, which we will refer to as (fossil) energy. As for all variables in this book, it is useful to think about it as an aggregate, that is an index of all relevant resources that are exhaustible and non-renewable. The variable E represents the *flow* of energy, for example the quantity of the energy resource that is used during, say, one year. The corresponding stock variable is denoted by S and can be understood as the total remaining (extractable) quantity of the resource in the ground.

Since energy here is a non-renewable resource, the decline in the remaining stock equals the current use. Formally, this is described by

$$\dot{S} = -E.$$

At the starting point of time, $t = 0$, there is an initially given stock of energy, S_0. We will treat the time horizon as infinite, which makes

$$S_0 = \int_0^\infty E(t)dt \tag{6.1}$$

a natural constraint on the economy. This means that the sum of the uses of the resource over all points of time must equal the initially given stock.[3] The economy should, of course, not be forced to use all of the resource, so it would be more appropriate to say that the use is less than, or equal to, the initial stock. However, by the equality sign in (6.1) we impose an assumption that the use of the resource is always economically interesting.[4]

As for all productive inputs, energy should be chosen optimally by the firm (and supplied optimally by the owners of the resource). To avoid too many complications we will, however, use a result from more extensive analyses as a rule-of-thumb.[5] It typically turns out that the optimal use of energy declines at a constant exponential rate, at least in the long run. We therefore assume that the use of energy is

$$E(t) = E_0 e^{-s_E t} \tag{6.2}$$

---

[3] If there are some new discoveries, $D(t)$, as time runs, then the constraint is

$$S_0 + \int_0^\infty D(t)dt = \int_0^\infty E(t)dt,$$

with the obvious qualification that no part of the resource can be used before it is discovered.

[4] With the exception of Section 6.5, the cost of using E is zero, and energy always has a positive marginal product. It will therefore always be economically interesting to use it.

[5] This can be derived from the so-called Hotelling rule. See, for instance, Dixit (1976) for an exposition.

at any point of time, where E_0 is the use of energy at time 0 and s_E is a positive constant. This equation can be differentiated with respect to time, to get

$$\frac{\dot{E}}{E} = -s_E.$$

The assumption in (6.2) thus implies that the energy use declines at the constant rate s_E. As already mentioned, this will put an additional break on economic growth in the models of this chapter.

There is now an additional limitation that must be taken into account. At a given initial stock of the resource, the economy cannot afford to choose E_0 and s_E freely. This is quite obvious: an extremely high initial use, together with a very moderate decline in the use, could easily lead to a plan for a total use that is larger than the stock, meaning a violation of (6.1). To see what the limitation is, the use of energy in (6.2) can be substituted into (6.1) to derive a relation between the parameters of the model, which must hold lest the constraint is violated. The substitution gives

$$S_0 = \int_0^\infty E_0 e^{-s_E t} dt = E_0 \int_0^\infty e^{-s_E t} dt.$$

To solve this integral, we need the anti-derivative of $e^{-s_E t}$. It is quite easy to see that this would be $-(1/s_E)\, e^{-s_E t}$, because the former is the (time) derivative of the latter. Thus, we compute the integral and the equation becomes

$$S_0 = E_0 \left[\frac{-1}{s_E} e^{-s_E t} \right]_0^\infty = E_0 \left[\frac{-1}{s_E} e^{-s_E \cdot \infty} - \frac{-1}{s_E} e^{-s_E \cdot 0} \right] = \frac{E_0}{s_E}.$$

It is natural to consider S_0 as exogenously given by nature and history, whereas both E_0 and s_E are chosen by the actors of the economy. If, for instance, the value of s_E has been decided, this version of the constraint can be used to pin down the necessary initial use of energy as

$$E_0 = S_0 s_E.$$

This means that the initial use of energy can be higher if the initial stock is larger or if the use declines at a higher rate. We substitute this into (6.2):

$$E(t) = S_0 s_E e^{-s_E t}. \tag{6.3}$$

This is a description of how much energy can be used at different points of time, given that the "sum" of use is equal to the total supply that is initially given, as required by (6.1). Some possible time paths for $E(t)$ are depicted in Figure 6.1. Since $s_E' > s_E''$, E starts at a higher level but declines at a faster rate on the s_E'-path, compared to the time path where s_E'' applies. Equation (6.3) gives an expression for feasible uses of energy at all points of time, and thereby describes the energy input in the production functions below.

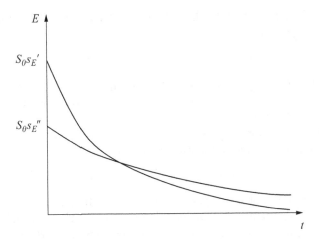

Figure 6.1. Time paths of energy use

6.2 **The general case**

6.2.1 DIRECTION OF TECHNOLOGICAL CHANGE

We now put the energy variable E into the aggregate production function and analyze the conditions for balanced growth. As demonstrated in Appendix 6.9.1, it must be possible to write the production function in the form

$$Y(t) = F[K(t), A(t)L_Y(t), B(t)E(t)]. \qquad (6.4)$$

Similarly to Chapter 5, this function is CRS in the three inputs K, L_Y, and E (so that there are DRS in K and L_Y). We here let B denote the the energy-augmenting technology factor. As before, no technology factor is allotted to capital.[6]

Balanced growth requires some special relations between the growth rates in this case too. To heuristically find what they are (relegating the proof to the appendix), it is again useful to divide the production function by K and use the CRS assumption. The result is

$$\frac{Y}{K} = F\left[1, \frac{AL_Y}{K}, \frac{BE}{K}\right]. \qquad (6.5)$$

We know from Chapter 4 that capital and output must grow at the same rate on a balanced growth path. Both sides of (6.5) must therefore be constant. Appendix 6.9.1 shows that this must be accomplished by the ratios AL_Y/K and

---

[6] The reason that we remove land here, as energy is added, is that it is useful to look at one complication at a time. Both factors are combined in Exercise 6.2.

BE/K both being constant. It follows that we must have the following relations between the growth rates:

$$g_A + n = g_K \quad \text{and} \quad g_B - s_E = g_K.$$

In analogy with Chapter 5, technological progress must here be labor- and energy-augmenting in the steady state, while no growing capital-augmenting factor can be allowed.

From the fact that $g_Y = g_K$ on the balanced growth path, it follows that the necessary relations between the various growth rates are

$$g_Y = g_K = n + g_A = g_B - s_E. \tag{6.6}$$

It should by now not be surprising that we find that $g_Y = n + g_A$, so that $g_y = g_A$, meaning that per capita income again grows at a rate equal to g_A. The following implication of the last equality in (6.6) is particularly interesting:

$$n + g_A + s_E = g_B. \tag{6.7}$$

Equation (6.7) reveals the important result that the growth rate of the productivity factor related to energy in steady state must equal the sum of three terms, namely the population growth rate, the rate of progress in labor productivity, and the rate of decline in energy use. This is a strong requirement on the rate of improvement in energy effectiveness; it clearly is stronger than the requirement on land productivity in Chapter 5 (cf. (5.3)), because E is declining whereas the amount of land was constant in the previous chapter. It could certainly be questioned whether this requirement can be permanently fulfilled.

6.2.2 IMPLICATIONS

What are the theoretical possibilities that equation (6.7) holds exactly? As long as the rates of growth of the technology factors depend on how much research of the two types is carried out, and if the conditions for technological progress are of the Romer type, it is fully possible to direct research efforts in such a way that (6.7) is actually fulfilled. To see this, we invoke the assumptions that define this special case, namely that $n = 0$ and that $\lambda_A = \phi_A = \lambda_B = \phi_B = 1$ in (4.12), so that

$$g_A = \eta_A s_A L \quad \text{and} \quad g_B = \eta_B s_B L.$$

Since the Romer model does not allow population growth, (6.7) reduces to $g_A + s_E = g_B$. Using the above expressions for the growth rates of the technology factors, the condition for balanced growth becomes

$$\eta_A s_A L + s_E = \eta_B s_B L.$$

This means that innovative entrepreneurs must choose a relation between s_A and s_B such that

$$s_B = \frac{\eta_A}{\eta_B} s_A + \frac{s_E}{\eta_B L}. \tag{6.8}$$

Given the values of the exogenous parameters, and of s_E, this equality points out a unique s_B, corresponding to any choice of s_A, which implies balanced growth. Naturally, more energy saving research is required if research to increase the productivity of labor is more extensive or if the productivity in energy-related research is low. In addition, more energy research is required if the use of energy declines faster (but a smaller *share* of labor in energy research is required if the population is larger).[7]

As noted after (6.6), per capita income grows at the same rate as the labor-augmenting technology factor, A, on the BGP. On the surface, this is reminiscent of the result in the Solow model, with its sustained per capita income growth. However, as in Chapter 5, it is important to note that productive labor here must be diverted from the production of consumption and investment goods and put into research activities, which of course lowers the level of growth. Moreover, the growth rate of A is constrained by the need to develop B. This effect is stronger here than in Chapter 5, because a higher growth rate of B (at given g_A) is necessary here. One can see this by comparing (6.8) and (5.4).

If we turn to the possibility that the conditions in the research sector are better described by the semi-endogenous model, we find that it is not unlikely that (6.7) can be fulfilled in this case as well. This implies a considerable difference between the present model and the corresponding case in Chapter 5, which is due to the extra degree of flexibility provided by the possibility of choosing s_E. We can see this by first recalling that $g_A = \frac{\lambda_A}{1-\phi_A} n$ and $g_B = \frac{\lambda_B}{1-\phi_B} n$ on the balanced growth path for this type of model. Substituting this into (6.7), we have

$$s_E = \left(\frac{\lambda_B}{1 - \phi_B} - \frac{\lambda_A + 1 - \phi_A}{1 - \phi_A} \right) n. \tag{6.9}$$

The corresponding equation in the previous chapter—(5.5)—contained only exogenous constants, and could therefore not be expected to hold in general. Here, however, s_E is endogenously chosen by the actors of the economy. If the parameters on the right hand side are such that the parenthesis is positive (implying that $g_B > n + g_A$) it is possible to choose a positive s_E that satisfies this equation.[8] To have $g_B > n + g_A$ it is necessary that λ_B and ϕ_B are large,

---

[7] On the other hand, a larger population leaves less energy to each person. This shifts the level of per capita income down at every point of time.

[8] The energy constraint (6.3) of course requires that the initial use of energy is adjusted so that $E_0 = S_0 s_E$.

compared to the corresponding parameters of the labor-saving research function, that is that there is a larger potential for the previous type of research than for the latter.[9]

In Chapter 5 we also looked at the possibility that $n = g_A = g_B = 0$. We then found a stationary state, without growth but also without decline in per capita income. We cannot have such a stationary state here, because E declines over time. This follows from an inspection of (6.5), with all variables but E constant. There will be more to say about this when we come to the explicit production functions in Sections 6.3 and 6.4 below.

Having examined the necessary relations between various growth rates in steady state, it is also relevant to ask whether the economy could be expected to find its way to it. This is the purpose of the next subsection.

6.2.3 TRANSITIONAL DYNAMICS

We now derive a differential equation in z along similar lines as in Section 5.3, to analyze the transitional dynamics of the present model. This analysis follows Section 5.3 very closely, and can therefore be made quite brief.

Appendix 6.9.2 shows that total output, when the production function is (6.4), grows at the rate

$$\frac{\dot{Y}}{Y} = \zeta_K \cdot \frac{\dot{K}}{K} + \zeta_L(n + g_A) + \zeta_E\left(g_B - s_E\right), \tag{6.10}$$

where ζ_E is the output elasticity (income share) of energy. We also reproduce the by now familiar expressions for the growth rates of z and K, respectively:

$$\frac{\dot{z}}{z} = \frac{\dot{K}}{K} - \frac{\dot{Y}}{Y} \quad \text{and} \quad \frac{\dot{K}}{K} = s\frac{1}{z} - \delta.$$

Combining these with (6.10) we get the differential equation in the capital–output ratio:

$$\frac{\dot{z}}{z} = s\frac{1}{z} - \delta - \zeta_K\left(s\frac{1}{z} - \delta\right) - \zeta_L(n + g_A) - \zeta_E\left(g_B - s_E\right).$$

We multiply both sides of this equation by z and collect terms. The result is

$$\dot{z} = (1 - \zeta_K)s - z\left[(1 - \zeta_K)\delta + \zeta_L(n + g_A) + \zeta_E\left(g_B - s_E\right)\right]. \tag{6.11}$$

Although there is a minus sign in the final term of the bracket, this term is positive, because $g_B > s_E$, by (6.7).

The dynamics of z implied by equation (6.11) is illustrated in Figure 6.2. It is clearly stable if the output elasticities are constant, as in the Cobb–Douglas

---

[9] If the conditions are such that $g_B \leq n + g_A$, there is no positive s_E that satisfies equation (6.9). A long-run balanced growth path with a declining use of energy is then not feasible.

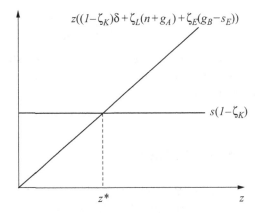

$$z((1-\zeta_K)\delta+\zeta_L(n+g_A)+\zeta_E(g_B-s_E))$$

$s(1-\zeta_K)$

z^*

z

Figure 6.2. Transitional dynamics

case, so that the curves stay where they are as z moves towards z^* (from above or from below). But, again, the lines should not be expected to remain still as the economy grows, since the output elasticities vary as the underlying variables are changing. Nevertheless, for similar reasons as in Chapter 5, it is not at all implausible that the economy converges to a steady state z, at which the income shares become constant. The analysis of the balanced growth path in the previous section is therefore interesting.

If there are reasons to assume that $n + g_A + s_E = g_B$ at all points of time (or after some early point of time), the model definitely is stable. To see this, we use this equality and $1 - \zeta_K = \zeta_L + \zeta_E$ (which holds because the output elasticities for a CRS function sum to unity) in (6.11). After some manipulations, we have

$$\dot{z} = (1 - \zeta_K)\left(s - z\left[\delta + n + g_A\right]\right). \tag{6.12}$$

The gap in the final parenthesis is always closing. Although the first parenthesis may vary during the transition, it cannot stop the entire expression from vanishing, and therefore $\dot{z}$ approaches zero.

The steady state capital–output ratio is given by putting $\dot{z} = 0$ in (6.12) and solving for[10]

$$z^* = \frac{s}{\delta + n + g_A}. \tag{6.13}$$

As before, there is no need for information about the production function to obtain this solution. Analogously to Chapter 5, we finally use (6.5) and (6.13) to get

---

[10] To get z^* we are allowed to use (6.12) in the general case too, because we assume that $n + g_A + s_E = g_B$ holds, at least in steady state.

$$\frac{\delta + n + g_A}{s} = F\left(1, \frac{AL_Y}{K}, \frac{BE}{K}\right). \tag{6.14}$$

This equation can (in principle) be used to determine the path of K, when the saving rate and the allocation of labor have been set, so that the development of A, B, and L_Y is determined.

6.3 Energy in the CES function

To get a more explicit example, which highlights the role of the elasticity of substitution, we now analyze the growth path when the production function is of the CES type. Perhaps more importantly, this also provides a convenient possibility of studying for growth paths that are non-balanced, that is not fulfilling (6.7) in the long run.

As in Chapter 5 we bundle capital and labor into a sub-production function, which here enters together with energy in the total production function. In the present context it reads:

$$Y = \left(\beta\left(\alpha K^\varepsilon + (1-\alpha)(AL_Y)^\varepsilon\right)^{\varrho/\varepsilon} + (1-\beta)(BE)^\varrho\right)^{1/\varrho}, \tag{6.15}$$

where it is assumed that $-\infty < \varepsilon \leq 1$ and $-\infty < \varrho \leq 1$. This implies that the elasticity of substitution between K and L is $1/(1-\varepsilon)$. The elasticity of substitution between the "service" provided by K and L together, on the one hand, and E on the other is $1/(1-\varrho)$.[11]

Let us first briefly investigate the growth path when the technology factors satisfy the balanced growth condition. In addition to being illuminating in its own right, this gives useful expressions for the analysis of non-balanced growth, which is the theme of Section 6.3.2.

6.3.1 BALANCED GROWTH

We start by computing the output–capital ratio for the CES case, by dividing the production function by K. This yields[12]

$$\frac{Y}{K} = \left(\beta\left(\alpha + (1-\alpha)\left(\frac{AL_Y}{K}\right)^\varepsilon\right)^{\varrho/\varepsilon} + (1-\beta)\left(\frac{BE}{K}\right)^\varrho\right)^{1/\varrho}. \tag{6.16}$$

---

[11] It is left as an exercise for the reader to show this.

[12] Two intermediate steps are

$$\frac{Y}{K} = \frac{1}{K}\left(\beta\left(\alpha K^\varepsilon + (1-\alpha)(AL_Y)^\varepsilon\right)^{\varrho/\varepsilon} + (1-\beta)(BE)^\varrho\right)^{1/\varrho}$$

This expression is clearly constant along a path on which the growth rates are related as in (6.6), that is when $g_K = n + g_A$ and $g_K = g_B - s_E$. A constant capital–output ratio is then clearly feasible (which should be expected, since this is a special case of the general growth model in Section 6.2).

We then turn to the income shares of the three production factors. In Exercise 6.1 the following expressions are derived:

$$\zeta_K = \frac{\beta\,(\alpha + (1-\alpha)(AL_Y/K)^\varepsilon)^{\varrho/\varepsilon}}{\beta\,(\alpha + (1-\alpha)(AL_Y/K)^\varepsilon)^{\varrho/\varepsilon} + (1-\beta)(BE/K)^\varrho} \cdot$$

$$\cdot \frac{\alpha}{\alpha + (1-\alpha)(AL_Y/K)^\varepsilon},$$

$$\zeta_L = \frac{\beta\,(\alpha + (1-\alpha)(AL_Y/K)^\varepsilon)^{\varrho/\varepsilon}}{\beta\,(\alpha + (1-\alpha)(AL_Y/K)^\varepsilon)^{\varrho/\varepsilon} + (1-\beta)(BE/K)^\varrho} \cdot$$

$$\cdot \frac{(1-\alpha)(AL_Y/K)^\varepsilon}{\alpha + (1-\alpha)(AL/K)^\varepsilon},$$

and

$$\zeta_E = \frac{(1-\beta)\varrho(BE/K)^\varrho}{\beta\,(\alpha + (1-\alpha)(AL_Y/K)^\varepsilon)^{\varrho/\varepsilon} + (1-\beta)(BE/K)^\varrho}.$$

They are all constant if $g_K = n + g_A$ and $g_K = g_B - s_E$. As expected, a CES-based economy can attain a balanced growth path.[13]

6.3.2 NON-BALANCED GROWTH

We saw in Chapter 5 how useful the CES function can be in exemplifying scenarios where the economy does not follow a balanced growth path. For an additional example of this, we now consider the possibility that the energy-augmenting technological progress stops short of fulfilling the condition for balanced growth in (6.7). We assume that this is because the Romer technology function (4.6) does not apply to the development of B (but possibly to A). Instead, the Jones or the weak or absolute limits-to-growth technology production functions in Sections 4.3.2–4.3.4 rule the development of B. Thus, the long-run growth rate of B is either limited to an upper-bound (Jones) or there is even a monotonous decline in this growth rate.

and

$$\frac{Y}{K} = \left(\beta\frac{1}{K^\varrho}\left(\alpha K^\varepsilon + (1-\alpha)(AL_Y)^\varepsilon\right)^{\varrho/\varepsilon} + (1-\beta)\frac{1}{K^\varrho}(BE)^\varrho\right)^{1/\varrho}.$$

---

[13] The constancy of ζ_K and of K/Y imply a constant marginal product of capital, which was mentioned in Chapter 2 as another condition for balanced growth.

Specifically, we assume that the growth rate of the energy-augmenting technology factor is so low that

$$0 \leq g_B < n + g_A + s_E. \tag{6.17}$$

To see whether it is possible that Y/K approaches a positive constant in the long run, in spite of the inequality in (6.17), we analyze the dynamics of z under this assumption. For this, it is useful to rewrite (6.11) as

$$\dot{z} = (1 - \zeta_K)s - z\left[(1 - \zeta_K)(\delta + n + g_A) - \zeta_E\left(s_E + n + g_A - g_B\right)\right], \tag{6.18}$$

where we have used the fact that constant returns to scale in production imply that $1 - \zeta_K - \zeta_E = \zeta_L$.

A non-balanced growth of the kind that we analyze here will (depending on ϱ) imply that we either have $\zeta_E \to 0$ or $\zeta_E \to 1$ in the long run. Some observations about these two cases follow here.

1. If $\zeta_E \to 0$, (6.18) goes to (6.12). Therefore z approaches the steady state value $z^* = s/(\delta + n + g_A)$ in the long run. The model is then stable.
2. If $\zeta_E \to 1$, and thus $\zeta_K \to 0$, the differential equation in (6.18) approaches

$$\dot{z} = s - z\left[\delta + g_B - s_E\right]$$

in the long run. There are now two possibilities. If $\delta + g_B > s_E$, the dynamics is stable, with $z^* = s/(\delta + g_B - s_E)$. If $\delta + g_B < s_E$, the model is unstable, with an ever-growing capital–output ratio. Since s_E can be chosen to be very low (implying a low initial use of energy), stability is always feasible. Therefore we can also analyze this case under the assumption about stability.

We will now examine what limits the relatively poor development of B put to growth. It should, of course, be expected that the results depend crucially on the sign of ϱ.

6.3.2.1 High elasticity of substitution

Let us first examine a case when $\varrho > 0$, that is the elasticity of substitution between energy and the composite capital–labor input is high. We posit a scenario where $g_B - s_E < n + g_A = g_K$. The limiting value of output per capita would then be

$$\frac{Y}{K} = \left(\beta\left(\alpha + (1 - \alpha)\left(\frac{AL_Y}{K}\right)^{\varepsilon}\right)^{\varrho/\varepsilon} + 0\right)^{1/\varrho} > 0. \tag{6.19}$$

Is this scenario consistent with a stable behavior of the capital–output ratio? To answer this question, we first note from Section 6.3.1 that $\zeta_E \to 0$ in the long run, under the conditions that $g_B - s_E < n + g_A = g_K$ and $\varrho > 0$. As noted after equation (6.18), the model therefore is stable. Since both sides of the equality in (6.19) are constant in the long run, both K and Y grow at the rate $n + g_A$. The per capita income growth rate consequently is g_A.[14]

The somewhat remarkable result that the economy can maintain a constant capital–output ratio, in spite of the poor development of effective energy, follows from the fact that energy is not essential under the assumption that $\varrho > 0$. On the contrary, it is fairly easy to replace it (and the weak technological progress associated with it) by the service provided by capital and labor (including the labor-augmenting technology factor). As mentioned above, however, this scenario comes with the empirically questionable implication that the income share of energy approaches zero in the long run. Moreover, as discussed in Dasgupta (1993), it is doubtful that capital can literally be a substitute for energy to the extent that energy is inessential in production.

Despite the implausible implication, we end this sub-section by putting the role of substitutability even more in focus. The reason is that this provides useful insights into central mechanisms of the basic resource-and-growth model, which were pointed out by several papers in the early days of the limits-to-growth debate.[15] These papers gave much attention to a special case with zero population growth and zero technological progress.[16] The motivation for the first assumption was that the population cannot grow exponentially for very long periods of time, for space reasons if no other reasons. And resource problems are indeed problems for long periods of time. Technological progress was taken away because it was interesting to examine the extent to which capital accumulation can cover up for the inevitable decline in E.

These assumptions are succinctly expressed as $g_A = n = 0$, which means that capital accumulation is the only driver of economic growth. We also assume that $\varepsilon > 0$, so that capital substitutes well for the now constant factors L_Y and A. As K grows, the long-run capital–output ratio in (6.16) becomes

$$\frac{Y}{K} = \left(\beta \left(\alpha + (1-\alpha) \cdot 0 \right)^{\varrho/\varepsilon} + 0 \right)^{1/\varrho} = \left(\beta \, (\alpha)^{\varrho/\varepsilon} \right)^{1/\varrho} = \beta^{1/\varrho} \alpha^{1/\varepsilon} > 0.$$

It is clear that the capital–output ratio *falls* toward this value as K grows. If it is sufficiently high, the rate of capital (and output) growth approaches the positive value

$$\frac{\dot{K}}{K} = s\beta^{1/\varrho} \alpha^{1/\varepsilon} - \delta$$

---

[14] This gives the impression that the economy can benefit from allocating labor so that g_A is high and g_B is low. It should, however, be remembered that a small B shifts the level of income down.

[15] See, for instance, Dasgupta and Heal (1974).

[16] This case was quickly made within Chapter 5 on land, since we could easily confirm that a stationary state was feasible in the general case.

in steady state. This example illustrates a good growth potential when there are very strong substitution possibilities. It suffers, however, from implying that the income share of capital goes to unity.

6.3.2.2 Low elasticity of substitution

If $\varrho < 0$, we have the case where the joint labor-and-capital input in (6.15) does not substitute well for energy. It is now suitable to analyze the long-run development of income by dividing both sides of the production function (6.15) by BE, and using the CRS property. This eventually gives

$$Y = \left(\beta \left(\alpha \left(\frac{K}{BE} \right)^{\varepsilon} + (1 - \alpha) \left(\frac{AL_Y}{BE} \right)^{\varepsilon} \right)^{\varrho/\varepsilon} + (1 - \beta) \right)^{1/\varrho} \cdot BE.$$

Let us again consider a scenario with $g_B - s_E < n + g_A = g_K$. Since $\varrho < 0$, we then have that

$$Y \to (1 - \beta)^{1/\varrho} BE \tag{6.20}$$

(from below) as $K/(BE) \to \infty$ and $AL_Y/(BE) \to \infty$. This means that output in the long run is proportional to BE and thus bounded by the development of the amount of effective energy.

Does this case allow a development of z such that it approaches a steady state? To answer this question, we first note that $\zeta_E \to 1$ in the long run. The closer inspection of (6.18) above revealed that the model is stable if and only if $\delta + g_B > s_E$. This is possible with a sufficiently low s_E, although it requires that E_0 is chosen low as well, implying a low initial level of income. It is thus not unreasonable to assume that stability holds, so we will do so from here.

Since equation (6.20) implies that Y grows in step with BE in the long run, we have $g_y = g_B - s_E - n$. A poor development of energy-related productivity does not therefore necessarily imply that per capita income must decline over time. But if the potential to make B grow is very limited, so that $g_B < s_E + n$, then y is forced to fall as time runs,[17] Sustainable development is thus in jeopardy. In particular, if $g_B < n$, there is no way to choose s_E low enough to get sustainability.

Let us also here consider the case with zero technological change and zero population growth. Then $g_y = -s_E < 0$, so per capita income is bound to decline when $(g_A =)g_B = n = 0$, which was not the case in the preceding subsection. This can also be compared to the findings in Chapter 5, where it was possible to have a constant per capita income under similar assumptions, because the use of land did not have to decline over time.

---

[17] Note that a high g_A does not help the economy away from this non-sustainability trap. It is the effective energy that sets the limit, when the substitutability between energy and capital–labor is low.

As in the case with good substitution possibilities, the present scenario implies an implausible value of the long-run income share of energy; now it tends to unity in the long run because of scarcity and essentiality of effective energy. The implausible long-run income shares bring the relevance of these examples into question, but they are nevertheless merited by giving some idea of what could happen if growth is non-balanced.

6.4 A Cobb–Douglas case

Finally, a neat exposition (albeit with limited generality) of the feasibility of sustainable development, when the trend in energy use is declining, is obtained by assuming that the production function takes a Cobb–Douglas form. In this case the production technology is represented by

$$Y = K^\alpha E^\gamma (AL_Y)^{1-\alpha-\gamma}. \qquad (6.21)$$

Since production obviously is zero when $E = 0$ (i.e. energy is essential in production), one could expect that output and consumption must eventually fall to zero. Somewhat surprisingly, this is not generally true. The reason is that the use of the resource, although it is limited, can be spread out over an entire infinite time horizon. One possibility to ensure this is to let the use of E follow the exponential decline that is given in equation (6.3). It would mean that only a fraction of the remaining stock is used at each point of time.

The analysis of the dynamics of the variable z in Section 6.2 is valid here as well, with the qualification that the income shares in equation (6.11) are now constant. The curves in Figure 6.2 therefore stay where they are during the transition to the steady state, so the model is stable. It is therefore appropriate to use the equality $\dot{Y}/Y = \dot{K}/K$ in the long-run analysis. As with the CES function, we examine the cases with and without technological progress in turn.

6.4.1 WITH TECHNOLOGICAL PROGRESS

To obtain the growth rate of Y, we start by taking the logarithm of both sides of equation (6.21), which gives that $\ln Y(t) = \alpha \ln K(t) + \gamma \ln E(t) + (1 - \alpha - \gamma) \ln A(t) + (1 - \alpha - \gamma) \ln L_Y(t)$. Differentiating both sides with respect to t yields

$$\frac{\dot{Y}}{Y} = \alpha \frac{\dot{K}}{K} - \gamma s_E + (1 - \alpha - \gamma)g_A + (1 - \alpha - \gamma)n. \qquad (6.22)$$

Since $\dot{K}/K = \dot{Y}/Y$ in the long run, we can eliminate $\dot{K}/K$ from equation (6.22) and obtain

$$\frac{\dot{Y}}{Y} = \frac{1}{1 - \alpha} \left(-\gamma s_E + (1 - \alpha - \gamma)g_A + (1 - \alpha - \gamma)n \right).$$

In contrast to the land version of this model there is now a drag even on the growth of total output, represented by the term capturing the decline in the use of energy. Like in the case with land, the total coefficient in front of $n + g_A$ is smaller than one, due to the diminishing returns to capital and labor.

As always, the growth in per capita income is at least as interesting as the growth rate of total income. Since $\dot{y}/y = \dot{Y}/Y - n$, it follows that

$$\frac{\dot{y}}{y} = \frac{1}{1 - \alpha} \left(-\gamma s_E + (1 - \alpha - \gamma)g_A + (1 - \alpha - \gamma)n \right) - n$$

$$\frac{\dot{y}}{y} = \frac{1}{1 - \alpha} \left(-\gamma s_E + (1 - \alpha - \gamma)g_A + (1 - \alpha - \gamma - 1 + \alpha)n \right)$$

$$\frac{\dot{y}}{y} = \frac{1}{1 - \alpha} \left((1 - \alpha - \gamma)g_A - \gamma(s_E + n) \right). \tag{6.23}$$

Like in the Cobb–Douglas example of Chapter 5, there is a race between a term driving per capita income growth and a drag on growth. The latter now consists of two terms. The first is due to the fact that a growing number of people use the limited natural resource. This effect was already present in the previous chapter, where the natural resource was a constant quantity of land. The new effect, captured by s_E, appears because the use of the resource has to decrease over time.[18]

From the description of the race between technological progress and the drag in (6.23) we can obtain the condition for sustained growth in per capita income as

$$\frac{\dot{y}}{y} > 0 \quad \Leftrightarrow \quad (1 - \alpha - \gamma)g_A > \gamma(s_E + n).$$

The more important energy is in production (i.e. the higher γ) the lower is the long-run growth rate, because the decreasing returns to capital and labor become more severe. The drag is also large if s_E is high, that is if the use of energy has to decline rapidly. Recall that the use has to decline quickly if the initial use of the resource is high. Working in the opposite direction is the technological progress. If entrepreneurs in the innovation sector are sufficiently rewarded for their efforts (so that g_A is high), and if the output elasticity of the technology factor is large, the growth in per capita income will be positive.

The importance of technological progress becomes even more evident if we look at the case when it is not there, that is when $g_A = 0$. Then the growth rate in (6.23) becomes negative and equals

---

[18] If $\gamma = 0$ then, by (6.23), $g_y = g_A$ as in the basic Solow model. By letting energy be inessential for production it naturally follows that both drags on growth are alleviated.

$$\frac{\dot{y}}{y} = -\frac{\gamma(s_E + n)}{1 - \alpha} < 0. \tag{6.24}$$

This means that y approaches 0 asymptotically. The increasing population pressure on the declining exhaustible resource leads to an ever-declining marginal product of labor, and capital accumulation cannot fully offset this effect. As emphasized in Chapter 5, however, population growth may be slowed down (or even reversed to population decline) when per capita income falls. This would tend to put a break on the decline in (6.24). As opposed to (5.18), however, per capita income will here fall steadily even if population growth approaches zero, due to the decline in the use of energy.

From (6.23) one could jump to the suggestion that s_E should be lowered toward zero, so that the drag is significantly reduced and g_y increases. It should then be recalled, however, that the energy constraint (6.3) requires a balancing lower use level of energy. We therefore encounter a problem of optimization over time: What is the optimal s_E, in the sense that the sum of the well-being over the entire time horizon is the highest possible? The answer to this question is beyond the scope of this book and belongs to graduate studies.

6.4.2 WITHOUT TECHNOLOGICAL PROGRESS

In this sub-section we come back to the question of whether it is possible to sustain a strictly positive consumption in the long run, even if there is no technological change, and when the population is constant. To simplify the notation (and without loss of generality) we make the normalization $AL = 1$, so that the production function (6.21) becomes $Y = K^\alpha E^\gamma$. Although energy clearly is essential in this production function, we will demonstrate that a positive and non-declining consumption can be sustained if $\alpha > \gamma$, that is, if capital is more important than energy in production, in the sense that capital has a higher output elasticity. We will also briefly show that this cannot happen if $\gamma \geq \alpha$.

6.4.2.1 The good Cobb–Douglas case

In this sub-section we assume that $\alpha > \gamma$, which implies that capital is relatively important in production. If capital accumulation is at all able to replace the resource to a degree sufficient to generate sustainable development, it should be in this case.

We will construct an example in which consumption is at the constant level $\bar{C}$ at all points of time from zero to infinity. This, of course, is a kind of sustainable development (and a stationary state). We saw in equation (6.24) that, in the absence of technological progress, per capita income would decline toward zero even if there is no population growth. To come around this obstacle to sustainable development, we have to drop the assumption about a constant saving ratio. Instead, we will follow Solow (1974) and assume an accumulation "policy" in which capital grows linearly with t:

$$K(t) = K_0 + mt, \tag{6.25}$$

where $m > 0$. The time derivative of K is therefore constant: $\dot{K} = m$. We also neglect the physical depreciation of capital in this sub-section.[19]

These assumptions imply that the differential equation of capital, $\dot{K} = K^\alpha E^\gamma - C$, simply becomes $m = K^\alpha E^\gamma - \bar{C}$, or

$$m + \bar{C} = K^\alpha E^\gamma. \tag{6.26}$$

Since both m and $\bar{C}$ are constant, we examine the possibility that the production level is constant as well. We are therefore looking for the feasibility of a growth path along which K^α grows as fast as E^γ declines, at all points of time. Since the capital stock at any point of time is given by (6.25), equation (6.26) will tell us what the implied necessary energy use levels are at different points of time. Given that, we will finally check if together they are sufficiently low that their sum is equal to the initial stock of the resource.

We thus start by solving equation (6.26) for E. The first step is to divide both sides by K^α, which gives $E^\gamma = K^{-\alpha}(m + \bar{C})$. We then raise both sides by $1/\gamma$ and use (6.25) to replace K. This gives

$$E(t) = (\bar{C} + m)^{1/\gamma} (K_0 + mt)^{-\alpha/\gamma}.$$

This is an expression for $E(t)$, which tells us how much of the resource must be taken out at time t, in order to fulfill (6.26). The amount of energy that is necessary to keep output constant clearly declines with time.

The growth path described here is feasible only if the sum of all extractions is equal to the initial stock, that is if (6.1) is fulfilled. In the present context, this constraint is specified to

$$S_0 = \int_0^\infty E(t)dt = \int_0^\infty (\bar{C} + m)^{1/\gamma} (K_0 + mt)^{-\alpha/\gamma} dt.$$

We pull the constant part of the integrand out in front of the integral sign and get the energy constraint

$$S_0 = (\bar{C} + m)^{1/\gamma} \int_0^\infty (K_0 + mt)^{-\alpha/\gamma} dt. \tag{6.27}$$

The central question now is whether this equality can hold. A necessary requirement is that the integral is bounded. In Appendix 6.9.3 it is demonstrated that we get a finite expression on the right hand side only if $\alpha > \gamma$. Computation of the integral then yields

---

[19] Solow (1974) interpreted the production function as net-of-depreciation.

$$S_0 = (\bar{C} + m)^{1/\gamma} \frac{1}{m} \cdot \frac{\gamma}{\alpha - \gamma} \cdot K_0^{\frac{\gamma - \alpha}{\gamma}}. \tag{6.28}$$

We thus arrive at the important conclusion that the total use of the resource, expressed by the right hand side, is a finite quantity if capital has the highest output elasticity. A positive consumption forever is thus feasible, despite the bounded supply of the resource, if $\bar{C}$ is chosen low enough. In other words, sustainable development is possible if $\alpha > \gamma$.

It is informative to rewrite the last equality, so that an expression for the stationary level of production emerges. The result is

$$\bar{C} + m = m^\gamma \left(\frac{\alpha - \gamma}{\gamma}\right)^\gamma S_0^\gamma K_0^{\alpha - \gamma} = Y.$$

It is obvious that $\bar{C}$ can be chosen higher if K_0 and S_0 are higher, that is if the economy is well endowed from the start. The relation between $\bar{C}$ and m is ambiguous. On the one hand, there is rivalry between consumption and investment over current production. On the other hand, a more ambitious capital accumulation means higher production levels at all points of time, which may or may not allow for higher consumption.[20]

6.4.2.2 The bad Cobb–Douglas case

We will not examine the other possibility, that is $\gamma \geq \alpha$, in detail, but just state the results.[21] In this case, a positive and constant output level cannot be maintained forever with a finite resource base, even if all output is saved. (Of course, the conclusion must hold even more strongly if $s < 1$.)

To sketch the reason for this, we start by noting that the resource extraction at time t, needed to provide constant consumption, will now be

$$E(t) = (A + m)^{1/\gamma} (K_0 + mt)^{-\alpha/\gamma},$$

where A is a constant. This is very similar to the expression for extraction obtained in the previous sub-section, although the derivation here is different. The important difference is that, because $\gamma \geq \alpha$, the sum of the required extractions is infinite:[22]

---

[20] The derivative of $\bar{C}$ with respect to m is

$$\frac{d\bar{C}}{dm} = \frac{\gamma}{m}\left(\bar{C} + m - \frac{m}{\gamma}\right).$$

This is positive if $\bar{C} > m\left(\frac{1-\gamma}{\gamma}\right)$.

[21] For details, see Dasgupta and Heal (1979), Chapter 7.

[22] As noted in Appendix 6.9.3, $[m(1 - \alpha/\gamma)]^{-1}(K_0 + mt)^{1-\alpha/\gamma}$, the anti-derivative of $(K_0 + mt)^{-\alpha/\gamma}$, now has a positive exponent. When it is evaluated at $t = \infty$ it becomes infinite.

$$\int_0^\infty E(t)dt = \int_0^\infty (A + m)^{1/\gamma} (K_0 + mt)^{-\alpha/\gamma} dt = \infty > S_0.$$

Hence, the finite resource stock does not suffice to keep production positive forever. This means that consumption eventually must fall to zero. Sustainable development is thus not feasible when $\gamma \geq \alpha$.

6.5 Transition to renewable energy

In this section we take into account the fact that renewable energy can be substituted for non-renewable energy. The focus is thus shifted from scarcity of energy[23] toward an optimal balance in the use of the different sources of energy. The change in the representative firm's optimal relative use of these two types of energy over time, is driven by the change in their relative price. Economic policy and innovations may influence the development of the prices. One reason that we are interested in this transition is that fossil fuels are polluting. This example thereby links the present part of the book to the next, where the focus is on the polluting consequences of economic activity. In particular, Section 8.4 will connect back to this section and analyze the process of phasing out of fossil energy, which is motivated by its polluting character.[24]

6.5.1 FIRM OPTIMIZATION

We denote the two types of energy by N (non-renewable) and R (renewable), respectively. For example, we may think of N as gasoline or diesel and R as biogas or ethanol. Assume that the energy service that enters the production function is given by the energy function

$$E(N, R) = \left(bN^\varepsilon + (1 - b)R^\varepsilon\right)^{1/\varepsilon}. \tag{6.29}$$

The two types of energy may be less than perfect substitutes because they are more difficult to substitute in some parts of the economy than in others. This can be explained by different needs for complementary investments, which are not explicitly modeled here.[25] As before, it is easier to substitute between the two inputs if ε is high.

---

[23] Non-renewable fossil fuel is actually available in huge quantities if coal and shale oil are included; see Smil (2003). Although these sources of energy are very polluting, they contribute to making fossil fuels less scarce.

[24] This section draws on Eriksson (2013).

[25] For instance, low costs of clean electricity (from e.g. wind turbines or solar panels) is not sufficient for it to be widely used in the transport sector. First, electric cars need to be developed, not least the batteries. In addition, charging posts must be installed at many different places, so that the cars

The aggregate production function now has this energy service as an input, along with capital and labor. In the general case, it can be written as

$$Y = F(K, AL_Y, B_1 \cdot E(N, R)). \qquad (6.30)$$

As usual, A is the technology factor attached to labor, whereas energy-related technological progress is represented by B_1.[26]

A full growth model is analyzed in the next sub-section. At this point, we will just examine the evolution of the optimal combination of N and R for the representative firm. The profit function of this firm is

$$\Pi = F(K, AL_Y, B_1 \cdot E(N, R)) - rK - wL - w_N N - w_R R, \qquad (6.31)$$

where w_N and w_R are the prices of the two types of energy. It is assumed that w_N grows at the constant exogenous rate g_{w_N}, which could be explained by increasing scarcity.[27] In addition, we assume that the price of renewable energy is inversely related to the technology factor B, that is $w_R = w_R^0/B$, where w_R^0 is a constant. This implies that $g_{w_R} = -g_B$. Thus the economy can take research efforts to make the renewable energy cheaper. We summarize these assumptions as

$$\frac{\dot{w}_N}{w_N} = g_{w_N} > 0 \quad \text{and} \quad \frac{\dot{w}_R}{w_R} = -g_B < 0. \qquad (6.32)$$

There can, of course, also be technological progress that lowers the cost of the non-renewable energy. What is important, however, is the relative price between the two types of energy, which means that the analysis is interesting enough even with just the technology factors that we have introduced here.

The remainder of this sub-section looks more closely at the representative firm's profit maximization problem, with the purpose of describing how the optimal relative demand for N and R changes over time. The optimality conditions with respect to the uses of N and R, are that their prices must equal the values of their marginal products. Mathematically, this reads

$$w_N = F_E \cdot E_N \quad \text{and} \quad w_R = F_E \cdot E_R. \qquad (6.33)$$

The right hand sides contain the outer derivative with respect to E, followed by the inner derivatives of E with respect to N and R, respectively. Taking the ratios of these expressions gives

---

can be recharged where and when it is convenient for the users. There is also a need for electricity transportation grids, for instance to transport solar-based electricity from Sahara to continental Europe.

[26] We will drop B_1 later, but include it here for conformity with earlier production functions. The letter B is here reserved for the technology factor that lowers the price of renewable energy, which is introduced in the next paragraph.

[27] An alternative explanation could be derived from the so-called Hotelling rule. See, for instance, Dixit (1976).

$$\frac{w_N}{w_R} = \frac{F_E \cdot E_N}{F_E \cdot E_R} = \frac{E_N}{E_R}. \tag{6.34}$$

Since both types of energy are found in the same sub-function[28] of (6.30), the marginal products have the same outer derivative, both of which are cancelled out in this ratio.

At this point it is useful to invoke the explicit expression for E in (6.29) above. This allows us to compute

$$E_N = \left(bN^\varepsilon + (1-b)R^\varepsilon\right)^{\frac{1}{\varepsilon}-1} bN^{\varepsilon-1}$$

and

$$E_R = \left(bN^\varepsilon + (1-b)R^\varepsilon\right)^{\frac{1}{\varepsilon}-1} (1-b)R^{\varepsilon-1}.$$

We can now use (6.29) to find that $\left(bN^\varepsilon + (1-b)R^\varepsilon\right)^{\frac{1}{\varepsilon}-1} = E^{1-\varepsilon}$. The partial derivatives of the energy function can therefore be simplified to

$$E_N = E^{1-\varepsilon} bN^{\varepsilon-1} \tag{6.35}$$

and

$$E_R = E^{1-\varepsilon}(1-b)R^{\varepsilon-1}. \tag{6.36}$$

Using this in the ratio of marginal products in (6.34) above, we finally have that

$$\frac{w_N}{w_R} = \frac{E^{1-\varepsilon} bN^{\varepsilon-1}}{E^{1-\varepsilon}(1-b)R^{\varepsilon-1}} = \frac{b}{(1-b)} \cdot \frac{N^{\varepsilon-1}}{R^{\varepsilon-1}} = \frac{b}{(1-b)} \cdot \frac{R^{1-\varepsilon}}{N^{1-\varepsilon}}.$$

The simplicity of the final ratio, of course, arises because the partial derivatives of E have identical outer derivatives, as in the general case of (6.34).

Our goal (in this sub-section) is to find the optimal relative demand of the two types of energy. We therefore cross-multiply with the constants and get

$$\frac{w_N(1-b)}{w_R b} = \left(\frac{R}{N}\right)^{1-\varepsilon}.$$

On the right hand side, the numerator and the denominator have the same exponent, which has been pulled outside the parenthesis. The final step is to release the factor ratio from the exponent, which can be done by raising both sides to $1/(1-\varepsilon)$:

$$\frac{R}{N} = \left(\frac{w_N(1-b)}{w_R b}\right)^{\frac{1}{1-\varepsilon}} = \left(\frac{w_N(1-b)}{w_R b}\right)^{\sigma}. \tag{6.37}$$

In the far right equality we have used the definition of the elasticity of substitution: $1/(1-\varepsilon) = \sigma$.

---

[28] The function is termed *weakly separable*.

To see how the ratio in (6.37) changes over time, it is useful to first factorize the right hand side of this equation:

$$\frac{R}{N} = \left(\frac{w_N}{w_R}\right)^{\sigma} \cdot \left(\frac{(1-b)}{b}\right)^{\sigma}. \tag{6.38}$$

Since $\sigma > 0$, and because our assumptions in (6.32) imply that w_N/w_R increases as time runs, R/N will increase over time.

The time path of the relative demand of the two types of energy is described by the time derivative of (6.38). Starting by computing the logarithm gives us

$$\ln(R/N) = \sigma \ln(w_N/w_R) + \sigma \ln((1-b)/b).$$

The final term is a constant and we can therefore leave it as it is. It is, however, useful to split the other terms, so that

$$\ln R(t) - \ln N(t) = \sigma \ln(w_N(t)) - \sigma \ln(w_R(t)) + \sigma \ln((1-b)/b).$$

By differentiating both sides with respect to time, we then have the important relation between the changes:

$$\frac{\dot{R}}{R} - \frac{\dot{N}}{N} = \sigma \left(\frac{\dot{w}_N}{w_N} - \frac{\dot{w}_R}{w_R}\right). \tag{6.39}$$

The assumptions in (6.32) about the trends in the two energy prices imply that the parenthesis on the right hand side is positive. The representative firm therefore gradually increases the share of renewable energy. A higher elasticity of substitution makes this process faster, that is, the easier it is to substitute the two types of energy, the more rapid is the change. Moreover, the more resources society puts into research that reduces the costs of renewable energy, the faster w_R falls and the quicker is the transition to renewable energy.

Equation (6.39) does, however, only tell us how the two types of energy change in relative terms. In the growth process it may or may not be that both R and N grow. To see what the absolute trends are, we must analyze a full growth model.

6.5.2 THE FULL GROWTH MODEL

To keep the extension of the analysis to a full growth model tractable, we here assume that the production function in (6.30) takes the Cobb–Douglas form $Y = K^{\alpha} E^{\gamma} (AL_Y)^{1-\alpha-\gamma}$, as given in (6.21). A difference is, of course, that we here use $E(N, R) = (bN^{\varepsilon} + (1-b)R^{\varepsilon})^{1/\varepsilon}$ instead of (6.3). Although A seems to be attached only to labor, it actually augments all inputs, as always for the Cobb–Douglas function.

Let us first analyze the transitional dynamics in this case. The usual procedure of first taking the logarithm of the production function, and then differentiating with respect to time, now gives

$$\frac{\dot{Y}}{Y} = \alpha\frac{\dot{K}}{K} + \gamma\frac{\dot{E}}{E} + (1 - \alpha - \gamma)g_A + (1 - \alpha - \gamma)n. \tag{6.40}$$

Note that this equation differs from (6.22) only by having $\gamma\dot{E}/E$ instead of $-\gamma s_E$. Now we need an expression to substitute for $\dot{E}/E$. Appendix 6.9.4 shows that

$$\frac{\dot{E}}{E} = \frac{\dot{Y}}{Y} - \zeta_N\frac{\dot{w}_N}{w_N} - \zeta_R\frac{\dot{w}_R}{w_R}, \tag{6.41}$$

where

$$\zeta_N = \frac{b}{b + (1 - b)(R/N)^\varepsilon} \quad \text{and} \quad \zeta_R = \frac{(1 - b)}{b(R/N)^{-\varepsilon} + (1 - b)}. \tag{6.42}$$

In addition to the time differentiation of $E(N, R)$, the derivation of (6.41) uses the (time derivatives of the) optimality conditions with regard to N and R of a profit-maximizing firm. Note that (6.38) determines the development of ζ_N and ζ_R when the time paths of w_N and w_R are given.

We now use (6.41) to eliminate the rate of change of energy, $\dot{E}/E$, from (6.40). The result is

$$\frac{\dot{Y}}{Y} = \alpha\frac{\dot{K}}{K} + \gamma\left(\frac{\dot{Y}}{Y} - \zeta_N\frac{\dot{w}_N}{w_N} - \zeta_R\frac{\dot{w}_R}{w_R}\right) + (1 - \alpha - \gamma)g_A + (1 - \alpha - \gamma)n.$$

Collecting $\dot{Y}/Y$ terms and simplifying, yields the following expression for output growth:

$$\frac{\dot{Y}}{Y} = \frac{1}{1 - \gamma}\left(\alpha\frac{\dot{K}}{K} - \gamma\left(\zeta_N\frac{\dot{w}_N}{w_N} + \zeta_R\frac{\dot{w}_R}{w_R}\right) + (1 - \alpha - \gamma)(g_A + n)\right). \tag{6.43}$$

Recall now that R/N in ζ_N and ζ_R can be replaced by the factor prices and constants, according to (6.38). Equation (6.43) therefore expresses the growth rate of output as a function of the growth rate of capital and expressions that are constant or determined by other equations.

Now we follow the usual procedure to get a differential equation in the capital–output ratio, z. Combining (6.43) with

$$\frac{\dot{z}}{z} = \frac{\dot{K}}{K} - \frac{\dot{Y}}{Y} \quad \text{and} \quad \frac{\dot{K}}{K} = s\frac{1}{z} - \delta,$$

gives

$$\frac{\dot{z}}{z} = s\frac{1}{z} - \delta$$
$$- \frac{1}{1 - \gamma}\left[\alpha s\frac{1}{z} - \alpha\delta - \gamma\left(\zeta_N\frac{\dot{w}_N}{w_N} + \zeta_R\frac{\dot{w}_R}{w_R}\right) + (1 - \alpha - \gamma)(g_A + n)\right].$$

This can be rearranged to

$$\dot{z} = s \cdot \frac{1 - \alpha - \gamma}{1 - \gamma}$$

$$-z \frac{1}{1 - \gamma} \left[(1 - \alpha - \gamma)(g_A + n + \delta) - \gamma \left(\zeta_N \frac{\dot{w}_N}{w_N} + \zeta_R \frac{\dot{w}_R}{w_R} \right) \right]. \quad (6.44)$$

As before, stability of z requires that the (final) bracket on the right hand side is positive. There is some ambiguity because of the final part of (6.44), which contains the rates of change of the resource prices.

To examine this matter further, remember that we have assumed that w_R is non-increasing, while w_N is non-declining. Recalling (6.42), there are thus two possible scenarios as $R/N \to \infty$, depending on the elasticity of substitution between non-renewable and renewable energy:

$$\varepsilon > 0 \quad \Rightarrow \quad \zeta_N \frac{\dot{w}_N}{w_N} + \zeta_R \frac{\dot{w}_R}{w_R} \to \frac{\dot{w}_R}{w_R} \quad \leq 0 \quad (6.45)$$

and

$$\varepsilon < 0 \quad \Rightarrow \quad \zeta_N \frac{\dot{w}_N}{w_N} + \zeta_R \frac{\dot{w}_R}{w_R} \to \frac{\dot{w}_N}{w_N} \quad \geq 0. \quad (6.46)$$

Thus, if there are good substitution possibilities between the two types of resources ($\varepsilon > 0$), the final term in (6.44) is negative, at least eventually. The dynamics are then stable. In the opposite case ($\varepsilon < 0$), there is a slight risk of instability, but that is ruled out if

$$(1 - \alpha - \gamma)(g_A + n + \delta) > \gamma \frac{\dot{w}_N}{w_N}.$$

It is not unreasonable to assume that this inequality holds (or that $\varepsilon > 0$). Therefore, we will from here take the model to be stable.

6.5.3 LONG-RUN GROWTH

Given that the capital–output ratio eventually settles at a constant value, the variables K and Y grow at the same rate in the long run. Using this in (6.43) gives

$$\frac{\dot{Y}}{Y} = \frac{1}{1 - \gamma} \left(\alpha \frac{\dot{Y}}{Y} - \gamma \left(\zeta_N \frac{\dot{w}_N}{w_N} + \zeta_R \frac{\dot{w}_R}{w_R} \right) + (1 - \alpha - \gamma)(g_A + n) \right).$$

After some rearrangements we get

$$\frac{\dot{Y}}{Y} = g_A + n - \frac{\gamma}{1 - \alpha - \gamma} \left(\zeta_N \frac{\dot{w}_N}{w_N} + \zeta_R \frac{\dot{w}_R}{w_R} \right). \quad (6.47)$$

The long-run growth rate of total income deviates from the growth rate of the basic Solow model, $g_A + n$, which it is convenient to call the *reference growth rate* here. The deviation is due to the changes in the energy prices, which influence the profit-maximizing demands of the two types of energy, and thereby the total output and its growth rate.

For instance, (6.45) implies that $\dot{Y}/Y > g_A + n$ in the long run if $\varepsilon > 0$. This follows from the fact that R gets cheaper, and that this input is a good substitute for the energy input that gets more expensive. The optimal use of R thus shows a steep upward trend, as we will see below, and therefore tends to pull the output growth rate above the reference growth rate. On the other hand, $\dot{Y}/Y < g_A + n$ in the long run if $\varepsilon < 0$, according to (6.46). Now the low elasticity of substitution makes the (optimal) trend in R less steep and the rising w_N holds the growth of N back (as in the previous case).

The steady state growth rate of per capita income is in this case easily computed as

$$\frac{\dot{y}}{y} = g_A - \frac{\gamma}{1 - \alpha - \gamma}\left(\zeta_N \frac{\dot{w}_N}{w_N} + \zeta_R \frac{\dot{w}_R}{w_R}\right). \tag{6.48}$$

As for total income growth, the long-run expressions depend on the elasticity of substitution between renewable and non-renewable energy. If $\varepsilon > 0$, we have (recalling (6.45)) that

$$\frac{\dot{y}}{y} \quad \rightarrow \quad g_A - \frac{\gamma}{1 - \alpha - \gamma}\frac{\dot{w}_R}{w_R} > g_A.$$

The economy benefits from the decreasing price of an energy source that can easily dominate the use of energy. It is noteworthy that per capita income will grow even if $g_A = 0$, which is due to a very rapid growth of R in this case. Poor substitution possibilities, that is $\varepsilon < 0$, lead to an opposite result, namely that

$$\frac{\dot{y}}{y} \quad \rightarrow \quad g_A - \frac{\gamma}{1 - \alpha - \gamma}\frac{\dot{w}_N}{w_N} < g_A,$$

where we have used (6.46). In this case, the economy suffers from the rising price of an energy input that it cannot easily do without. Note that we here can have a declining per capita output even if $g_A > 0$, which would be caused by poor growth in both types of energy.

6.5.4 LONG-RUN ENERGY PATHS

Given the solution for steady state income growth, we can retrieve the growth rates of E, N, and R. First, substitution of (6.47) into (6.41) yields

$$\frac{\dot{E}}{E} = g_A + n - \frac{\gamma}{1 - \alpha - \gamma}\left(\zeta_N \frac{\dot{w}_N}{w_N} + \zeta_R \frac{\dot{w}_R}{w_R}\right) - \zeta_N \frac{\dot{w}_N}{w_N} - \zeta_R \frac{\dot{w}_R}{w_R},$$

which boils down to

$$\frac{\dot{E}}{E} = g_A + n - \frac{1 - \alpha}{1 - \alpha - \gamma}\left(\zeta_N \frac{\dot{w}_N}{w_N} + \zeta_R \frac{\dot{w}_R}{w_R}\right). \tag{6.49}$$

At this point, the working of the model may be illuminated by taking a brief look at the case with constant energy prices. If $\dot{w}_N = \dot{w}_R = 0$, we have $\dot{E}/E = \dot{Y}/Y = g_A + n$, that is energy use grows in lock step with output. The rising use of energy is motivated by its tendency to increase marginal productivity as the other inputs grow. (Recall that we have ruled out scarcity of energy in this section.)

If, however, the energy prices change according to our basic assumptions in (6.32), equations (6.45) and (6.46) imply that the long-run growth rates of energy are

$$g_E > g_A + n \quad \text{if} \quad \varepsilon > 0 \qquad \text{and} \qquad g_E < g_A + n \quad \text{if} \quad \varepsilon < 0.$$

Not surprisingly, the use of energy grows faster than $g_A + n$ if Y does so. For both E and Y this is because the conditions of energy supply (and use) are beneficial. Conversely, bad substitution possibilities (together with the divergence of energy prices) put a break on both energy and output growth.

Finally, the growth rates of the two types of energy are derived in Appendix 6.9.5. They read

$$\frac{\dot{N}}{N} = g_A + n + \sigma \frac{\varepsilon(1 - \alpha) - \gamma}{1 - \alpha - \gamma} \cdot \zeta_R \frac{\dot{w}_R}{w_R}$$

$$+ \sigma \cdot \frac{\dot{w}_N}{w_N} \cdot \frac{(\varepsilon(1 - \alpha) - \gamma)\zeta_N - (1 - \alpha - \gamma)}{1 - \alpha - \gamma} \tag{6.50}$$

and

$$\frac{\dot{R}}{R} = g_A + n + \sigma \frac{\varepsilon(1 - \alpha) - \gamma}{1 - \alpha - \gamma} \cdot \zeta_N \frac{\dot{w}_N}{w_N}$$

$$+ \sigma \cdot \frac{\dot{w}_R}{w_R} \cdot \frac{(\varepsilon(1 - \alpha) - \gamma)\zeta_R - (1 - \alpha - \gamma)}{1 - \alpha - \gamma}. \tag{6.51}$$

As for the other growth rates, the elasticity of substitution between N and R influences how they are related to the reference growth rate.

We look at the two possibilities of a high and low σ, respectively. First, by (6.45), we have that

$$\frac{\dot{N}}{N} \rightarrow g_A + n + \sigma \frac{\varepsilon(1 - \alpha) - \gamma}{1 - \alpha - \gamma} \cdot \frac{\dot{w}_R}{w_R} - \sigma \cdot \frac{\dot{w}_N}{w_N} < g_A + n \quad \text{if} \quad \varepsilon > 0$$

and

$$\frac{\dot{R}}{R} \to g_A + n - \frac{\dot{w}_R}{w_R} \cdot \frac{1-\alpha}{1-\alpha-\gamma} > g_A + n \quad \text{if} \quad \varepsilon > 0.$$

Since $g_E > g_A + n$ here, it is natural that the energy input that exhibits a decreasing price (and that does not have to be much complemented by the other energy input) grows faster than the reference rate. When it comes to the non-renewable energy, it might even be that $\dot{N}/N < 0$, because it is easy to substitute for.

In the opposite case, with bad substitution possibilities, (6.46) applies, and we have that

$$\frac{\dot{N}}{N} \to g_A + n - \frac{\dot{w}_N}{w_N} \cdot \frac{1-\alpha}{1-\alpha-\gamma} < g_A + n \quad \text{if} \quad \varepsilon < 0$$

and

$$\frac{\dot{R}}{R} \to g_A + n + \sigma \frac{\varepsilon(1-\alpha)-\gamma}{1-\alpha-\gamma} \cdot \frac{\dot{w}_N}{w_N} - \sigma \cdot \frac{\dot{w}_R}{w_R} > g_A + n \quad \text{if} \quad \varepsilon < 0.$$

Even though $g_E < g_A + n$, R grows faster than $g_A + n$. The reason that the high growth rate of R does not pull the growth rate of E above the reference growth rate, is that R does not substitute well for N. Finally, one can show that N falls slower here than when $\varepsilon > 0$.[29] It thus less likely that $\dot{N}/N < 0$ here, because of the low substitution possibility.

6.6 The resource curse

Given the well-functioning economy that we have assumed throughout this book, we can expect that natural resources provide good opportunities for economic growth and development. There are indeed many examples of countries that have been "blessed" by natural resources, such as Botswana (diamonds) and Norway (oil). However, remarkably many economies have been "cursed" by natural resource wealth, expressed in bad macroeconomic performance and growing inequality among its citizens.[30]

---

[29] Comparing the two rates of change of N, we find that

$$\sigma \frac{\varepsilon(1-\alpha)-\gamma}{1-\alpha-\gamma} \cdot \frac{\dot{w}_R}{w_R} - \sigma \cdot \frac{\dot{w}_N}{w_N} < -\frac{\dot{w}_N}{w_N} \cdot \frac{1-\alpha}{1-\alpha-\gamma},$$

where the left hand side is the negative part of $\dot{N}/N$ when $\varepsilon > 0$, and the right hand side is the corresponding expression when $\varepsilon < 0$. The inequality holds because the $\sigma > 1$ on the left hand side, while $(1-\alpha)/(1-\alpha-\gamma) < 1$ on the right hand side.

[30] This section builds on van der Ploeg (2011).

6.6.1 NEGATIVE AND POSITIVE EXPERIENCES OF NATURAL RESOURCES

A very dramatic example of a country that has experienced a resource curse is Nigeria. Although oil revenues per capita have increased considerably over the recent 4–5 decades, there has been a stagnation in per capita income, putting an increasing share of the population below the poverty line. At the same time, small minorities have enriched themselves, often under military dictatorships. Even though there was a high growth rate of physical capital, the total factor productivity declined, with capacity utilization often being as low as one third. It thus seems that oil wealth has led to bad politics and governance in Nigeria.

Nigeria is not the only oil-exporting country with a negative growth experience during the recent few decades. Other examples are Iran, Venezuela, Libya, Iraq, Kuwait, and Qatar. There has been a decline in per capita GNP in OPEC as a whole. Another negative resource experience was suffered by South Africa, after a boom in gold prices. This resulted in an appreciation of the real exchange rate in the 1970s, which led to de-industrialization and disappointing growth.

Positive scenarios related to natural resources have, however, also played out. One of the most famous comes from Botswana (which has been called "an African success story"), a country that had minimal investment and substantial inequality at the time it was decolonized. Botswana takes some 40% of its GDP from diamonds, but it has shown the world's highest growth rate since 1965, with a very high public expenditure on education as a fraction of GNP. Moreover, Botswana's per capita GDP is at least ten times that of Nigeria.

Some other good examples are Indonesia, Malaysia, and Thailand, where high growth rates were achieved by economic diversification and industrialization. However, the growth performances of their less resource-endowed neighbors Hong Kong, Singapore, and South Korea were even better.

Norway is one of the largest oil exporters in the world, but it has managed to keep a high growth rate in manufacturing and the rest of the economy compared with its neighbors. An explanation for its ability to avoid a resource curse is probably that there is very little corruption in Norway. The country has good institutions, and so is well managed and the economic policy relies heavily on the market forces.

6.6.2 EXPLANATIONS OF THE NATURAL RESOURCE CURSE

Given the wide diversity in experience among resource-rich countries, many explanations for the resource curse have been suggested. Here we will mention some of the most common.

6.6.2.1 Dutch disease

According to the Dutch disease[31] theory, the revenues from a natural resource gives higher income and wealth, which boosts demand and leads to an appreciation of the real exchange rate. Domestic manufacturing products thus become more expensive on the world market, and so the economy experiences a contraction of the industry sector. (This is the short-run effect; there are several possibilities when it comes to the long-run effect.)

Macroeconomic and sectoral empirical studies offer some support for Dutch disease effects. There is also some quasi-experimental, within-country evidence for Brazil, which provides further evidence for this hypothesis.

6.6.2.2 Temporary loss in learning-by-doing

When an economy experiences a natural resource windfall, it gets a comparative advantage in that sector. One can then expect that this sector expands, at the cost of a sector that was earlier dominant in the economy's trade. This seems socially optimal (and is a natural market outcome), since the economy now specializes in the sector where it has recently obtained a comparative advantage.

Suppose, however, that the previously dominant trade sector was an "engine of growth," because there were considerable learning-by-doing effects there, that is the mere activity in this sector produced insights that led to higher productivity (partly as "positive externalities"). Then, the resource windfall, by worsening the competitiveness of this sector, can cause a fall in growth (at least temporarily).

Early cross-country studies provide (quite robust) support for this hypothesis. However, they have later been subject to some criticism on econometric grounds. Due to this, researchers have moved on to panel data studies, where the results still put the hypothesis into question. These studies also point to the necessity of taking the quality of institutions (e.g. the degree of democracy), or financial development into account.

6.6.2.3 Institutions

A dictator in a country with a wealth of natural resources has greater possibilities of staying in power, by buying off political challengers. For instance in Congo, President Mobuto was able to do so thanks to the generous supplies of copper, diamonds, zinc, gold, silver, and oil. In such a process the quality of institutions is often worsened and modernization is resisted.

---

[31] This label stems from the relative decline of manufacturing experienced by the Netherlands, following the export of natural gas found in Slochteren.

In corrupt countries public sectors are often expanded and supporters are offered well paid but unproductive jobs. The political elite in a resource-rich and non-democratic country may also want to block technological and institutional improvements, to the extent that their power is expected to be weakened by this. All this corruption, of course, hampers growth. For example, talents turn to rent-seeking activities (trying to become bureaucrats, oligarchs, war lords etc.) instead of productive entrepreneurship.

However, recent empirical research indicates that the resource curse can be turned into a blessing if the country is able to develop good institutions that drastically reduce corruption. In fact institutions that encourage productive entrepreneurship seem to have more explanatory power of per capita income than geography and trade. For example, the poor economic performances of "oil-rich states such as Angola, Nigeria, Sudan, and Venezuela, diamond rich Sierra Leone, Liberia, and Congo, and drug states Colombia and Afghanistan" are likely explained by weak institutions (van der Ploeg, 2011, p. 382).

6.6.3 SUMMARY ON THE RESOURCE CURSE

From the various experiences of countries with resources it becomes obvious how important institutions are. Modern economic growth research is therefore increasingly taking them into account. See, for instance, Chapters 22 and 23 in Acemoglu (2009). We will nevertheless continue to assume that the institutions of the economies that we analyze work well, leaving the analysis of the relation between growth and institutions for later studies.

6.7 **Conclusion**

In this chapter the remaining stock and the use of the natural resource decline over time. For sustained growth, there is now a very strong requirement for innovations that make the use of the depletable resource more effective. The required diversion of labor from ordinary production and labor-augmenting research is therefore more pronounced than in Chapter 5. Consequently, the growth rate and level are lower than in the case with land, if everything else is unchanged.

If the research sector can only provide resource-saving technological progress at a low (or zero) rate in the long run, sustained growth can still be feasible, if there are generous substitution possibilities between the resource and the other inputs of production. However, the usual problem with implausible long-run income shares arises here as well. In the case with poor substitution possibilities, the upper bound of Y is given by a neat function of BE. Even if the maximum growth rate of B is small, there is a tiny possibility for sustained per capita income growth, in particular if the population growth is low.

The substitution of renewable energy for non-renewable energy was described as a natural outcome, when we followed the profit-maximizing behavior of a representative firm. The driving forces were the increasing price of the latter input and a decreasing price of the former. There was for sure a substitution in the relative sense, but it was unclear whether the absolute trend of non-renewable energy was negative or not. We come back to this in Chapter 8, where one reason for the increase in the price of non-renewable energy is an environmental tax, which is motivated by the polluting effect of this input.

■ FURTHER READING

Chapter 14 in Perman et al. (2011) contains a good discussion about the role of natural resources in the growth process, in particular on the substitutability between natural resources and human-made capital. There are also elements of intertemporal optimization for the reader who feels tempted to take that step. A classic book is Dasgupta and Heal (1979), which is (technically) quite accessible. An interesting discussion on different views of sustainability (with a focus on exhaustible resources) is found in Neumayer (2010), especially Chapter 3.

6.8 **Exercises**

6.1 CES income shares
Derive the income shares in Section 6.3.
6.2 Land and energy
Suppose that both land and labor are inputs in the production function, that is

$$Y = K^\alpha T^\beta E^\gamma (AL)^{1-\alpha-\beta-\gamma}.$$

(1) Show that the model is stable, by deriving and analyzing a differential equation for z in this case.
(2) What is the long-run growth rate of y in this case?

6.9 **Appendix**

6.9.1 BALANCED DIRECTION

To analyze the conditions for a balanced growth path when energy is included in the general growth model, we follow the same steps as in Chapter 5 (and

Section 4.5). In the aggregate production function, capital and labor are now joined by energy (from (6.3)) and a vector of technology factors:

$$Y = \tilde{F}(K, L_Y, E, \tilde{A}), \tag{6.52}$$

where $\tilde{A}$ may consist of technology factors other than those in Chapter 5. In line with our earlier assumptions, this function exhibits constant returns to scale in K, L_Y, and E.

As before, our starting point is the assumption that the economy is on a path with constant growth rates after some point of time, $\tau < \infty$. This means again that

$$Y(t) = Y(\tau)e^{g_Y(t-\tau)}, \quad K(t) = K(\tau)e^{g_K(t-\tau)}, \quad \text{and} \quad C(t) = C(\tau)e^{g_C(t-\tau)}.$$

from $t = \tau$ and onwards. Assuming again that there is always a strictly positive investment, and using the capital accumulation equation, we can obtain the result that $g_Y = g_K = g_C$ in the long run, by the same steps as in Section 4.5.

What is the necessary character of technological progress along the long-run growth path? To answer this question, we note that the production function (6.52) at $t = \tau$ is $Y(\tau) = \tilde{F}\left[K(\tau), L_Y(\tau), E(\tau), \tilde{A}(\tau)\right]$, where $E(\tau) = E_0 e^{-s_E \cdot \tau}$. As in the Chapter 5, it is here useful to replace quantities indexed by τ by quantities indexed by t. Therefore we note that one possible way to write the quantity of energy from τ on is

$$E(t) = E_0 e^{-s_E t} \cdot e^{-s_E \cdot \tau} \cdot e^{s_E \cdot \tau} = E(\tau)e^{-s_E(t-\tau)}.$$

This means that $E(\tau) = E(t)e^{s_E(t-\tau)}$.[32] Consequently, the aggregate production function can be written as

$$Y(t)e^{-g_Y(t-\tau)} = \tilde{F}\left[K(t)e^{-g_K(t-\tau)}, L_Y(t)e^{-n(t-\tau)}, E(t)e^{s_E(t-\tau)}, \tilde{A}(\tau)\right],$$

for $t \geq \tau$. Upon division of both sides by $e^{-g_Y(t-\tau)}$, using the assumption of constant returns to scale with respect to capital, labor, and energy, we have

$$Y(t) = \tilde{F}\left[K(t), L_Y(t)e^{(g_Y-n)(t-\tau)}, E(t)e^{(g_Y+s_E)(t-\tau)}, \tilde{A}(\tau)\right].$$

By the previous finding that $g_Y = g_K$ the exponential function vanishes in the first variable place. Noting that $\tilde{A}(\tau)$ is constant, since it is evaluated at a certain point of time, it can be suppressed in the description of the production function, which therefore can be represented by (6.4), that is

$$Y(t) = F[K(t), A(t)L_Y(t), B(t)E(t)],$$

---

[32] As in the corresponding section of Chapter 5 we can write $Y(\tau) = Y(t)e^{-g_Y(t-\tau)}$, $K(\tau) = K(t)e^{-g_K(t-\tau)}$ and $L(\tau) = L(t)e^{-n(t-\tau)}$.

with

$$\frac{\dot{A}}{A} = g_A = g_Y - n \quad \text{and} \quad \frac{\dot{B}}{B} = g_B = g_Y + s_E.$$

6.9.2 OUTPUT GROWTH

To get an expression for the proportional growth rate of total output we first take logs of (6.4) and differentiate with respect to time. The result is

$$\frac{\dot{Y}}{Y} = \frac{F_K}{F} \cdot \dot{K} + \frac{F_2}{F} \cdot (\dot{AL_Y}) + \frac{F_3}{F} \cdot (\dot{BE}).$$

Next, we multiply the first right hand term by K/K, the second by AL_Y/AL_Y, and the third by BE/BE. Note also that $F_2 A = F_{L_Y}$ and that $F_3 B = F_E$. This gives the result

$$\frac{\dot{Y}}{Y} = \frac{F_K K}{F} \cdot \frac{\dot{K}}{K} + \frac{F_{L_Y} L_Y}{F} \cdot \left(\frac{\dot{A}}{A} + \frac{\dot{L_Y}}{L_Y}\right) + \frac{F_E E}{Y} \cdot \left(\frac{\dot{B}}{B} + \frac{\dot{E}}{E}\right).$$

Finally, using the notation for income shares and more compact expressions for growth rates, this simplifies to (6.10), that is:

$$\frac{\dot{Y}}{Y} = \zeta_K \cdot \frac{\dot{K}}{K} + \zeta_L (n + g_A) + \zeta_E \left(g_B - s_E\right).$$

6.9.3 INTEGRATING THE RESOURCE CONSTRAINT

To compute the integral in (6.27), it is useful to start with a finite time horizon, between $t = 0$ and $t = \bar{t}$, with the plan to let $\bar{t} \to \infty$ later. The use of energy during this period is

$$\int_0^{\bar{t}} E(t)dt = \int_0^{\bar{t}} (\bar{C} + m)^{1/\gamma} (K_0 + mt)^{-\alpha/\gamma} dt$$

$$= (\bar{C} + m)^{1/\gamma} \int_0^{\bar{t}} (K_0 + mt)^{-\alpha/\gamma} dt.$$

To develop the right hand side, we note that the anti-derivative of $(K_0 + mt)^{-\alpha/\gamma}$ is

$$[m(1 - \alpha/\gamma)]^{-1} (K_0 + mt)^{1-\alpha/\gamma} = \frac{1}{m} \cdot \frac{\gamma}{\gamma - \alpha} \cdot (K_0 + mt)^{\frac{\gamma-\alpha}{\gamma}}.$$

As always this can easily be checked by differentiating the latter expression with respect to time, and then confirming that the result is the initial expression. Using this in the integral above, we have

$$\int_0^{\bar{t}} E(t)dt = (\bar{C} + m)^{1/\gamma} [m(1 - \alpha/\gamma)]^{-1} [(K_0 + mt)^{1-\alpha/\gamma}]_0^{\bar{t}}.$$

Evaluating the integral at the two endpoints, we have

$$\int_0^{\bar{t}} E(t)dt = (\bar{C} + m)^{1/\gamma} \left[m\left(\frac{\gamma - \alpha}{\gamma}\right) \right]^{-1} \left[(K_0 + m\bar{t})^{1-\alpha/\gamma} - K_0^{1-\alpha/\gamma} \right].$$

Letting now $\bar{t} \to \infty$, we note that the first term in the last bracket then goes to zero only if $\alpha > \gamma$, which we have assumed. (If $\alpha < \gamma$, $(K_0 + m\bar{t})^{1-\alpha/\gamma} \to \infty$ as $\bar{t} \to \infty$. If $\alpha = \gamma$, $[m(1 - \alpha/\gamma)]^{-1} = \infty$.)

We thus obtain

$$\int_0^{\infty} E(t)dt = (\bar{C} + m)^{1/\gamma} \left[m\left(\frac{\gamma - \alpha}{\gamma}\right) \right]^{-1} \left[-K_0^{1-\alpha/\gamma} \right].$$

Rewriting this slightly, and recalling the constraint that the use should equal the initial stock, we have

$$\int_0^{\infty} E(t)dt = (\bar{C} + m)^{1/\gamma} m^{-1} \left(\frac{\gamma}{\alpha - \gamma}\right) K_0^{1-\alpha/\gamma} = S_0,$$

which is equivalent to (6.28) in the main text.

6.9.4 TIME DERIVATIVE OF E

To get an expression for $\dot{E}/E$, we note that $\ln E = \frac{1}{\varepsilon} \ln(bN^\varepsilon + (1 - b)R^\varepsilon)$. Differentiation with respect to time gives

$$\frac{\dot{E}}{E} = \frac{1}{\varepsilon} \cdot \frac{1}{bN^\varepsilon + (1 - b)R^\varepsilon} \left(b\varepsilon N^{\varepsilon-1}\dot{N} + (1 - b)\varepsilon R^{\varepsilon-1}\dot{R}\right)$$

$$\frac{\dot{E}}{E} = \frac{bN^\varepsilon}{bN^\varepsilon + (1 - b)R^\varepsilon} \frac{\dot{N}}{N} + \frac{(1 - b)R^\varepsilon}{bN^\varepsilon + (1 - b)R^\varepsilon} \frac{\dot{R}}{R}.$$

Now define

$$\zeta_N = \frac{bN^\varepsilon}{bN^\varepsilon + (1 - b)R^\varepsilon} = \frac{b}{b + (1 - b)(R/N)^\varepsilon}$$

and

$$\zeta_R = \frac{(1 - b)R^\varepsilon}{bN^\varepsilon + (1 - b)R^\varepsilon} = \frac{(1 - b)}{b(R/N)^{-\varepsilon} + (1 - b)}.$$

Thus

$$\frac{\dot{E}}{E} = \zeta_N \frac{\dot{N}}{N} + \zeta_R \frac{\dot{R}}{R}. \tag{6.53}$$

The next step is to eliminate the growth rates on the right hand side, by using two profit-maximization conditions.

For this, we use the optimum condition (6.33), and note that $F_E = \gamma E^{-1} Y$ in the Cobb–Douglas case. We therefore have the following necessary conditions for profit maximization:

$$\gamma E^{-1} E_N Y = w_N \quad \text{and} \quad \gamma E^{-1} E_R Y = w_R.$$

Recalling (6.35) and (6.36), these two expressions read

$$\gamma \cdot \frac{b N^{\varepsilon-1}}{E^\varepsilon} \cdot Y = w_N \quad \text{and} \quad \gamma \cdot \frac{(1-b) R^{\varepsilon-1}}{E^\varepsilon} \cdot Y = w_R. \tag{6.54}$$

Since we want to eliminate the growth rates of the energy inputs on the right hand side of (6.53), we now take the logs of (6.54):

$$\ln(\gamma b) + (\varepsilon - 1) \ln N - \varepsilon \ln E + \ln Y = \ln w_N$$

and

$$\ln(\gamma(1-b)) + (\varepsilon - 1) \ln R - \varepsilon \ln E + \ln Y = \ln w_R.$$

The time derivatives are

$$(\varepsilon - 1)\frac{\dot{N}}{N} - \varepsilon \frac{\dot{E}}{E} + \frac{\dot{Y}}{Y} = \frac{\dot{w}_N}{w_N} \quad \text{and} \quad (\varepsilon - 1)\frac{\dot{R}}{R} - \varepsilon \frac{\dot{E}}{E} + \frac{\dot{Y}}{Y} = \frac{\dot{w}_R}{w_R}.$$

Rearranging:

$$(1 - \varepsilon)\frac{\dot{N}}{N} = \frac{\dot{Y}}{Y} - \frac{\dot{w}_N}{w_N} - \varepsilon \frac{\dot{E}}{E} \quad \text{and} \quad (1 - \varepsilon)\frac{\dot{R}}{R} = \frac{\dot{Y}}{Y} - \frac{\dot{w}_R}{w_R} - \varepsilon \frac{\dot{E}}{E}.$$

Divide by $1 - \varepsilon$ and recall that $1/(1 - \varepsilon) = \sigma$:

$$\frac{\dot{N}}{N} = \sigma \frac{\dot{Y}}{Y} - \sigma \frac{\dot{w}_N}{w_N} - \sigma \varepsilon \frac{\dot{E}}{E} \quad \text{and} \quad \frac{\dot{R}}{R} = \sigma \frac{\dot{Y}}{Y} - \sigma \frac{\dot{w}_R}{w_R} - \sigma \varepsilon \frac{\dot{E}}{E}. \tag{6.55}$$

By this we have obtained two useful expressions for the rates of change in the uses of the two types of energy.

The final step is to use this in (6.53):

$$\frac{\dot{E}}{E} = \zeta_N \left(\sigma \frac{\dot{Y}}{Y} - \sigma \frac{\dot{w}_N}{w_N} - \sigma \varepsilon \frac{\dot{E}}{E} \right) + \zeta_R \left(\sigma \frac{\dot{Y}}{Y} - \sigma \frac{\dot{w}_R}{w_R} - \sigma \varepsilon \frac{\dot{E}}{E} \right).$$

Since $\zeta_N + \zeta_R = 1$:

$$\frac{\dot{E}}{E} = \sigma \frac{\dot{Y}}{Y} - \sigma \varepsilon \frac{\dot{E}}{E} - \sigma \zeta_N \left(\frac{\dot{w}_N}{w_N} \right) - \sigma \zeta_R \left(\frac{\dot{w}_R}{w_R} \right).$$

Solve for $\dot{E}/E$:

$$\frac{\dot{E}}{E} + \sigma\varepsilon\frac{\dot{E}}{E} = \sigma\frac{\dot{Y}}{Y} - \sigma\zeta_N\left(\frac{\dot{w}_N}{w_N}\right) - \sigma\zeta_R\left(\frac{\dot{w}_R}{w_R}\right).$$

Since $1 + \sigma\varepsilon = 1 + \frac{\varepsilon}{1-\varepsilon} = \frac{1-\varepsilon+\varepsilon}{1-\varepsilon} = \frac{1}{1-\varepsilon} = \sigma$:

$$\sigma\frac{\dot{E}}{E} = \sigma\frac{\dot{Y}}{Y} - \sigma\zeta_N\left(\frac{\dot{w}_N}{w_N}\right) - \sigma\zeta_R\left(\frac{\dot{w}_R}{w_R}\right)$$

$$\frac{\dot{E}}{E} = \frac{\dot{Y}}{Y} - \zeta_N\frac{\dot{w}_N}{w_N} - \zeta_R\frac{\dot{w}_R}{w_R}.$$

This is (6.41) in the main text.

6.9.5 GROWTH RATES OF N AND R

To get the growth rates of N and R in steady state we rewrite (6.55) (from Appendix 6.9.4) as

$$\frac{\dot{N}}{N} = \sigma\left(\frac{\dot{Y}}{Y} - \varepsilon\frac{\dot{E}}{E}\right) - \sigma\frac{\dot{w}_N}{w_N} \quad \text{and} \quad \frac{\dot{R}}{R} = \sigma\left(\frac{\dot{Y}}{Y} - \varepsilon\frac{\dot{E}}{E}\right) - \sigma\frac{\dot{w}_R}{w_R}. \quad (6.56)$$

We now use (6.47) and (6.49) to compute

$$\frac{\dot{Y}}{Y} - \varepsilon\frac{\dot{E}}{E} = g_A + n - \frac{\gamma}{1-\alpha-\gamma}\left(\zeta_N\frac{\dot{w}_N}{w_N} + \zeta_R\frac{\dot{w}_R}{w_R}\right)$$

$$- \varepsilon\left(g_A + n - \frac{1-\alpha}{1-\alpha-\gamma}\left(\zeta_N\frac{\dot{w}_N}{w_N} + \zeta_R\frac{\dot{w}_R}{w_R}\right)\right).$$

This can be simplified to

$$\frac{\dot{Y}}{Y} - \varepsilon\frac{\dot{E}}{E} = (1-\varepsilon)(g_A + n) + \frac{\varepsilon(1-\alpha)-\gamma}{1-\alpha-\gamma}\cdot\left(\zeta_N\frac{\dot{w}_N}{w_N} + \zeta_R\frac{\dot{w}_R}{w_R}\right).$$

Inserting this in (6.56) gives (recall that $1/(1-\varepsilon) = \sigma$):

$$\frac{\dot{N}}{N} = (g_A + n) + \sigma\frac{\varepsilon(1-\alpha)-\gamma}{1-\alpha-\gamma}\cdot\left(\zeta_N\frac{\dot{w}_N}{w_N} + \zeta_R\frac{\dot{w}_R}{w_R}\right) - \sigma\frac{\dot{w}_N}{w_N}$$

and

$$\frac{\dot{R}}{R} = (g_A + n) + \sigma\frac{\varepsilon(1-\alpha)-\gamma}{1-\alpha-\gamma}\cdot\left(\zeta_N\frac{\dot{w}_N}{w_N} + \zeta_R\frac{\dot{w}_R}{w_R}\right) - \sigma\frac{\dot{w}_R}{w_R}.$$

Rearranging:

$$\frac{\dot{N}}{N} = (g_A + n) + \sigma \frac{\varepsilon(1-\alpha) - \gamma}{1 - \alpha - \gamma} \cdot \zeta_R \frac{\dot{w}_R}{w_R}$$

$$+ \sigma \cdot \left(\frac{(\varepsilon(1-\alpha) - \gamma)\zeta_N}{1 - \alpha - \gamma} - 1 \right) \cdot \frac{\dot{w}_N}{w_N}$$

and

$$\frac{\dot{R}}{R} = (g_A + n) + \sigma \frac{\varepsilon(1-\alpha) - \gamma}{1 - \alpha - \gamma} \cdot \zeta_N \frac{\dot{w}_N}{w_N}$$

$$+ \sigma \cdot \left(\frac{(\varepsilon(1-\alpha) - \gamma)\zeta_R}{1 - \alpha - \gamma} - 1 \right) \cdot \frac{\dot{w}_R}{w_R}.$$

These are equivalent to (6.50) and (6.51) in the main text.

Part III
Pollution

7 Pollution reduction by abatement

The remainder of this book will concern the emissions of toxic pollutants that are the consequences of economic activities. Common examples of such substances are sulfur dioxide, nitrogen dioxide, lead, DDT and so on. They harm human beings directly, or they harm nature to the eventual detriment of man. For variation the words emission and pollution will be used interchangeably, with no distinct connotation.

The central question in this part of the book is whether there can be non-increasing pollution along with non-decreasing per capita income. This gives the definition of sustainable development that we will use from here on. The wish to prevent pollution from increasing poses a new damper to income growth. In order to focus on the particular challenges that this implies, we take the scarce natural resources, such as land and energy, out of the analysis, and thereby the particular limits to growth that they brought with them in the preceding two chapters.

Pollution can be reduced at a cost. We will discuss two ways of taking action to lower the quantities of emissions. One is by directing research efforts so that the production technology becomes less polluting. This is the theme of Chapter 8. In the present chapter, by contrast, some of the currently produced gross output is used to abate pollution.[1] In our main example, the components of the production–pollution structure can be combined such that the net output is described *as if* it were a function of pollution (along with capital and labor). This makes it straightforward to derive a condition that relates the feasible rates of change in per capita income and pollution to each other, in a way that is (somewhat) familiar from previous chapters. Not surprisingly, we find that there exists a "sustainable region," in which income can grow while pollution declines, if there is sufficient technological progress.[2]

Before we come to this growth analysis in Section 7.4, there are some preparatory sections. We begin with a simple memory (or accounting) rule, which is obtained by a decomposition of the sources of pollution into Scale,

---

[1] One could say that we discuss "end-of-pipe" abatement in this chapter, whereas the next chapter is about "beginning-of-the-process" action against pollution (like developing technology in a direction that facilitates the switching to cleaner fuels).

[2] The words "decline" and "grow" can here be understood in the "weak" sense, that is including the absence of change.

Technology, and Composition effects. It is sometimes useful to classify the mechanisms of more elaborate models into these types of categories.

Then, in Section 7.2, we describe how pollution can be modeled as a stock, to which a flow of pollution is continuously added but which also undergoes a natural decay. Although the stock aspect is important, we argue that many interesting results can be obtained by focusing the analysis on whether the flow pollution can decline over time (as per capita income grows). This requires, however, that the stock starts from a sufficiently low level (i.e. at a safe distance from causing an ecological collapse).

Section 7.3 develops a way to represent the relation between production and pollution. Gross pollution is modeled as an increasing function (a side effect) of gross production. By setting aside some gross output for abatement, the net pollution can become lower. Some emphasis is put on the importance of the functional relationship between gross pollution, abatement, and the resulting net pollution. Not surprisingly, the prospects for sustainability can easily go from pessimistic to optimistic through slight adjustments in the parameter values.

This production–pollution–abatement structure is put into a growth model in Section 7.4. Confining the analysis to a Cobb–Douglas production function, a very tractable model is obtained. It is used to describe a trade-off between a growing income and a declining pollution in steady state. The section also pins down the condition for having the possibility of both, that is of sustainable development.

Section 7.5 then looks at one implication of the long-run growth path, namely how the share of gross output that goes to abatement changes over time. The finding is that it tends to unity in the long run (although at a rate that permits per capita net income growth). This suggests that our understanding of the sustainability problem would benefit from a complementary model with environmental innovation, which is the topic of Chapter 8.

Finally, Section 7.6 shows how firms can be induced to reduce pollution, by use of a pollution tax. Formulating a profit function that includes such a tax we show how the firm's optimal emission level is influenced by the tax. We find that a requirement for a downward trend in pollution is that the pollution tax grows at a rate that is higher than the growth rate of total income.

7.1 Scale, composition, and technology effects

We begin this part about growth and pollution with a simple but useful memory rule, which decomposes the change in polluting emissions into scale, composition, and technology effects. The emissions time path is not derived from a dynamic model. Instead the changes of the underlying variables are taken as exogenously given. This can therefore be seen as an exercise in pollution accounting, not entirely unlike the computation of the Solow residual, which was mentioned in Section 2.4.4.

In this section (and in this section only) the national output, $Y(t)$, is produced in n different sectors. Production in any sector i is denoted $Y_i(t)$. This disaggregation means that we can allow emissions to differ between the sectors, so that the total level of pollution in an economy is also explained by its industry structure. We let $b_i(t)$ signify the quantity of emission per unit of output produced in industry i. This means that the pollution from sector i is

$$X_i(t) = b_i(t)Y_i(t) \qquad i = 1, \ldots, n.$$

When $b_i(t)$ declines, so that $X_i(t)$ falls (*ceteris paribus*), it will interpreted as "green" technological change.

To describe structural change, we define the value share of industry i in national output as $\varsigma_i(t) \equiv Y_i(t)/Y(t)$. Consequently, the emission quantity from industry i is $X_i(t) = b_i(t)\varsigma_i(t)Y(t)$. We must, of course, have $\sum_{i=1}^{n} \varsigma_i = 1$, that is the sum of the shares of the sectors equals unity.

The total of emissions from all sectors in the economy is then the sum over all X_i, that is $X(t) = \sum_{i=1}^{n} X_i(t)$, or

$$X(t) = Y(t) \sum_{i=1}^{n} b_i(t)\varsigma_i(t), \qquad (7.1)$$

where $Y(t)$ is pulled out from the sum because it is independent of i. This sum expresses how total pollution depends on the different components. As mentioned above, we will here assume that they are all changing at exogenous rates, leaving the endogenization of the variables to later models. Here we just study what direction total pollution takes over time, under various assumptions about b_i and ς_i (Y is just steadily growing).

The time derivative of equation (7.1), computed in Exercise 7.1, shows that the rate of change of pollution consists of three effects:

$$g_X = \underbrace{g_Y}_{\text{Scale effect}} + \underbrace{\sum_{i=1}^{n} \pi_i g_{b_i}}_{\text{Technology effect}} + \underbrace{\sum_{i=1}^{n} \pi_i g_{\varsigma_i}}_{\text{Composition effect}}, \qquad (7.2)$$

where we have defined $\pi_i(t) = X_i(t)/X(t)$ as the share of total pollution that comes from sector i. This accounting identity has several interesting implications.

A first possibility is that there is no technological or structural change, so that $g_{b_i} = g_{\varsigma_i} = 0$ for all i. With the Technology and Composition effects thus taken out, there would be a serious conflict between economic growth and the environment, because equation (7.2) now reduces to

$$g_X = g_Y.$$

Pollution would then grow in step with output and sustainable development would clearly not be feasible. While this example appears overly pessimistic, it serves as a benchmark that can be mitigated by adding counteracting effects, which may or may not invert the pollution trend.

If we start by considering the possibility of structural change, but still assume that $g_{b_i} = 0$ for all sectors, equation (7.2) becomes

$$g_X = g_Y + \sum_{i=1}^{n} \pi_i g_{\varsigma_i}.$$

The structural adjustment can affect the total pollution in either direction. If $\sum_{i=1}^{n} \pi_i g_{\varsigma_i} < 0$, then dirty industries on average lose shares, while clean branches gain. For example, it could be that traditional industries yield to service sectors. In this case the composition of the industry gets cleaner over time. This means that pollution does not grow as much as output, that is $g_X < g_Y$, possibly even with pollution declining at times. It is, however, questionable whether this effect can be strong enough to sustain a long-run pollution decline. In particular, when all production takes place in the cleanest sector, there is no room for making production even cleaner by structural change. The possibilities for counteracting pollution by structural change are thus limited, unless some sectors do not pollute at all and the economy is eventually active only in such sectors. It should also be noted that the trend toward a cleaner composition of the industries in some (mainly rich) countries to some extent has been made possible by movements of dirty production to poorer countries (so-called "pollution havens"; see Copeland and Taylor (2003)).

The final, and not the least important, possibility to decrease pollution is to make production cleaner, for instance by using cleaner inputs (biogas instead of fossil fuels) or by capturing and storing the poisonous byproducts of production (carbon-capturing coal power plants).[3] To simplify the exposition, we assume that there is no structural change, that is $g_{\varsigma_i} = 0$ for all sectors. Then (7.2) becomes

$$g_X = g_Y + \sum_{i=1}^{n} \pi_i g_{b_i}.$$

If Y grows continuously, then an increase in X can be avoided only if the b_i:s declines sufficiently fast, due to environmentally friendly innovations. The condition for non-increasing pollution can be formulated as follows:

---

[3] In this section, these technological changes come to the economy at no cost. Endogenous environmental innovations, which require the use of a scarce resource, are the theme of Chapter 8.

$$g_X \leq 0 \quad \Leftrightarrow \quad g_Y \leq -\sum_{i=1}^{n} \pi_i g_{b_i}.$$

This is the kind of condition that we will encounter several times below. Adapting the jargon of earlier chapters, the direction of the pollution trend is determined by a race between a Scale effect and a Technology effect.

To make this example more similar to what we find in the one-sector growth models below, we can rephrase it under the assumption that all sectors are polluting equally much per unit of output. This means that we impose $b_i(t) = b(t)$ and thus $g_{b_i} = g_b$ for all i. The sum representing the technology effects is therefore simplified: $\Sigma_{i=1}^{n} \pi_i g_b = g_b \Sigma_{i=1}^{n} \pi_i = g_b$. Equation (7.2) thus boils down to

$$g_X = g_Y + g_b,$$

and consequently the condition for avoiding pollution growth is simply reduced to

$$g_X \leq 0 \quad \Leftrightarrow \quad g_Y \leq -g_b.$$

This means that the emission per unit of output must decline at a faster rate than the aggregate output grows.

It may be useful to illustrate the relation between the rates of change of income and pollution in a figure. To this end, we rewrite the previous equation as $g_Y = -g_b + g_X$. More interestingly,

$$g_y = -g_b + g_X - n,$$

where we have used $g_y = g_Y - n$. In Figure 7.1, where we measure g_X and g_y on the axes, this equation is shown as a positively sloping straight line. It

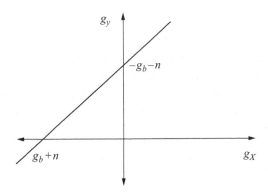

Figure 7.1. Trade-off between pollution and income

has a slope equal to 1 due to the simple structure of the model.[4] The positive slope means that a higher income growth can be obtained if pollution is allowed to grow faster. If $-g_b > n$, that is pollution per value unit of output declines faster than the population growth rate, a part of this line is found in the second quadrant. This part can be said to constitute the *sustainability region*, because here it is possible to choose a rising per capita income along with falling pollution, which is to say that sustainability is feasible. If $-g_b$ gets higher, this region is expanded, so the set of possible choices is improved. For instance, a faster income growth can be had at an unchanged rate of decline in pollution.

7.2 **Stock pollution**

For most environmental problems it is natural to regard pollution as a *stock* variable, built up by a history of emission *flows*, which have been added to the stock over many years. For example, the atmosphere contains large quantities of methane, CO_2, and other greenhouse gases, which contribute to global warming.[5] The concentrations of these substances have reached their present levels partly by the contributions generated by human economic activities, mostly since the beginning of industrialization. New units are continuously added, tending to increase the stocks, but there are also natural decay processes. Some other long-lasting pollutants are: (i) heavy metals, for example lead and mercury; and (ii) persistent synthetic chemicals, such as PCB, DDT, and dioxines.

To model the dynamics of a pollution stock, we denote it by Q and form a differential equation that describes the change of this stock over time.[6] The stock tends to grow due to new emissions, X, whereas the natural decay can be represented by the term $-\phi Q$, where ϕ is the rate of decay. We thus have the equation

$$\dot{Q} = X - \phi Q. \tag{7.3}$$

The change in the pollution stock can thus be either positive, negative, or zero, depending on the magnitudes of the two right hand side terms. Note that the natural decay term is stronger the higher ϕ and Q are. The latter would mean that nature has a greater capacity to break down the pollutant, or that the pollutant is easier to break down, when the stock is large. This is obviously

[4] In Section 7.4 the slope of a similar line will depend on the parameters from the production-pollution structure of the model.

[5] See Stern (2007) and Nordhaus (2008) for two prominent analyses of the climate problem. There has been an extensive debate around the different conclusions that they come to.

[6] This stock may be seen as an aggregate of many (even all relevant) pollutants.

questionable and therefore we will look at an example with non-linear decay toward the end of this section.

To give the simplest possible illustration of how equation (7.3) works, we start by assuming that X is constant, at the level X_1. Then the dynamics of the pollution stock can be described by Figure 7.2, where the two right hand terms of (7.3) are represented by one line each. We see that there is an intersection between the horizontal X_1 line and the positively sloping ϕQ line at one and only one point. Furthermore, it is clear that Q is drawn to this point: to the left of it $\dot{Q} > 0$, whereas $\dot{Q} < 0$ to the right of it. At this unique intersection $\dot{Q} = 0$ and we have $X_1 = \phi Q$, which implies that the long-run stock of pollution is

$$Q^* = \frac{1}{\phi}X_1.$$

There is thus a limit to how large the pollution stock will be in the long run, given that there is a constant flow of emission. As can be expected, the steady state pollution stock will be small if the rate of decay is high or if the pollution flow is low.

The reason that Q eventually stops growing is that the natural decay increases as the stock grows, that is ϕQ is higher at a larger Q. This part of the formulation in (7.3) has been subject to criticism, however. It implicitly assumes away any limitations to nature's capacity to break down toxic substances. On the contrary, the model assumes that nature becomes stronger through high strain from pollution. This is hardly realistic. If nature is consistently overloaded there is instead likely to be a major breakdown of the ecological system upon which economic activity rests. One way to take into account that there is a limit to how much the environment can endure is to assume that there will be an ecological

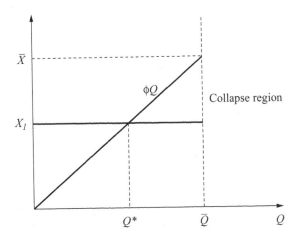

Figure 7.2. Stock pollution dynamics

collapse if the pollution stock surpasses a critical level, say $\bar{Q}$. A consequence of such a collapse would be a very drastic reduction of the economy's productive capacity (along with deteriorated living conditions). This border is illustrated by the vertical line at $\bar{Q}$ in Figure 7.2.

Although the model involves a clear risk of an ecological collapse, there is a somewhat encouraging message from this analysis, namely that it is fully possible to avoid a collapse, provided that X is chosen low enough. There is a critical value of X, such that the steady state pollution stock is on the border of the collapse region. We denote this quantity of pollution by $\bar{X}$, which is shown in the figure. It is defined by the equality

$$\bar{X} = \bar{Q}\phi,$$

which describes a steady state where the steady state pollution stock is $Q^* = \bar{Q}$. By keeping X at least a bit lower than $\bar{X}$ it is possible to establish an environmental quality that allows a functioning ecological system on a long term, given that $Q(0) < \bar{Q}$.

The prospects become bleaker if we introduce a stronger limitation in nature's ability to break down pollution. For example, let us change (7.3) to

$$\dot{Q} = X - \varphi(Q), \tag{7.4}$$

where the function $\varphi(Q)$ is first growing, but with a declining slope, which eventually turns negative. This equation is illustrated in Figure 7.3, where the curve that represents $\varphi(Q)$ is hump shaped. We first note that the long-run pollution flow now must be lower than $\bar{X}$, because the decay curve bends down and never reaches $\bar{X}$. Moreover, if Q has found its way far to the right, it is necessary to choose X very low. For instance, if $Q = Q_2$, the pollution flow

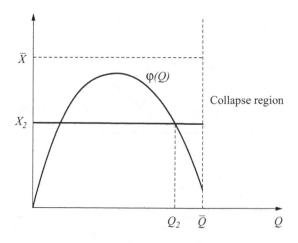

Figure 7.3. Non-linear pollution stock dynamics

cannot be higher than X_2[7] otherwise the pollution stock will grow into the collapse region. This means that the environment has become very weak in its capacity to make toxic substances less harmful when the pollution stock has grown large. It can therefore only recover if it gets some rest, that is low pollution inflows.

Let us now drop the assumption that the pollution flow is constant, and at the same time go back to the simpler formulation in (7.3). As the inhabitants of an economy experience higher incomes, it is possible that they prefer an increasingly better environment (at the cost of slower income growth). That is, they may want to decrease X from X_1 to X_2 and so on, all the way down to X_n in Figure 7.4.[8] Consequently Q will follow the indicated path downward, and ultimately end up at the steady state value Q_n.

Another scenario, which some people might regard as an illustration of what is happening in the world today, begins with initial emissions higher than $\bar{X}$. Because Q starts at a moderately high level, it will remain below $\bar{Q}$ for some time. Thus, there is still time to lower X so that the growth of the pollution stock comes to a halt (and possibly turns down) before it enters the collapse region. This means that we can have a scenario where measures will, or will not, be taken to reduce the emission flow to $X < \bar{X}$ before Q reaches $\bar{Q}$. Figure 7.5 illustrates two paths. One successfully brings the pollution stock down toward X_n, while the other leads into the collapse region because of a too slow reduction of the pollution flow.

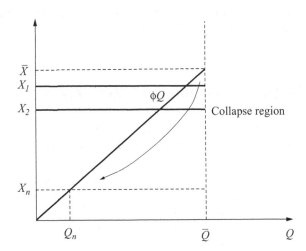

Figure 7.4. Stock pollution dynamics with changing emissions

---

[7] The intersection point at Q_2 is unstable: to the left of it (above the other intersection point) $\varphi(Q) > X_2$ and thus (by (7.4)) $\dot{Q} < 0$; to the right of it $\varphi(Q) < X_2$ and thus $\dot{Q} > 0$.

[8] It may not be optimal to push pollution all the way down to zero, because that is likely to be extremely costly.

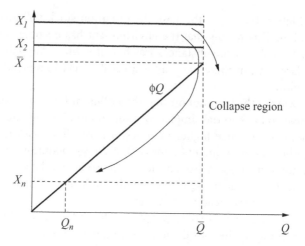

Figure 7.5. The race

While this analysis shows that it is important to take the stock property of pollution into account, it also points to a possibility of analyzing the question of sustainability in terms of the pollution flow only. For example, we can assume that X is initially lower than $\bar{X}$, or at least ends up below this level before the stock goes into the collapse region. Ensuring in this way that there will be no ecological breakdown, we can leave the dynamics of Q in the background and concentrate on the conditions for a non-increasing X. This is the simplification that we will allow ourselves from here on.[9]

7.3 Production, pollution, and abatement

This section develops a production–pollution–abatement structure in which economic activity generates pollution jointly with ordinary gross output, and where some gross output can be used for abatement in order to bring the net pollution down. For example, abatement can take the form of installations of scrubbers, which reduce sulfur emissions, or catalytic converters in cars, which transform toxic exhaust gases into less damaging substances.

The relations between production, pollution, and abatement, and in particular the paths they take over time when we place them in a growth model, clearly depend much on the assumptions that we make here. This motivates a somewhat lengthy discussion of the mathematical forms that we use and

---

[9] The reader is, however, encouraged to look at Xepapadeas (2005) for more examples with stock pollution.

their implications. One version of this structure, which we judge as neither too optimistic nor too pessimistic, is put into a growth model in the next section.

We now make a distinction between gross output and net output. Gross output is produced according to the function

$$Y^G = F(K, AL_Y),$$

which is a standard neo-classical function, with constant returns to scale in capital and labor.

Jointly with the ordinary output, some gross pollution, X^G, is generated, since more output is likely to imply a higher material throughput, for example more use of materials and energy. We will simply assume that

$$X^G = Y^G.$$

In words, gross pollution is proportional to gross output, and for simplicity the constant of proportionality is chosen to be unity here. This could be motivated by the choice of units.[10]

It is assumed that the share ϑ of gross output is used in pollution abatement. This share is not necessarily constant over time. The production output that remains after the setting aside for abatement is then the net output

$$Y = (1 - \vartheta)F(K, AL_Y). \tag{7.5}$$

Of course, only this part of the gross output is available for investment[11] and consumption.

When we formulate a function for net pollution, X, it is natural to assume that it rises with gross pollution, X^G, and that it falls if abatement, ϑY^G, gets higher. The net pollution can thus be described by the function

$$X = H\left(\vartheta Y^G, Y^G\right), \tag{7.6}$$

which is decreasing in its first argument and increasing in the second. The mathematical properties of this function can be specified further in different ways. The choices we make in this step will, of course, have crucial implications for the feasibility of sustainable development. We will illustrate this by three examples, which have some (but not full) similarities with the production functions that we have studied above. The examples do not aspire to full coverage, but they nevertheless show how much the results can change, following slight variations in the parameter values.

---

[10] For example, if one unit of output generates 5 kilograms of pollution, we can define 5 kilograms of pollution as one unit of pollution.

[11] There is no explicit modeling of abatement as an *investment* here. Abatement can thus best be considered a flow activity in this chapter. The "green" technological change in Chapter 8 captures the investment aspect more explicitly.

7.3.1 SPECIFIC FORM I

As a first example, we assume that the function in (7.6) takes a log-linear form, like $X = x^I \left(\vartheta Y^G\right)^{-a} \left(Y^G\right)^b$, where x^I, a, and b are positive constants. One could say that this function is a Cobb–Douglas in the two variables $(\vartheta Y^G)^{-1}$ and Y^G, but not necessarily with constant returns to scale. This clearly means that net pollution increases in gross pollution and declines in abatement. To analyze how X might change over time, we rewrite the previous expression as

$$X = x^I \cdot \frac{\left(Y^G\right)^{b-a}}{\vartheta^a}. \tag{7.7}$$

Let us first discuss the implications of this equation under the assumption that ϑ is constant. It is then clear that net pollution depends entirely on the difference $b - a$. If $b > a$, it is unavoidable that net pollution increases as gross production grows. Although the growth rate may be low, because the exponent $b - a$ can be small, the growth is continuously ongoing. This case is thus not reconcilable with sustainable development. An underlying assumption, driving this scenario, could be that more advanced production techniques create more difficult abatement problems. While this is not entirely implausible, we will not consider such an outcome to be the most likely one.

The possibility that $b = a$ does not seem implausible either (at least at first sight).[12] It would mean that net pollution is $X = x^I/\vartheta^a$, and therefore can be maintained at a constant level as gross output grows, if a constant share is used in abatement.[13] In this case, total abatement would grow at the same rate as gross output, which would be the explanation for the possibility of keeping X constant. It is, however, questionable that pollution is entirely independent of the gross production volume, and therefore this particular case seems a bit unlikely.

Allowing ϑ to now increase over time, not much is added. This is most easily seen by going back to the case where $b > a$. It is clear the the time path of net pollution is the result of a race between gross output and the abatement share. The latter has an upper limit at $\vartheta = 1$, however (which implies that consumption is zero). Beyond that, X will unambiguously grow because Y^G grows. This leaves us with a pessimistic outcome that is not very different from the case with a constant ϑ. Similar results can be obtained under other assumptions about the difference $b - a$.

A preliminary conclusion is therefore that the net pollution function suggested here is sufficiently flexible to generate a wide variety of implications.

---

[12] We leave the case $b < a$, implying a steady decline in X, for the very strong optimists. This is probably only possible if there also is technological progress in the abatement technology, which we do not analyze until the next chapter.

[13] The constant x^I would then be the minimum amount of pollution, that is the result of putting $\vartheta = 1$.

It may therefore be useful, but a potential weakness is that it is not possible to drive X all the way down to zero by use of ϑ alone. In fact, the limited role of ϑ makes the (opportunity) cost of abatement less important for the time path of pollution. Instead, it depends on the quite arbitrary parameters a and b, which makes the outcome very dependent on "luck." We therefore now turn to an example that more explicitly requires that consumption and investment must be foregone in order to have substantial abatement.

7.3.2 SPECIFIC FORM II

In the previous example, we essentially assumed that it was possible to pull out both Y^G factors in (7.6) from the H function, so that only ϑ remained in it. We now assume something similar for a general function, but with quite different possibilities with respect to the effects of varying ϑ. More specifically, we look at the case when (7.6) can be written as

$$X = H(\vartheta Y^G, Y^G) = H(\vartheta, 1) \cdot Y^G.$$

We can simplify this by defining the more condensed function $h(\vartheta) \equiv H(\vartheta, 1)$. Thus

$$X = h(\vartheta) \cdot F(K, AL_Y). \tag{7.8}$$

This means that net pollution increases in step with production if ϑ is constant. But h is decreasing in ϑ, that is $h'(\vartheta) < 0$, because H is declining in its first argument. Thus, as in (7.6), pollution is lower if a larger fraction of the gross output is set aside for abatement activities, at constant gross production.

We assume that $h(\vartheta) \leq 1$, with $h(0) = 1$. The implication is then that $X = Y^G$, that is pollution is at its maximum level and equals gross output if there is no abatement, that is if $\vartheta = 0$.

As ϑ increases, $h(\vartheta)$ falls, and a very important question then is whether it falls toward zero or not. If it does not, that is if $h(1) > 0$, then we have a pessimistic scenario, in which net pollution will be strictly positive even if all gross output is used in abatement. An implication is also that net pollution is bound to grow at the same rate as gross output in the long run (albeit possibly on a low level).

As many times before, we can change the outcome drastically by varying an assumption. For instance, let us say that there is some $\tilde{\vartheta} < 1$, such that $h(\tilde{\vartheta}) = 0$, that is it is possible to entirely choke pollution without using all gross output in abatement. This implies very beneficial conditions for abatement, which make it possible to (for instance) have a growth path with $X = 0$ and $Y = (1 - \tilde{\vartheta})F(K, AL_Y)$, where the latter is forever growing. It is thus feasible to have an entirely clean environment, given that one is prepared to pay a certain fraction of gross income for it (a fraction which can be large).

Finally, there is the possibility of a middle ground case, in which $h(\vartheta) \to 0$ when $\vartheta \to 1$. This is the case that we will eventually use in a growth model in the next section, but in a somewhat more specific version. We now turn to this.

7.3.3 SPECIFIC FORM III

The functional form that will be applied from here (used in Copeland and Taylor, 2003) is neither very pessimistic nor optimistic. The assumption now is that $h = (1 - \vartheta)^{1/\beta}$, where $0 < \beta < 1$. This formulation implies that $h = 0$ only when $\vartheta = 1$.[14] The pollution function (7.8) is then modified to

$$X = (1 - \vartheta)^{1/\beta} \cdot F(K, AL_Y). \tag{7.9}$$

The parameter β influences the effect of an increased ϑ on X. At given gross pollution and abatement share, a higher β implies more net pollution, that is less beneficial conditions for abatement activities.[15]

To analyze the full growth model, it is useful to derive a production function, where pollution enters *as if* it were an input. To this end, we solve (7.9) for $1 - \vartheta = X^\beta \cdot [F(K, AL_Y)]^{-\beta}$ and substitute this into (7.5). The result is

$$Y = X^\beta \cdot [F(K, AL_Y)]^{-\beta} \cdot F(K, AL_Y),$$

or

$$Y = X^\beta \cdot [F(K, AL_Y)]^{1-\beta}. \tag{7.10}$$

We have thus transformed the function such that pollution is like a factor of production. The production function exhibits constant returns to scale in X, K, and L_Y together. If β is high, pollution is like an important input in the net production function. As we will see below, a high β makes sustainable development less likely. In the process of deriving (7.10) we have eliminated the important variable ϑ, but once we understand the dynamics of the other variables, we will go back and describe how it changes over time (see Section 7.5).

---

[14] This example could be extended to more optimistic and pessimistic cases if the function is modified to $h = (1 - \vartheta + \varpi)^{1/\beta}$, where ϖ is a constant. If $\varpi > 0$, h will be positive even if $\vartheta = 1$, so that pollution can never be fully choked. If $\varpi < 0$, on the other hand, $h = 0$ when $\vartheta = 1 + \varpi < 1$, implying zero pollution even if not all gross output is used in abatement.

[15] Equation (7.9) can be rewritten as $X = e^{\frac{1}{\beta} \ln(1-\vartheta)} \cdot F(K, AL_Y)$. The derivative with respect to β is

$$\frac{\partial X}{\partial \beta} = -\frac{1}{\beta^2} \ln(1 - \vartheta) e^{\frac{1}{\beta} \ln(1-\vartheta)} \cdot F(K, AL_Y) = -\frac{1}{\beta^2} \cdot \ln(1 - \vartheta) \cdot X > 0,$$

since $1 - \vartheta < 1$.

7.4 **The growth model**

This section places the production–pollution–abatement structure just presented in an economic growth model. From the analysis in the previous section it is clear that the substitutability between capital and labor is not central for the feasibility of sustainable development in the present context. Instead, the relation between gross output, on the one hand, and abatement/pollution, on the other, is very important. Therefore, we will confine ourselves to the tractable case where the technology for gross production can be described by a Cobb–Douglas function, namely $Y^G = K^{\tilde{\alpha}}(AL_Y)^{1-\tilde{\alpha}}$, where $0 < \tilde{\alpha} < 1$. This gives the following modified version of (7.10):

$$Y = X^{\beta}(K^{\tilde{\alpha}}(AL_Y)^{1-\tilde{\alpha}})^{-\beta} \cdot K^{\tilde{\alpha}}(AL_Y)^{1-\tilde{\alpha}} = X^{\beta}K^{\tilde{\alpha}(1-\beta)}(AL_Y)^{(1-\tilde{\alpha})(1-\beta)}.$$

We can simplify the notation by putting $\tilde{\alpha}(1 - \beta) = \alpha$, which implies that $(1 - \tilde{\alpha})(1 - \beta) = 1 - \alpha - \beta$. The result is that net output is given by the function

$$Y = K^{\alpha}X^{\beta}(AL_Y)^{1-\alpha-\beta}. \tag{7.11}$$

This function could be understood as follows: to increase net output, at given quantities of capital and labor, the services of these factors in abatement activities have to decrease. The resulting increase in pollution is here visible in the production function. It may seem like a high β is a good thing, since a given value of X^{β} can then be obtained at a lower X. However, a high β means that α and $1 - \alpha - \beta$ get smaller, giving the "real" production factors lower impact on net output, and we will see that this jeopardizes sustainablity later in this section. Moreover, as we saw in connection to (7.9) a high β implies a low productivity of abatement.

By familiar reasoning, the dynamics of the growth model is such that $z = K/Y$ approaches a unique steady state value, wherever it starts from (unless X falls very rapidly). It is left as an exercise for the reader to show this (see Exercise (7.2)). As before, we will use the implied steady state equality $g_Y = g_K$ when we now look at the feasible relation between the long-run rates of change of central variables, which here are income and pollution.

As usual we start by taking the logarithm of the production function. In this case (7.11) is transformed to

$$\ln Y = \alpha \ln K + \beta \ln X + (1 - \alpha - \beta)\ln A + (1 - \alpha - \beta)\ln L_Y.$$

By differentiating both sides of this equation with respect to time, we find that the relation between proportional growth rates is

$$g_Y = \alpha g_K + \beta g_X + (1 - \alpha - \beta)g_A + (1 - \alpha - \beta)n.$$

The growth of output is as always a weighted sum of the rates of change of the inputs where pollution is now one of them. At this point we use the fact that $g_Y = g_K$ in the long run, to eliminate the growth rate of capital. The result is

$$g_Y = \frac{1}{1 - \alpha} \left(\beta g_X + (1 - \alpha - \beta)g_A + (1 - \alpha - \beta)n \right). \tag{7.12}$$

Note that total output can grow even if pollution is not allowed to increase, due to the growth in A and L_Y.

Following the steps that we have gone through several times before, that is using the fact that $g_y = g_Y - n$ and simplifying, we obtain the rate of growth of per capita income as[16]

$$g_y = \frac{1}{1 - \alpha} \left((1 - \alpha - \beta)g_A - \beta(n - g_X) \right). \tag{7.13}$$

The interpretation of this expression can again be phrased in terms of a race between a driver and a drag on growth. If we require that pollution should decline over time, so that $g_X < 0$, then the drag consists of two terms, and it is more severe if β is large. A higher β means that abatement efforts are less effective in reducing pollution, as mentioned above. Note that equation (7.13) is very similar to the corresponding expressions in the chapters with natural resources in a Cobb–Douglas production function (cf. equation (6.23)). This is not surprising, given the similarity of the production functions.

Is this model economy able to exhibit sustainable development, which here it is natural to define by the two requirements that $g_y \geq 0$ and $g_X \leq 0$? To see the available options, it is useful to separate the right hand side of (7.13) into two terms such that:

$$g_y = \frac{(1 - \alpha - \beta)g_A - \beta n}{1 - \alpha} + \frac{\beta}{1 - \alpha} g_X. \tag{7.14}$$

This equation is depicted as a positively sloping straight line in Figure 7.6. At given values of the parameters and g_A, this line describes the feasible long-run combinations of g_y and g_X. When one of these rates of change is chosen, equation (7.14) gives the other. The positive slope of this line means that a faster decline in pollution has a "cost" in terms of a lower growth rate in per capita income, which can be illustrated by a movement down to the left along the line.

If there are good conditions and good incentives to carry out research, there is a trade-off between growth and an improved environment, not an unresolvable conflict.[17] To see this, we note that the condition

---

[16] The pollution variable X is not expressed in per capita terms. This is because it is regarded as a perfect public "bad," which means that there is no rivalry in the suffering from it. For further discussions about this, see Baumol and Oates (1988), Chapter 3.

[17] In analogy with our previous analyses, one technology factor is sufficient here, because the production function is a Cobb–Douglas.

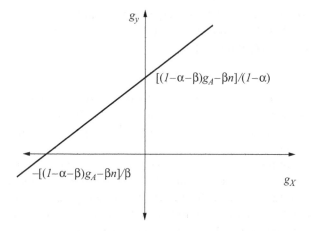

Figure 7.6. Trade-off between increasing income and declining pollution

$$(1 - \alpha - \beta)g_A > \beta n, \tag{7.15}$$

which clearly can be satisfied if g_A is high enough, is sufficient for the line to go through the second quadrant in Figure 7.6. This segment is especially interesting, since here $g_y \geq 0$ and $g_X \leq 0$. Like in Section 7.1, we will call it the *sustainability region*. To develop an understanding of this region, it may be useful to start by looking at the two intersections with the axes, that is the points where either income or pollution are constant.[18]

Consider first the possibility that society decides to accept a constant pollution, that is $g_X = 0$.[19] Then (7.14) is reduced to

$$g_y = \frac{(1 - \alpha - \beta)g_A - \beta n}{1 - \alpha}.$$

Provided that technological progress is sufficiently strong to fulfill (7.15), growth in per capita income is feasible. In fact this expression is identical to equation (5.17) in Chapter 5. The constant production factor, land, is here replaced by the "production factor" pollution, which is also unchanged in this paragraph. Like in Chapter 5, the constant factor causes diminishing returns to labor and capital, making the growth rate in per capita income lower than g_A.

---

[18] There is no reason to assume that the inhabitants of the economy find one of them the most preferred choice; we are just exploring the possible choices.

[19] By the production function, the *level* of X can be freely chosen, with an implied level of income for each X (at given K, A, and L_Y).

Next, assume a hypothetical society that gives high priority to an improved environmental quality and instead accepts zero income growth, that is $g_y = 0$. Then equation (7.14) implies that

$$g_X = - \left[(1 - \alpha - \beta)g_A - \beta n \right] / \beta.$$

For a declining pollution it is then, of course, required that (7.15) is fulfilled (so that the sustainability region exists). The more forceful the growth-promoting technological change is, in the race against the drag on growth, the faster the pollution decline will be here.

Any point in the sustainability region could, of course, be preferred.[20] The more important a good environmental quality is for the inhabitants of the economy, the further down to the left the chosen point will be. To be able to say what the best long-run combination of g_y and g_X is, we would need to formulate an intertemporal optimization problem, with utility of consumption and disutility of pollution. As explained earlier, however, such an analysis is beyond the scope of this book. We do introduce a utility function in Chapter 9, though, but not in an intertemporal optimization problem.

A higher g_A expands the sustainability region, that is the line in Figure 7.6 takes a parallel upward shift (because the constant term in (7.14) gets higher). If the research technology is of the Romer type, such a change can be accomplished by a reallocation of labor (possibly following improved incentives to do research) such that L_A becomes higher and L_Y lower.[21] At a higher rate of technological progress the set of feasible choices is thus improved, in the sense that income can grow and pollution can decline at higher rates. A movement in the opposite direction (though not parallel) will happen if β increases, so that the growth drag becomes stronger. Of course, the conditions may be so bad that the sustainability region will not exist. This happens if $(1 - \alpha - \beta)g_A < \beta n$, so that the middle term of (7.14) is negative. The line does not then go through the second quadrant, which means that a constant pollution would require declining per capita income.

It is interesting to note the formal similarity between equation (7.14) and equation (6.23). In both cases there are two drags on growth. The difference is that the necessarily declining amount of energy in Chapter 6 is here replaced by the possibly falling pollution. Moreover, the downward trend in pollution is a good thing, which is not necessarily true for the declining energy (unless energy is polluting).

---

[20] Points outside the sustainability region can perhaps not be entirely ruled out as undesirable. However, when we take the stock aspect of pollution and the collapse region from Section 7.2 into account, a growing pollution flow cannot be permitted in the long run.

[21] The latter of course means that income growth occurs at a lower level, and thus we have a trade-off between the present and the future. Again, an intertemporal optimization problem is required to find the right balance.

7.5 **Abatement share**

The long-run dynamics of y and X described above is tied to an underlying time path of ϑ, the share of gross output used in abatement. From Section 7.3 it seems necessary that the abatement share tends to unity in the long run, if pollution is to be held in check. We now examine this closer.

To reintroduce the variable ϑ, we substitute the gross production function that we used in the previous section, $Y^G = K^{\tilde{\alpha}}(AL_Y)^{1-\tilde{\alpha}}$, into (7.9). This gives the net pollution

$$X = (1 - \vartheta)^{1/\beta} \cdot K^{\tilde{\alpha}}(AL_Y)^{1-\tilde{\alpha}}. \tag{7.16}$$

Computing the logarithm of both sides of equation (7.16), we have $\ln X = \frac{1}{\beta} \ln(1-\vartheta) + \tilde{\alpha} \ln K + (1-\tilde{\alpha})\ln(AL_Y)$. We then differentiate both sides with respect to time and obtain

$$g_X = -\frac{1}{\beta}\frac{\dot{\vartheta}}{1-\vartheta} + \tilde{\alpha}g_K + (1-\tilde{\alpha})(g_A + n).$$

Since we will combine this with one other equation, it is useful to eliminate $\tilde{\alpha}$. This is done by noting that the assumption in the previous section (just before (7.11)) implies that $\tilde{\alpha} = \frac{\alpha}{1-\beta}$ and $1 - \tilde{\alpha} = \frac{1-\alpha-\beta}{1-\beta}$. Therefore we have

$$g_X = -\frac{1}{\beta}\frac{\dot{\vartheta}}{1-\vartheta} + \frac{\alpha}{1-\beta}g_K + \frac{1-\alpha-\beta}{1-\beta}(g_A + n).$$

To reduce the number of variables, we use equation (7.12) and the steady state condition $g_Y = g_K$ to eliminate g_K, so that

$$g_X = -\frac{1}{\beta}\frac{\dot{\vartheta}}{1-\vartheta} + \frac{\alpha}{1-\beta}\frac{1}{1-\alpha}\left(\beta g_X + (1-\alpha-\beta)g_A + (1-\alpha-\beta)n\right)$$

$$+\frac{1-\alpha-\beta}{1-\beta}(g_A + n).$$

This equation can be simplified by collecting terms:

$$\dot{\vartheta} = [1 - \vartheta]\frac{\beta}{1-\beta}\frac{1}{1-\alpha}(1-\alpha-\beta)\cdot\left((g_A + n)(1-\alpha+\alpha\beta) - g_X\right). \tag{7.17}$$

See Exercise 7.3 for a demonstration of this.

Let us now focus on the dynamics of ϑ, and just assume that g_X is a given constant. One possibility to have ϑ constant is when $(g_A + n)(1-\alpha+\alpha\beta) = g_X$. Since this implies that pollution is increasing over time, however, we shall not devote much attention to this possibility. Instead, we examine the case with $(g_A + n)(1 - \alpha + \alpha\beta) - g_X > 0$, preferably with pollution declining.

The vital part of equation (7.17) is then the brackets with $1 - \vartheta$, since what follows after it is just a positive constant. For all values of ϑ smaller than unity, ϑ is growing and the growth stops only when $\vartheta = 1$. Abatement thus tends to swallow all gross output in the long run. However, ϑ approaches unity only asymptotically and never actually gets there. There is thus always some output to consume and invest, and it can continuously grow, due to the growth in A, as described in the previous section.

According to Brock and Taylor (2010) abatement's share of GDP is relatively constant and rather low in developed countries. The model does not at all seem consistent with this stylized fact. However, we need to recall that ϑ is the share of *gross* output that is used for abatement. The conclusion is modified when we relate the sum of pollution taxes to net output in Section 7.6.

7.6 **Environmental policy**

Polluting emissions are typically negative external effects, and unregulated firms seldom have the incentives to take the costs of reducing them all the way down to a socially optimal level. Therefore, there are pollution taxes. We now look at how such a tax can influence a representative profit-maximizing firm's decisions. Since we have not introduced a utility function, we will not be able to say whether the pollution reaches its socially optimal level. The analysis is thus only positive, not normative.

We will let the tax on pollution be τ_X. Using the production function in (7.11), we can form the profit function,

$$\Pi = K^\alpha X^\beta (AL_Y)^{1-\alpha-\beta} - rK - wL - \tau_X X,$$

for a representative firm. A necessary condition for profit maximization with respect to X is that

$$K^\alpha \beta X^{\beta-1} (AL_Y)^{1-\alpha-\beta} = \tau_X.$$

This, of course, means that it is optimal for the firm to increase the amount of pollution up to the point where its marginal product equals the pollution tax.

By using the production function itself, this optimality condition can be simplified to

$$\beta \cdot \frac{Y}{X} = \tau_X. \tag{7.18}$$

An immediate implication of this version of the optimality condition is that the firm finds it optimal to let the quantity of pollution grow in step with output, if the environmental tax is constant. To understand why this is so, note that the marginal productivity of pollution increases if the other inputs grow, while

X remains constant. The marginal product of pollution then comes to exceed the pollution tax rate. It is therefore optimal to raise X to the point where the equality in (7.18) is restored. We thus learn that the tax rate cannot be constant if income grows and we want pollution to be non-increasing.

To get an expression for the optimal development of pollution over time, from the firm's perspective, we take the logs of (7.18) and differentiate with respect to time. The result is $g_Y - g_X = g_{\tau_X}$, or

$$g_X = g_Y - g_{\tau_X}. \tag{7.19}$$

To make pollution fall as time runs, it is required that the tax grows faster than total output.

The necessity of a permanently increasing pollution tax rate may seem to distort business to a very serious extent. However, equation (7.18) implies that $\tau_X X / Y = \beta$. This means that the total pollution tax sum that the firm pays in optimum will always be a constant share of the net output, irrespective of the tax rate. This does not directly correspond to the empirical observations of Brock and Taylor (2010), that abatement expenditure as a share of GDP is fairly constant over time. However, it is much less to the contrary of these facts than the impression that is given by just looking at ϑ, as we did in Section 7.5.

Finally, the reader should be alerted to the fact that we here assume optimization only in one dimension, namely the firm's optimal choice of pollution, and examine how it is influenced by economic policy. Recall, however, that we have replaced other aspects of optimization with rule-of-thumb behavior, notably savings and research efforts. If optimization were to be introduced in these respects as well, the policy implications would be enriched, but with condition (7.18) being one of them.

7.7 **Conclusion**

In this chapter we introduce a link between economic activity and pollution. The link is constructed here such that the pollution flow in the end appears as an input in production. From there, the analysis is remarkably analogous to the Cobb–Douglas cases in the preceding two chapters. Thus, the condition for sustainability can be phrased as a technology effect winning a race against dampers of growth. In this case, the latter are due to population growth and the decline in pollution.

Although the stock aspect of pollution is admittedly important, we argued that the analysis can be concentrated on the flow of pollution, given that the stock is kept small enough to avoid an ecological collapse. This is a fairly safe strategy if we focus on growth paths with non-increasing pollution flows (and with the initial pollution stock not being in the collapse region), which we do here. The reader is nevertheless encouraged to go further to references with stock pollution (see below). For instance, a serious analysis of climate change cannot be done without modeling the greenhouse gases in the atmosphere as a stock.

▓ FURTHER READING

The reviews by Brock and Taylor (2005) and Xepapadeas (2005) are strongly recommended, although the reader might find some parts of them difficult. The reader might also find parts of Chapter 5 in Aghion and Howitt (1998) interesting, as well as parts of Chapter 16 in Aghion and Howitt (2009). See also Perman et al. (2011), Chapter 16.

7.8 **Exercises**

7.1 **Scale, Technology, and Composition effects**
Derive equation (7.2).

7.2 z **Dynamics**
Show that the dynamics of z is globally stable in the model of Section 7.4.

7.3 **Abatement share**
Derive equation (7.17).

8 Pollution reduction by directed technological change

In this chapter we reintroduce the concept of directed technological change. In addition to the labor-augmenting technology factor A, we will have the technology factor B, which in one way or another makes the production technology cleaner. The latter factor thus captures environmental or (for variation) green technological change.[1]

In a first example, developed over Sections 8.1 through 8.3, it is assumed that gross pollution is proportional to output.[2] The environmental technology factor helps reduce a certain quantity of gross pollution to a lower quantity of net pollution. The higher B is, the larger this reduction. A central issue is how gross pollution and green technology interact in the determination of net pollution. Even if there is a strong growth in the green technology factor, the question still remains how able it is to counteract the environmental consequences of production. Central to the results are the properties of the function describing the interplay between output and the environmental technology factor in determining the net pollution level.

We analyze the implications of two forms of this *net pollution function*, bearing similarities to the Cobb–Douglas and CES functions, respectively. In the former case, declining pollution is possible if the environmental technology improves at a sufficiently high rate, compared to the growth rate of the labor-augmenting technology factor (and the labor growth rate). If the function is of the CES type, the outcome goes more to the extreme cases: either it is very easy to counteract pollution by development of environmental technology, or it is a very demanding task to do so.[3] This analysis thus points to the importance of making a distinction between the rates of growth of various technology factors, on the one hand, and their ability to influence the outcome of the model, on the other.

In Section 8.4 we connect back to Section 6.5, where renewable energy was successively substituted for non-renewable energy. Here we will add the

---

[1] There is now a large literature on growth with environmental technological change; see, for instance, Acemoglu et al. (2012) and Grimaud and Rouge (2008), which both provide many references. Much of this literature is inspired by Acemoglu's work on *directed technological change*; see, for example, Acemoglu (2002).

[2] In contrast to Chapter 7, there is no difference between gross and net output here, because no output is used in abatement.

[3] If the analysis of Chapter 7 could be understood as end-of-pipe abatement, we here consider a beginning-of-the process activity to reduce pollution, captured by the technology factor B.

assumption that the latter is polluting, and analyze how pollution changes over time, as the relative use of the polluting input is declining. It is not at all safe to assume that the absolute use of the polluting energy falls, because a growing economy tends to use more energy.[4] The result will, of course, depend on the development of the relative prices of these two types of energy (which is influenced by the environmental technology factor), and on the elasticity of substitution between them. The trend of the polluting non-renewable energy is also determined by the general growth path of the economy, in particular by the time paths of A and L.

8.1 A model with environmental technology

The model that we introduce here extends over Sections 8.1 through 8.3. In this section, we describe the production function and the growth model, which is familiar material. We also introduce the function that determines the net pollution, and finally examine the implications of a simple version of this function.

8.1.1 OUTPUT AND GROWTH

The production side of the economy is now much like that which we had at the beginning of this book, in particular Chapter 4. Production is neither a function of natural resources nor of pollution. It just depends on capital, labor, and the technology factor A. Therefore the capital accumulation is

$$\dot{K} = sF[K, AL_Y] - \delta K.$$

The productive capacity of the economy is here not influenced by the state of the environment. The influence only goes in the other direction: produced output generates pollution. We can therefore analyze the capital accumulation process separately, and then use the result of this in the analysis of pollution.

The first step can in fact be done rather quickly, based on the results in Chapter 4. First, the production function can, by the assumption about constant returns to scale, be rewritten as $Y = AL_Y f\left(\tilde{k}\right)$, where we recall that $\tilde{k} \equiv K/(AL_Y)$. Differentiating this with respect to time, we have

$$g_Y = g_A + n + \frac{f'\tilde{k}}{f} \cdot \frac{\dot{\tilde{k}}}{\tilde{k}}. \tag{8.1}$$

---

[4] Recall that we dropped the assumption about scarcity of energy in Section 6.5.

From Chapter 4 we know that the dynamics of the model is stable, that is the final term eventually vanishes, because $\tilde{k}$ approaches the constant $\tilde{k}^*$. If the economy starts at a $\tilde{k}$ that is lower than the steady state value, the growth rate of Y will be higher during the transition period than it will be in steady state. In the long run, the total output is $Y = AL_Y f\left(\tilde{k}^*\right)$, and the growth rate of output will be $g_Y = g_A + n$. We will therefore often simply substitute this fact into the expressions below.

As in the later part of Chapter 4, the labor constraint is $L = L_Y + L_A + L_B$, since there are two technology factors. Equation (4.12), with its three special cases, again describes how the growth rates of these technology factors depend on the choices of labor allocation to the two types of research, L_A and L_B, respectively. We will not discuss the absolute limits to growth from Section 4.3.4 in detail, but it will be quite obvious what the results would be if B were tending toward an upper bound. The focus is instead on the possible limitation of B in its *ability* to make production clean, not its growth rate, and therefore we will mostly assume the Romer version of (4.12).

8.1.2 POLLUTION

The total quantity of net pollution is an increasing function of gross pollution. We assume that gross pollution is proportional to Y, with the constant of proportion normalized to unity for simplicity. It is possible to mitigate the polluting consequences of a large output by investing in environmental technology, which here is represented by the variable B. Starting at the general level, we simply assume that net pollution is given by

$$X(t) = G(Y(t), B(t)). \tag{8.2}$$

This function is increasing in the first argument and decreasing in the second, that is $G_Y > 0$ and $G_B < 0$. The first variable causes a scale effect, while the second is a technology effect. A "greening" of technology is thus captured by an increase in B.

To follow the evolution of pollution,[5] we differentiate (8.2) with respect to time and get

$$g_X = \frac{G_Y Y}{G} g_Y + \frac{G_B B}{G} g_B \tag{8.3}$$

(see Exercise 8.1). This provides yet another illustration of the race between the scale and technology effects, with the first right hand term being positive and the second being negative, thus leaving the total effect unclear. It is obvious that

---

[5] We will here onwards use "pollution" and "net pollution" interchangeably.

the change in pollution is determined not only by the growth rates of Y and B. It also depends on the elasticities of G with respect to these variables. We cannot take for granted that these elasticities are constant as Y or B change. Therefore we analyze the implications of having them varying with these variables in Section 8.3. However, assuming that they *are* constant still gives an opportunity to analyze some important aspects of the model, and therefore we start by doing just that in Sections 8.1.3 and 8.2.

8.1.3 THE SIMPLEST CASE

In some of the literature on growth and pollution,[6] the function in (8.2) has been assumed to take the simple form

$$X = \frac{Y}{B}. \tag{8.4}$$

This can be regarded as a Cobb–Douglas function in the variables Y and B^{-1}, that is $X = Y \cdot B^{-1}$. In that sense, it is an easy-to-handle special case of the Cobb–Douglas net pollution function that we will analyze in Section 8.2.

One way to illustrate the relation between the three variables in equation (8.4) is to draw *iso-pollution curves* in a figure with Y and B on the axes. One such curve would describe combinations of gross pollution and the environmental technology factor that give the same level of net pollution. To obtain the mathematical expression for an iso-pollution curve, we first fix pollution at some level X_1, and then solve (8.4) for

$$Y = X_1 \cdot B. \tag{8.5}$$

This curve is a straight line in this section, due to the simple form of the net pollution function, and it is illustrated in Figure 8.1. Since the curve is a positively sloping ray from the origin, it means that B must grow in proportion to Y (with X_1 as the constant of proportionality) in order to keep pollution constant.

At a lower pollution level, say X_2, equation (8.5) is modified to $Y = X_2 \cdot B$. This equation is also depicted in Figure 8.1, and has a lower slope than the curve representing (8.5). The implication is, of course, that a situation with less pollution can be obtained only at the cost of lower output, at given B. Alternatively, pollution can decline at constant output if B increases, and of course there are many possible combinations in between.

---

[6] See, for instance, Brock and Taylor (2010) (which, however, assumes exogenous technological change).

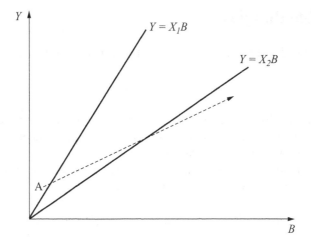

Figure 8.1. The simplest iso-pollution curve

To describe the various possibilities of change in pollution over time, let us take the logs of both sides in equation (8.4). The result is $\ln X(t) = \ln Y(t) - \ln B(t)$, which means that the relation between the rates of change is

$$g_X = g_Y - g_B. \tag{8.6}$$

An immediate consequence of this equation is that pollution declines if and only if the environmental technology factor grows faster than output. Thus, in contrast to (8.3), only the growth rates matter for the direction of the change of pollution, because both elasticities in (8.3) here equal unity (with opposite signs). This means that obtaining sustainable development is only a matter of putting a sufficient amount of effort into improving environmental technologies. In other words, the economy must allocate labor into research in such a way that $g_A + n \le g_B$.[7] Sustainability is thus feasible, but comes (as several times in earlier chapters) at the cost of holding back the growth rate and level of income, because L_A and L_Y must be kept low if L_B is high.

In Figure 8.1, a possible time path is illustrated by the dotted arrow starting at A. In this case B grows faster than Y, so that the path goes to lower and lower pollution levels, and thus lower iso-pollution curves.

We now turn to the possibility that the iso-pollution curves are not straight lines. That is, we follow an old habit in economics and generalize (8.4) (or specify (8.2)) to the Cobb–Douglas and CES forms, respectively, in the next two sections.

---

[7] As usual, there might be some obstacle to having this condition fulfilled if the research sector is best described by the Jones model.

8.2 **Cobb–Douglas**

A Cobb–Douglas version of the net pollution function (8.2) can, for example, be formulated as [8]

$$X = Y^a B^{-b}. \tag{8.7}$$

At this point we do not specify any values of the exponents a and b, except that they are positive. Actually, the purpose here is to examine the implications of various magnitudes of these parameters.[9]

One way to understand the implications of (8.7) is to look at the derivatives. Differentiating twice with respect to B, we have

$$\frac{\partial X}{\partial B} = -bY^a B^{-b-1} < 0 \quad \text{and} \quad \frac{\partial^2 X}{\partial B^2} = b(b+1)Y^a B^{-b-2} > 0.$$

The development of environmental technology thus lowers pollution, as expected. The positive second-order derivative means that additional units of the green technology factor produce smaller reductions in pollution, that is the returns to the green technology factor (in terms of reduced net pollution) are decreasing, irrespective of the magnitude of b.

As always for Cobb–Douglas functions, the exponents are elasticities, with straightforward interpretations. For instance

$$\frac{\partial X}{\partial B} \frac{B}{X} = -b,$$

which says how many percent net pollution declines if the green technology factor grows by 1 percent. Thus, a large b indicates that there are good conditions for making production cleaner.

The derivatives of the net pollution function in (8.7) with respect to Y are

$$\frac{\partial X}{\partial Y} = aY^{a-1} B^{-b} > 0 \quad \text{and} \quad \frac{\partial^2 X}{\partial Y^2} = a(a-1)Y^{a-2} B^{-b} \lessgtr 0.$$

The first derivative confirms that a higher output (gross pollution) raises net pollution, *ceteris paribus*. As long as $0 < a < 1$, the marginal increase of net pollution, following an additional unit of gross pollution, is declining. If $a > 1$,

---

[8] Toward the end of Section 8.3 we will specify this further to $X = Y^a B^{-(1-a)}$, because this is easier to compare with the CES function that we analyze there. However, it is also useful to allow more flexibility in the values of the exponents, not least for the discussion about the possible implications, and therefore we use the formulation in (8.7) here.

[9] There are some similarities between (8.7) and (7.7), but there are also considerable differences. For instance, the share of abatement in (7.7) has an upper limit (at unity), while B in (8.7) can grow without bound. Moreover, we do not make a difference between gross and net production here, because none of the output is used in abatement.

however, the "marginal product" is increasing, which would represent some kind of accelerating polluting effects of production.[10] Finally,

$$\frac{\partial X}{\partial Y}\frac{Y}{X} = a.$$

This constant elasticity shows the percentage increase in net pollution due to a 1 percent growth in gross pollution. A high a thus means that the conditions for keeping net pollution down are poor.

The logarithmic version of equation (8.7) is $\ln X(t) = a \ln Y(t) - b \ln B(t)$. Differentiating this with respect to time gives the growth rate of pollution as a weighted average of growth rates (with constant weights, in contrast to (8.3)):

$$g_X = a(g_A + n) - bg_B. \tag{8.8}$$

We have here used the steady state growth rate of output; the transitional dynamics will be discussed toward the end of this section.

In contrast to (8.6), equation (8.8) implies that the direction of change in X is not only determined by how fast the green technology factor grows compared to output. The necessary and sufficient condition for a non-increasing trend in pollution can be expressed as follows:

$$g_X \leq 0 \quad \Leftrightarrow \quad a(g_A + n) \leq bg_B. \tag{8.9}$$

We maintain a definition of sustainable development that can be succinctly expressed as $g_X \leq 0$ and $g_A \geq 0$, where the latter (implying non-declining per capita income) is assumed throughout. Thus, the possibility of such a development depends on the *ability* of the environmental technology factor to mitigate the polluting effects of the growing Y, which is captured by the parameters a and b. The larger b is, the more the greening of technology can accomplish. By contrast, a high value of a enforces the tendency of gross pollution to raise net pollution.[11]

The distinction between the magnitude of B and its actual effect on X may be understood as follows. The technology factor B itself captures the ability of the green dimension of technology (e.g. a chemical) to neutralize a toxic substance under ideal (lab) conditions. To the extent that the actual effect of B falls short of this potential ability in real applications, via the function in (8.7) (and more generally the G function in (8.2)), it can be explained by the green technology factor being applied to complex situations where many environmental problems are interacting. For instance, if several toxic substances are mixed at one place, a chemical that is designed to make one of them harmless may be

---

[10] The first unit of pollution may be easier to neutralize than later units.

[11] In the special case when $a = b$, we have that $g_X = a\left[(g_A + n) - g_B\right]$. Obviously, the possibility of $g_X < 0$ now depends only on the growth rates. Sustainable development is feasible if and only if $(g_A + n) < g_B$, as in (8.6).

partially destroyed by some of the others. The actual ability of B described in (8.7) thus refers to real ("field") conditions.

Sustainability can (as in many places above) clearly be seen as matter of choice for society. This is particularly obvious if the process of technological change is of the Romer type. Then we have $g_A = \eta_A s_A L$, $g_B = \eta_B s_B L$, and $n = 0$. Substituting this into the condition for sustainable development (8.9), gives

$$g_X \leq 0 \quad \Leftrightarrow \quad s_B \geq \frac{a}{b} \cdot \frac{\eta_A}{\eta_B} \cdot s_A. \tag{8.10}$$

It is clear that there will be sustainable development if the economy provides sufficiently strong incentives to conduct environmental research: if the share of labor that is allocated into environmental research is as high as required here, pollution will decline over time, and per capita income will rise if we assume that $s_A > 0$. Less effort in environmental research is necessary for sustainable development if a lower rate of income growth is chosen. The ratio a/b indicates the relative impact of gross pollution and green technology on net pollution. The higher it is, the stronger the efforts to develop green technology must be. This means that the amount of labor in production or in A-related research must be smaller, implying lower income growth (level, rate, or both).

For graphical illustrations of possible development paths, it is again useful to draw iso-pollution curves in the $Y - B$ plane. To this end, we solve equation (8.7) for

$$Y = X_1^{\frac{1}{a}} B^{\frac{b}{a}},$$

where we have fixed X at the specific level X_1. This equation gives a curve that describes combinations of Y and B for which net pollution is constant at X_1.

To see what shape such a curve can take, we examine the first- and second-order derivatives with respect to B. We have

$$\frac{dY}{dB} = X_1^{\frac{1}{a}} \frac{b}{a} B^{\frac{b-a}{a}} > 0.$$

The positive slope (again) means that a higher B allows for some increase in output, without net pollution being raised.

Whether the restriction of constant net pollution means that output can grow faster, or must grow slower, than the green technology factor is seen from the second-order derivative

$$\frac{d^2 Y}{dB^2} = X_1^{\frac{1}{a}} \frac{b}{a} \frac{b-a}{a} B^{\frac{b-2a}{a}}.$$

The sign of this expression depends entirely on the difference $b - a$. If $a > b$ the slope is decreasing, implying that the proportion Y/B falls along an iso-pollution curve. This means that it gets more difficult to counteract pollution as the scale of the economy grows. In (8.8) this corresponds to the environmental factor B having to grow faster than output, in order to keep X unchanged. On the other hand, if $a < b$ a constant X is reconcilable with an increasing Y/B ratio. The conditions are then so good that relatively less of environmental effort is needed to keep X constant as the scale of the economy grows. Finally, in the bordering case when $a = b$ the curve becomes a straight line. As the economy grows, environmental measures become neither less nor more difficult to undertake. Figures 8.2 and 8.3 illustrate the two cases with increasing and decreasing slopes of the iso-pollution curves, respectively.[12] It is clear that sustainable development is feasible in both cases. The difference is that the drag on income growth is more severe when $a > b$.

Let us finally consider transitional dynamics, that is the pollution path outside the steady state. Thus, we use (8.1) instead of $g_A + n$ for the grow rate of output in (8.8). The result is

$$g_X = a\left(g_A + n + \frac{f'\tilde{k}}{f} \cdot \frac{\dot{\tilde{k}}}{\tilde{k}}\right) - bg_B.$$

If we concentrate on the case in which $\tilde{k}$ is growing during the transition, we now have an additional positive term. During the transition this makes the first right hand term larger. It is therefore possible that the positive term

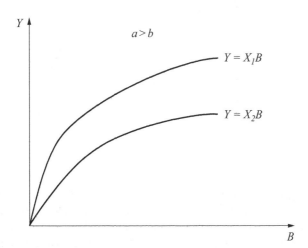

Figure 8.2. Cobb–Douglas iso-pollution curve 1

[12] We have already illustrated the case of a straight line in Section 8.1.3, for the special case $a = b = 1$.

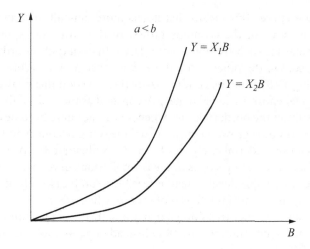

Figure 8.3. Cobb–Douglas iso-pollution curve 2

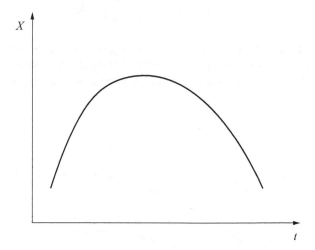

Figure 8.4. An environmental Kuznets curve

is dominating for the part of the period during which $\tilde{k}$ is growing fast, but yielding to the negative term as the steady state comes closer. In other words, it can happen that pollution is first increasing and then decreasing. We would then see an environmental Kuznets curve (EKC). Such a time path is depicted in Figure 8.4.[13]

---

[13] The original EKC curve (see Grossman and Krueger (1995)) related pollution to per capita income (not time). See Section 9.5 for more about this.

8.3 **CES**

We now turn to a second specific example of the G function in (8.2).[14] In this case it takes the CES form in Y and B^{-1}. More precisely,

$$X = \left[aY^{\varepsilon} + (1 - a)B^{-\varepsilon}\right]^{1/\varepsilon}, \qquad (8.11)$$

where $0 < a < 1$. In contrast to the CES production function, there are at this point no obvious reasons to assume any limitations on the parameter ε. We therefore just allow it to take any possible value, that is $-\infty < \varepsilon < \infty$.

To see how X evolves, we differentiate (8.11) with respect to time (see Exercise 8.2) and get the relations between the rates of proportional change as

$$g_X = \frac{a}{a + (1 - a)(BY)^{-\varepsilon}}(g_A + n) - \frac{(1 - a)}{a(YB)^{\varepsilon} + (1 - a)}g_B, \qquad (8.12)$$

where we have used the fact that $g_Y = g_A + n$ in steady state. Note that the product YB goes to infinity as time runs, because both these variables are steadily growing. It will therefore make a big difference whether ε is positive or negative, because this greatly influences the values that the weights in front of the growth rates in (8.12) tend to in the long run.[15]

Consider first the case when $\varepsilon > 0$. Then the factor in front of g_B in (8.12) falls toward zero over time, while the other weight tends to unity. Consequently, we have that

$$g_X \rightarrow g_A + n > 0$$

as time goes to infinity. No matter how fast the green technology factor develops, it will not be powerful enough to prevent the growth of the (production and pollution) scale from dominating the determination of the long-run pollution trend. An increasing net pollution then appears to be unavoidable as Y grows.[16]

This case is, however, not quite as gloomy as it may seem. To see why, let us for a moment relax the assumption about constant allocation of labor between the two kinds of research. In a model with optimization one would expect research to be increasingly directed toward green innovation in this case, because of a desire to avoid the strong positive trend in pollution. This would imply that B eventually grows faster than Y (at least in the Romer case).

---

[14] This section builds on Eriksson (2008).

[15] Given our previous experiences with the CES function, this should not be surprising. Compare, for instance, the CES case of Chapter 5: it is not only the growth rate of A that matters but also the effect that it has on output. This in turn depends on whether land is essential or not. Recall also the very different shapes of the average-product-of-capital curve, depending on ε, in Section 2.5.2.

[16] The result could also be interpreted in terms of essentiality: according to (8.11) X is growing with Y, even if $B^{-1} \rightarrow 0$, when $\varepsilon > 0$.

As a benchmark, we examine what is necessary for a constant pollution in the long run. We therefore rewrite (8.12) under the assumption that $g_X = 0$:

$$\frac{a}{a + (1 - a)(BY)^{-\varepsilon}} \cdot g_Y = \frac{(1 - a)}{a(YB)^{\varepsilon} + (1 - a)} \cdot g_B.$$

Here $g_A + n$ is replaced by g_Y, because we are not considering the steady state with constant proportional growth rates (in this paragraph). This equation can be rewritten as

$$\frac{\dot{Y}}{\dot{B}} = \frac{(1 - a)}{a} \cdot \frac{a + (1 - a)(BY)^{-\varepsilon}}{a(YB)^{\varepsilon} + (1 - a)} \cdot \frac{Y}{B}.$$

The right hand side clearly declines as time runs (because $\varepsilon > 0$ and Y/B falls), so the increase in Y, relative to B, has to decline. There is, however, no need for $\dot{Y}$ to go all the way down to zero, since $\dot{B}$ grows without bound.[17] This scenario would therefore allow for some income growth along with a constant (and even declining) pollution; income can just not grow at a constant proportional rate. There might, however, still be a problem with sustainable development: per capita income growth is less likely. On the other hand, if the population level eventually stabilizes, sustainability seems to be feasible.

Turning to the case when $\varepsilon < 0$, the prospects for the economy (including the environment) are very bright. The factor in front of $g_A + n$ in (8.12) falls toward zero over time, while the weight of the green technology factor tends to one. Consequently, we have that

$$g_X \rightarrow -g_B < 0$$

as $t \rightarrow \infty$. The scale effect is now dominated by the environmental technology effect. No matter how fast gross pollution grows, a tiny improvement of the environmental technology standard will guarantee declining net pollution.

This is a scenario that many people judge as too good to be true, but there may be some who find it plausible. Such a point of view could build on a vision where production in the future tends to use mainly brainpower, to make things smarter, for instance by use of better logistics and to develop computer games. If so, there would be less need for polluting physical inputs in production—growth would largely be "intangible."

To understand these results better, it is again useful to examine the iso-X curve in $B - Y$ space. We therefore start by noting that equation (8.11) can be solved for

$$Y = \left[\frac{1}{a}\left(X^{\varepsilon} - (1 - a)B^{-\varepsilon}\right)\right]^{1/\varepsilon}.$$

---

[17] If the growth rate $\dot{B}/B$ is positive and non-decreasing, both B and $\dot{B}$ grow over time.

As in the Cobb–Douglas case, it can be confirmed that $dY/dB > 0$. The curve is thus positively sloping, which means that a constant X can be maintained along with a larger Y if B increases.[18]

More important for the interpretation is the change in the slope, that is the second-order derivative. This expression is easier to read if we put it in elasticity terms:[19]

$$\epsilon_{Y'B} \equiv \frac{d^2 Y}{dB^2} \cdot B \cdot \left[\frac{dY}{dB}\right]^{-1} = (1 - \varepsilon)\frac{1}{(YB)^\varepsilon}\frac{1 - a}{a} - (\varepsilon + 1). \qquad (8.13)$$

This elasticity says how many percent the slope of the curve must change, when B increases by 1 percent, for unchanged pollution. This means that it is harder (easier) to prevent pollution from growing as the scale of economic activity grows if $\epsilon_{Y'B}$ is low (high).

The findings above, indicating that the results are more dramatic in the CES case, can be understood by the fact that the elasticity $\epsilon_{Y'B}$ is more bounded when the net pollution function takes the Cobb–Douglas form. This means that the iso-pollution curve bends less sharply, in relative terms, in the Cobb–Douglas case. To see this, we start by looking at the Cobb–Douglas version of the elasticity, which is obtained when $\varepsilon = 0$.[20] This results in the constant

$$\epsilon_{Y'B} = \frac{1 - 2a}{a}. \qquad (8.14)$$

Consider first the benchmark case when $a = 1/2$.[21] We then have $\epsilon_{Y'B} = 0$ and so the iso-X curve is a straight line, like in Figure 8.1. This would mean that it is neither more nor less difficult to counteract pollution with environmental innovations as the scale increases (as in Section 8.1.3). Whenever a deviates from $1/2$, however, the slope changes along the iso-X curve (which we also saw in Section 8.2, but without examining the elasticity $\epsilon_{Y'B}$). If $a > 1/2$ ($a < 1/2$), the slope of the iso-X curve decreases (increases) as the scale grows. Thus, B must grow faster (slower) than Y if pollution is to be kept constant. This corresponds to the cases when $a > b$ and $a < b$, respectively, in Section 8.2, as illustrated in Figures 8.2 and 8.3.

If the net pollution function takes the Cobb–Douglas form, the elasticity $\epsilon_{Y'B}$ is thus constant. This means that there is some limitation to how much more difficult (or easy) it becomes to mitigate pollution as the scale of the economy grows. The corresponding limits are less narrow when net pollution is given by the CES function, because YB grows over time. This can, for instance,

---

[18] This is actually an implication of the assumptions about the general net pollution function in (8.2).

[19] The derivation of (8.13) is left as an exercise for the reader.

[20] For the same reason as in Chapter 2 the function in (8.11) approaches $X = Y^a B^{-(1-a)}$ as $\varepsilon \to 0$. Note that we need to have the sum of exponents equal to unity here. That is, we cannot allow a and b to be chosen freely, which we did in (8.7).

[21] This would correspond to $a = b$ in Section 8.2, and also the case in Section 8.1.3, where $a = b = 1$.

be seen in the case when $\varepsilon < 0$, because then $\epsilon_{Y'B} \to \infty$ as $YB \to \infty$. The slope of the iso-pollution curve is thus rapidly increasing and tending to infinity when we move out along the curve. This implies that the ratio of B/Y, which is necessary to keep X constant, decreases quickly as the scale grows.[22] This is just another way of saying that environmental innovations can be very powerful in mitigating the polluting effects of production when $\varepsilon < 0$.

For $\varepsilon > 0$, the elasticity tends to $-(\varepsilon + 1)$, and thereby approaches a smaller value than it ever can take in the Cobb–Douglas version of the net pollution function.[23] A constant X then requires that the slope decreases more in percent than B increases. Hence, when Y grows, much more of B is needed to keep X constant; as the scale of the economy gets higher, it becomes much more difficult to counteract pollution by green technological change.

To sum up, the iso-pollution curve (eventually) changes slope faster (in relative terms), if the G function in (8.2) takes the form of a CES function, than it would do for a Cobb–Douglas net pollution function. This explains why the prospects for the environment become either very bright, or very gloomy, in the CES case.

Taking stock in the above analysis, the example with $\varepsilon < 0$ seems quite implausible. It is hardly realistic that the environmental problem should rapidly become easier to solve when the scale of the economic activity expands. While the case with $\varepsilon > 0$ is hopefully unnecessarily pessimistic, it cannot be ruled out entirely. Therefore, it is somewhat comforting that this case at least allows for some income growth, though less than exponential, along with non-increasing pollution.

The analysis in this section suggests some caution in assuming that the environmental technology effect can always be made strong enough to guarantee non-increasing pollution, along with exponential income growth. Since the empirical knowledge about the G function in (8.2) is scant, it is probably wise to keep the door open for several functional forms and with significant variations in the values of the parameters. Consequently, various scenarios, with quite different long-run outcomes must be regarded as possible.

8.4 **Phasing out a polluting input**

We end this chapter by introducing pollution in the model from Section 6.5.[24] The assumption that we add here is that the use of the non-renewable energy, N,

---

[22] There is a possibility that $\epsilon_{Y'B} \to \infty$ also in the Cobb–Douglas case, but only if $a \to 0$. This possibility is present in the CES function as well, and is there reinforced by the growth of the YB factor.

[23] In the Cobb–Douglas case, $\epsilon_{Y'B} > -1$, since $0 < a < 1$.

[24] This section draws on Eriksson (2013). It is inspired by Tahvonen and Salo (2001).

generates an emission flow that is proportional to N. For simplicity, we just put

$$X = N,$$

where the unitary factor of proportion can again be motivated by the choice of units. As in Section 6.5, the relative price of energy is changing such that the optimal relative use, N/R, falls over time (recall that R is renewable energy). However, the use of total energy, E, may well increase over time, and it is therefore an open question whether N will show a negative trend or not. To look deeper into the answer to this question, we start by recollecting some central implications of the model. Sections 8.4.2 and 8.4.3 then show how the results, regarding sustainability or not, depend on the substitutability between N and R.

8.4.1 RECOLLECTION OF THE MODEL

From Section 6.5 we first recall that the total service provided by energy was $E = (bN^\varepsilon + (1 - b)R^\varepsilon)^{1/\varepsilon}$. This joint energy input was substituted into the production function

$$Y = K^\alpha E^\gamma (AL_Y)^{1-\alpha-\gamma}.$$

There are two counteracting effects influencing the use of the polluting type of energy. On the one hand the optimal use of total energy typically increases over time, because the complementary factors capital, labor, and the productivity factor A all grow. This tends to raise the marginal productivity of both types of energy, and thereby increase the optimal use of them both. Working in the opposite direction is the fact that the relative price of the polluting energy is increasing. If the elasticity of substitution between the two types of energy is high, the use of the dirty energy may well decline over time.

The analysis of the dynamics in Chapter 6 indicated that the model is stable in most circumstances. Given stability, the steady state growth rate of per capita income was found to be (cf. (6.48))

$$\frac{\dot{y}}{y} = g_A - \frac{\gamma}{1-\alpha-\gamma} \left(\zeta_N \frac{\dot{w}_N}{w_N} + \zeta_R \frac{\dot{w}_R}{w_R} \right), \tag{8.15}$$

where

$$\zeta_N = \frac{b}{b + (1-b)(R/N)^\varepsilon} \quad \text{and} \quad \zeta_R = \frac{(1-b)}{b(R/N)^{-\varepsilon} + (1-b)}.$$

The values that these weights tend to in the long run depend on ε and R/N. Concerning the latter, we had (cf (6.38)):

$$\frac{R}{N} = \left(\frac{w_N}{w_R}\right)^{\sigma} \cdot \left(\frac{(1-b)}{b}\right)^{\sigma}. \tag{8.16}$$

This (optimal) relative demand is inversely related to the relative price, w_R/w_N, since $\sigma \equiv 1/(1 - \varepsilon) > 0$. The energy prices are assumed to change at the following rates (cf (6.32)):

$$\frac{\dot{w}_N}{w_N} = g_{w_N} \geq 0 \quad \text{and} \quad \frac{\dot{w}_R}{w_R} = -g_B < 0. \tag{8.17}$$

The former can mainly be considered exogenous, changing due to a rising pollution tax or increasing scarcity. The latter is endogenous, since the price of the renewable energy falls due to the growth of the technology factor B, as explained in Section 6.5.

From (8.16) and (8.17) it follows that the ratio R/N will rise over time. This gives two very different sets of trends for the weights in (8.15), depending on the substitutability between N and R. First,

$$\zeta_N \to 0 \quad \text{and} \quad \zeta_R \to 1 \quad \text{as} \quad R/N \to \infty \quad \text{if} \quad \varepsilon > 0. \tag{8.18}$$

Conversely, we have that

$$\zeta_N \to 1 \quad \text{and} \quad \zeta_R \to 0 \quad \text{as} \quad R/N \to \infty \quad \text{if} \quad \varepsilon < 0. \tag{8.19}$$

The value of ε will therefore influence the trends of the central variables of the analysis below (which we also saw in Section 6.5).

The proportional rate of change of the composite energy input was in Section 6.5 shown to be (cf. (6.49)):

$$\frac{\dot{E}}{E} = g_A + n - \frac{1-\alpha}{1-\alpha-\gamma}\left(\zeta_N \frac{\dot{w}_N}{w_N} + \zeta_R \frac{\dot{w}_R}{w_R}\right). \tag{8.20}$$

This growth rate can clearly be larger or smaller than the growth rate $g_A + n$, which we refer to as the *reference growth rate* (as in Section 6.5).

We also found that the optimal rates of change of the two types of energy were (cf. (6.50) and (6.51)):

$$\frac{\dot{N}}{N} = g_A + n + \sigma \frac{\varepsilon(1-\alpha) - \gamma}{1-\alpha-\gamma} \cdot \zeta_R \frac{\dot{w}_R}{w_R}$$
$$+ \sigma \cdot \frac{\dot{w}_N}{w_N} \cdot \frac{(\varepsilon(1-\alpha) - \gamma)\zeta_N - (1-\alpha-\gamma)}{1-\alpha-\gamma} \tag{8.21}$$

and

$$\frac{\dot{R}}{R} = g_A + n + \sigma \frac{\varepsilon(1-\alpha) - \gamma}{1-\alpha-\gamma} \cdot \zeta_N \frac{\dot{w}_N}{w_N}$$
$$+ \sigma \cdot \frac{\dot{w}_R}{w_R} \cdot \frac{(\varepsilon(1-\alpha) - \gamma)\zeta_R - (1-\alpha-\gamma)}{1-\alpha-\gamma}. \tag{8.22}$$

These growth rates can also deviate from the reference growth rate $g_A + n$, in both directions. We now examine the long-term trends more closely, by looking at what happens to the above expressions as $R/N \to \infty$, expecting that the results depend crucially on the elasticity of substitution between N and R. The central question is again whether there can be sustainable development, which here requires that $\dot{y}/y \geq 0$ and $\dot{N}/N \leq 0$.

8.4.2 GOOD SUBSTITUTION POSSIBILITIES

We first work under the assumption that it is easy to substitute renewable energy for non-renewable energy, that is $\varepsilon > 0$. By (8.15), (8.17), and (8.18) we then have that

$$\frac{\dot{y}}{y} \to g_A + \frac{\gamma}{1 - \alpha - \gamma} \cdot g_B > g_A,$$

as $R/N \to \infty$. The growth rate of the per capita income thus exceeds g_A. Here the economy benefits much from the decreasing price of renewable energy, because it can easily be the dominating energy input. It is worth noting that per capita income here can grow even if $g_A = 0$.

Turning to the long-run trend in the use of the non-renewable and polluting energy, we use (8.21) and (8.18) to get

$$\frac{\dot{N}}{N} \to g_A + n - \sigma \frac{\varepsilon(1 - \alpha) - \gamma}{1 - \alpha - \gamma} \cdot g_B - \sigma \cdot g_{wN} < g_A + n.$$

Analogously, (8.22) and (8.18) give

$$\frac{\dot{R}}{R} \to g_A + n + g_B \cdot \frac{1 - \alpha}{1 - \alpha - \gamma} > g_A + n.$$

As can be expected, the energy input that has an increasing price grows slower than the input which exhibits a decreasing price. The latter grows faster than the reference growth rate $g_A + n$, while the former grows slower.[25]

As for sustainablity, per capita income will clearly grow here, because we assume that there is at least a slight effort to make A grow.[26] But what is required for a downward trend in the polluting kind of energy? The vital condition for sustainability is

---

[25] By (8.20) and (8.18)

$$\frac{\dot{E}}{E} \to g_A + n + g_B \cdot \frac{1 - \alpha}{1 - \alpha - \gamma} > g_A + n \quad \text{if} \quad \varepsilon > 0.$$

Thus, total energy use also grows faster than $g_A + n$.

[26] Actually, as we saw above, it is not even necessary that $g_A > 0$.

$$\frac{\dot{N}}{N} \leq 0 \quad \Leftrightarrow \quad g_A + n \leq \sigma \frac{\varepsilon(1-\alpha) - \gamma}{1 - \alpha - \gamma} \cdot g_B + \sigma \cdot g_{w_N}.$$

Sustainability can be helped by substantial efforts in environmental research, and a steep increase in the pollution tax. (The latter has a negligible effect on per capita income growth in the long run, due to the high σ.) A large σ is of course helpful in this process. Finally, a realization of sustainability can be helped by allocating research efforts such that g_A is moderately high, that is by accepting a modest per capita income growth.

8.4.3 BAD SUBSTITUTION POSSIBILITIES

Poor substitution possibilities between N and R, that is $\varepsilon < 0$, would lead to a quite different result. To see this, we first note that (8.15) and (8.19) imply that long-run per capita income growth will now be

$$\frac{\dot{y}}{y} \to g_A - \frac{\gamma}{1 - \alpha - \gamma} \cdot g_{w_N} < g_A.$$

In this case, the economy suffers from the rising price of an energy input that it cannot easily replace. If γ and g_{w_N} are large, this drag on growth can lead to a declining per capita output, even if $g_A > 0$. This could be avoided by lowering the rate of change of the pollution tax, so that g_{w_N} becomes smaller. That could, however, be at the price of a positive trend in pollution, as we will see below.

As for the two energy inputs, the long-run rates of change are in this case obtained by combining (8.19) with (8.21) and (8.22), respectively. The results are

$$\frac{\dot{N}}{N} \to g_A + n - g_{w_N} \cdot \frac{1 - \alpha}{1 - \alpha - \gamma} < g_A + n$$

and

$$\frac{\dot{R}}{R} \to g_A + n + \sigma \frac{\varepsilon(1-\alpha) - \gamma}{1 - \alpha - \gamma} \cdot g_{w_N} + \sigma \cdot g_B > g_A + n.$$

The growth rate in N is here higher than in the previous case, because it is now more difficult to substitute for it. The fact that R grows faster than $g_A + n$ does not prevent E from growing slower than this reference rate, because the slower-growing N now puts a severe break on E.[27]

---

[27] By (8.20) and (8.19)

$$\frac{\dot{E}}{E} \to g_A + n - g_{w_N} \cdot \frac{1 - \alpha}{1 - \alpha - \gamma} < g_A + n \quad \text{when} \quad \varepsilon < 0.$$

Finally, addressing the issue about sustainability, there are two conditions that must be examined. First, for a non-decreasing per capita income it is required that

$$g_A \geq \frac{\gamma}{1 - \alpha - \gamma} \cdot g_{w_N}.$$

In addition, there is the condition for non-increasing pollution, which here reads

$$g_A \leq g_{w_N} \cdot \frac{1 - \alpha}{1 - \alpha - \gamma} - n.$$

The technology factor A must thus exceed a critical value, to ensure per capita income growth in the face of an increasing price of an energy input that cannot easily be substituted. On the other hand, a very high g_A tends to pull N upward, because more of the complementary factors raise the marginal product of N.

Sustainable development therefore requires that g_A can be found in an interval, which is described by a combination of the two preceding conditions, namely:

$$\frac{\gamma}{1 - \alpha - \gamma} \cdot g_{w_N} \leq g_A \leq g_{w_N} \cdot \frac{1 - \alpha}{1 - \alpha - \gamma} - n. \tag{8.23}$$

We must now examine whether such an interval exists. This will be the case if the inequality

$$\frac{\gamma}{1 - \alpha - \gamma} \cdot g_{w_N} < g_{w_N} \cdot \frac{1 - \alpha}{1 - \alpha - \gamma} - n$$

holds. This is equivalent to

$$n < g_{w_N}. \tag{8.24}$$

To get sustainability, a sufficiently steep time path of the pollution tax rate must be chosen (unless g_{w_N} is high enough without this). This must be combined with an allocation of research effort such that g_A can be found in the interval described by (8.23). Then pollution declines and per capita income grows. It is fairly remarkable that g_B is not influencing this interval. The formal explanation is, of course, that $\zeta_R \rightarrow 0$ in this case, so that the $\dot{w}_R / w_R$ term in (8.21) vanishes.

8.5 Conclusion

In the first three sections of this chapter, pollution is a function of production and an environmental technology factor, while production and capital accumulation follow the same lines as in Chapters 3 and 4. The pollution function is decreasing in the green technology factor and increasing in output. Under some assumptions, which are not unreasonable, sustainability arises if sufficient research effort is taken to "green the technology." By a slight adjustment of a parameter, however, the pollution function becomes a CES instead of a Cobb–Douglas. The possibilities for achieving sustainable development then change drastically; either it is very easy or it is extremely difficult. It is unclear what values of the parameters in the net pollution function are the most plausible ones empirically, so this latter case should be taken with a grain of salt. However, it might be regarded as a warning that there could be limits to what a green technology factor can achieve.

The final section of this chapter specifies the source of pollution further, by assuming that it comes from a particular input, namely non-renewable energy. There are forces acting towards a declining relative use of this type of energy. Since all other production factors are growing over time, however, there is a tendency to pull the use of the polluting energy up as well. Whether the net effect will imply a downward trend in this variable depends, as so often, on the elasticity of substitution and on the different growth rates of the technology factors.

▨ FURTHER READING

For suggestions of further reading, see Chapter 7.

8.6 Exercises

8.1 Pollution growth rate

Show that $X(t) = G(Y(t), B(t))$ implies that

$$g_X = \frac{G_Y Y}{G} g_Y + \frac{G_B B}{G} g_B.$$

8.2 CES pollution growth rate

Show that $X = \left[aY^\varepsilon + (1-a)B^{-\varepsilon} \right]^{1/\varepsilon}$ implies that

$$g_X = \frac{a}{a + (1-a)(BY)^{-\varepsilon}} g_Y - \frac{(1-a)}{a(YB)^\varepsilon + (1-a)} g_B.$$

9   Utility maximization

So far in this book we have not explicitly modeled any reason to keep the quantity of pollution down; we have just assumed that low and declining pollution is a good thing. This chapter introduces a representative consumer who experiences disutility of pollution, along with utility of consumption. He or she also faces a constraint, which implies that higher consumption only can be achieved at the cost of higher pollution, at a given level of technological development. The optimization problem of the representative consumer therefore amounts to choosing an optimal balance between the good and bad arguments of the utility function.

Over time, technological change shifts the constraint of the household, which leads to new optimal choices. We examine how the optimal level of pollution varies over time, under different assumptions about the utility function (or the abatement function). We are particularly interested to see what is required for a downward trend in pollution. In addition, we will see some examples of an environmental Kuznets curve (EKC), where the optimal pollution level first rises and then declines.

To facilitate the analysis, and thus to be able to clearly display the new features of this chapter, we simplify by assuming that there is no capital accumulation and no population growth. Moreover, technological progress is entirely exogenous. To emphasize that this chapter is quite different from all the previous ones, we switch to small letters for all variables.

An underlying assumption in the subsequent analysis is that the political system works well and so acts in the interest of the representative consumer. In particular the pollution externalities are internalized. One could model the accomplishment of this by introducing pollution taxes. For space reasons and for transparency, however, this will not be explicitly done here.

We start, in the next section, by presenting the most general version of the model analyzed in this chapter. A central finding is that the direction that pollution takes, in response to increasing productivity, depends much on how fast the marginal utility of consumption is decreasing as consumption grows. Section 9.2 then looks at a more specialized version of the same model, which provides a possibility to show some results in more detail.

Section 9.3 develops the model by introducing a variable that captures the environmental standard of the economy. It is thus a policy variable, which determines both environmental quality and income. This policy variable also provides a natural way to limit the income of a country at any point of time.

Section 9.4 looks at the implications of increasing returns to abatement. A consequence is that optimal abatement develops slowly at low income levels, but then rises faster as income grows, because of the increasing returns. Pollution is therefore first increasing in income, but then decreasing, which means that the model generates an EKC.

Due to a worldwide emergence of pollution data, the theoretical literature on the relation between pollution and per capita income has come to see an emerging empirical counterpart. We review this literature briefly in Section 9.5.

9.1 A general model

We now present a simple microeconomic model of optimization under a constraint. Following the optimal solution over time, as productivity exogenously increases, we focus primarily on the optimal development of pollution (and thus less on consumption).

9.1.1 THE MODEL

Assume that the representative consumer experiences utility from consumption c and disutility from pollution, x. The utility function is

$$U(c, x) = u(c) - v(x). \tag{9.1}$$

We adopt the following assumptions about the first sub-utility function: $u'(c) > 0$ and $u''(c) < 0$. This means that utility of consumption is increasing, but at a decreasing rate. This is to say that an incremental unit of consumption generates an additional amount of utility that is lower than the effects of the previous units. For the second part of (9.1) we assume that $v'(x) > 0$ and $v''(x) > 0$. In words, dis-utility of pollution is increasing, at an increasing rate. Thus, adding more pollution, when the level is already high, generates a lot of extra suffering.

The constraint that the household faces simply puts consumption equal to income, because nothing is saved. It can in general be described by the equation $c = af(x)$. Here $a(t)$ is a technology factor, growing with time, and f is an increasing function of x. We will, however, mostly consider the special case in which $f(x)$ is the power function x^α, leaving the general functional form to Exercise 9.1. The constraint then becomes

$$c = ax^\alpha. \tag{9.2}$$

We assume that $0 < \alpha \leq 1$, so that the function is concave in x. Thus, the economy can gain more consumption if it accepts more pollution, because more of the economy's gross income is transferred from abatement to consumption (as in Chapter 7). However, the higher consumption is, the more extra pollution must be accepted for an additional unit of consumption. In other words, the opportunity cost for consumption is increasing (unless $\alpha = 1$).

The growth in the technology factor a changes the feasible relation between c and x over time. When a increases, more consumption is possible at a given level of pollution. Alternatively, and perhaps more importantly, a certain volume of consumption can be had at a lower quantity of pollution when a gets higher. And, of course, the intermediate possibility is to use the growth in a to both increase consumption and decrease pollution.

We now have the ingredients for a simple optimization problem: to maximize the utility described in (9.1) subject to the constraint given in (9.2). This can be reformulated into a problem of one variable if we use (9.2) to eliminate c from (9.1):

$$U = u(ax^{\alpha}) - v(x).$$

The utility-maximizing level of pollution is obtained by putting the derivative of this function, with respect to x, equal to zero: $u'(ax^{\alpha})a\alpha x^{\alpha-1} - v'(x) = 0$. For an easier interpretation, we move the negative term over to the right hand side and get

$$(MB \equiv) \qquad u'(a(t)[x(t)]^{\alpha})a(t)\alpha[x(t)]^{\alpha-1} = v'(x(t)) \qquad (\equiv MC). \quad (9.3)$$

The left hand side of this equality is the marginal benefit of increasing pollution, which comes in the form of a higher consumption, whereas the right hand side captures the marginal cost, due to the disutility of an additional unit of pollution. Equation (9.3) is thus an instance of the famous rule that a marginal benefit in optimum should be equal to marginal cost.

9.1.2 OPTIMAL TIME PATH OF POLLUTION

We now examine how the optimal level of pollution implied by (9.3) evolves as a grows. This is done in two ways. The first uses only a little mathematics and mainly relies on a graphical analysis. The second approach builds entirely on a mathematical derivation.

9.1.2.1 A graphical approach

The first possibility to see how x changes over time starts from Figure 9.1. The positively sloping marginal cost curve, representing the right hand side of (9.3), is independent of a and will therefore stay put over time. The marginal benefit (the left hand side of (9.3)), on the other hand, changes when a grows, and we need to determine in which direction. The answer is given by the derivative

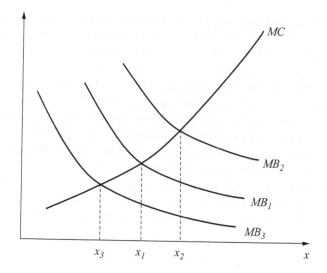

Figure 9.1. *MC* equals *MB*

$$\frac{\partial MB}{\partial a} = u'' x^\alpha a\alpha x^{\alpha-1} + u'\alpha x^{\alpha-1} = u'\alpha x^{\alpha-1}\left(\frac{u'' a x^\alpha}{u'} + 1\right). \qquad (9.4)$$

There are two effects on the marginal benefit from increased productivity, which are best seen in the middle part of (9.4). The first term is negative, because the marginal utility of consumption declines as a (and therefore consumption) increases. The second middle term is positive, simply because the increase in a gives a higher income and therefore a higher consumption.

This derivative of the marginal benefit can be simplified by defining the elasticity of the marginal utility of consumption:

$$\sigma(c) \equiv -\frac{u'' c}{u'}\left(=-\frac{du'}{dc}\cdot\frac{c}{u'}\right) > 0.$$

This elasticity tells us how many percent marginal utility falls when consumption increases by 1 percent. It thus gives an idea about how rapidly marginal utility diminishes. Using this elasticity in (9.4), and recalling that $ax^\alpha = c$, we have

$$\frac{\partial MB}{\partial a} = u'\alpha x^{\alpha-1}\left(1 - \sigma(c)\right).$$

We thus find that the direction of the shift in the marginal benefit curve depends on whether σ is larger or smaller than unity. This is summarized in the following two points:

- If $\sigma(c) < 1$ the marginal benefit gets higher at every x when productivity increases. The curve thus shifts up and the optimal level of pollution grows over time, for example from x_1 to x_2 in Figure 9.1.

- If $\sigma(c) > 1$ the marginal benefit curve shifts down when productivity grows. The optimal level of pollution therefore decreases over time, for example from x_1 to x_3.

The long-run trend in pollution is thus negative if and only if $\sigma(c) > 1$ at all consumption levels. An EKC would arise if $\sigma(c) < 1$ at low levels of development, while $\sigma(c) > 1$ at higher productivity levels.

9.1.2.2 A mathematical approach

An alternative way to reach the same conclusion as above builds on an entirely mathematical analysis. We start by taking the natural logarithms of both sides of the optimality condition in (9.3):

$$\ln[u'(a(t)[x(t)]^\alpha)] + \ln[a(t)] + \ln[\alpha] - (1-\alpha)\ln[x(t)] = \ln[v'(x(t))].$$

The next step is to differentiate both sides with respect to time. After the differentiation, we recall that the argument of the u function is simply c. The result is:

$$\frac{1}{u'(c)}u''(c)\left[\dot{a}x^\alpha + a\alpha x^{\alpha-1}\dot{x}\right] + \frac{1}{a}\dot{a} - (1-\alpha)\frac{1}{x}\dot{x} = \frac{1}{v'}v''\dot{x}.$$

To simplify this equation, we recall (9.2) and pull $ax^\alpha = c$ out from the bracket of the first term. On the right hand side, we multiply by x/x. Consequently, we have

$$\frac{u''c}{u'}\left[\frac{\dot{a}}{a} + \alpha\frac{\dot{x}}{x}\right] + \frac{\dot{a}}{a} - (1-\alpha)\frac{\dot{x}}{x} = \frac{v''x}{v'}\frac{\dot{x}}{x}.$$

At this point, we can make the expressions more condensed by recalling the definition of $\sigma(c)$ and defining the following elasticity:

$$\kappa(x) \equiv \frac{v''x}{v'} > 0.$$

We now use these elasticities, together with the notations $g_a \equiv \dot{a}/a$ and $g_x \equiv \dot{x}/x$. Collecting terms, we have

$$[1 - \sigma(c)]g_a = [\kappa(x) + (1-\alpha) + \sigma(c)\alpha]g_x.$$

The development of pollution, in response to the increase in a that takes place over time, is given if we solve this equation for g_x:

$$g_x = \frac{1 - \sigma(c)}{\kappa(x) + (1-\alpha) + \sigma(c)\alpha} \cdot g_a. \tag{9.5}$$

Since $g_a > 0$, the direction of change in x is determined entirely by $\sigma(c)$, because the denominator of the right hand side is positive. If $\sigma(c) < 1$, pollution increases when the economy becomes more productive, and therefore richer. In this case, the marginal utility of consumption falls quite slowly.

Therefore, the consumer chooses quite a steep consumption growth path, accepting increasing levels of pollution.

Conversely, $g_x < 0$ when $\sigma(c) > 1$. The marginal utility of consumption now falls rather rapidly. It therefore pays relatively little, in terms of utility, to increase consumption. Improvements in utility are therefore largely collected by a continuous improvement in environmental quality. However, as Exercise 9.2 shows, c is increasing in this case as well.

Finally, an EKC can arise if we combine these two scenarios. Assume that $\sigma(c)$ is monotonously rising in c, such that $\sigma(c) < 1$ at early phases of development, but $\sigma(c) > 1$ in later phases. Then pollution increases in the first period, but decreases in the latter. Thus, we have a kind of EKC, although pollution is related to productivity instead of income. It arises because the household wants it to be this way; it stems to a large extent from preference.

9.2 **A special case**

To further illustrate the role of preferences for the direction of change of pollution, we will here analyze a special case of the model above. Now the utility function is specified to

$$U = u(c) - v(x) = \delta(1 - e^{-\beta c}) - \gamma x. \tag{9.6}$$

The sub-utility function $u(c)$ approaches the upper bound δ when consumption goes to infinity, which is illustrated in Figure 9.2. The implication is that there is satiation in consumption. For simplicity, the sub-utility function $v(x)$ is just linear in pollution. This, of course, implies that $v'' = 0$ and consequently that $\kappa = 0$.

As for the constraint, we simplify by choosing $\alpha = 1$, so that the relation between consumption and pollution is linear:

$$c = ax. \tag{9.7}$$

Finally, we assume that technological change takes place at a constant exponential rate, that is $a = e^{gt}$. There are now two ways to see what the time path of pollution will be in this special case of the model.

9.2.1 USING THE FORMULA

The first possibility for giving a description of the development of x, is to examine what happens to the formula in (9.5), given the assumptions made here. First, note that in this case

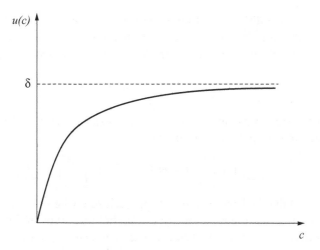

Figure 9.2. Bounded utility of consumption

$$\sigma(c) \equiv -\frac{u''(c) \cdot c}{u'(c)} = -\frac{-\delta \beta^2 e^{-\beta c} \cdot c}{\delta \beta e^{-\beta c}} = \beta c,$$

so $\sigma(c)$ is increasing in consumption. Furthermore, we use $\alpha = 1$, $\kappa = 0$, and $g_a = g$ in (9.5), which then is simplified to

$$g_x = \frac{1 - \beta c}{\beta c} \cdot g. \tag{9.8}$$

Suppose now that the economy initially has such a low productivity that the optimal consumption choice fulfills $\beta c < 1$.[1] Then there is an early phase during which $g_x > 0$. As productivity and consumption grow, however, βc eventually gets larger than unity and g_x becomes negative. The economy then switches from the upward-sloping to the downward-sloping part of the EKC.[2]

9.2.2 USING THE UTILITY-MAXIMIZATION CONDITION

For an alternative (and more detailed) description of the optimal development of pollution, we can solve an expression corresponding to the first-order condition in (9.3) for x. We therefore use (9.7) to eliminate c from (9.6):

$$U = \delta(1 - e^{-\beta a x}) - \gamma x.$$

---

[1] The condition for this to happen is given in footnote 4 below.
[2] For large βc we have $g_x \approx -g$. Almost all technological progress is used to improve the environmental quality when $u(c)$ is close to its upper limit δ.

The necessary condition for utility maximization is now $\delta\beta ae^{-\beta ax} - \gamma = 0$. We rewrite this as $e^{\beta ax} = \delta\beta a/\gamma$. To solve this equation for the optimal pollution level at any time t, we first take the logarithms of both sides, which gives

$$\beta ax = \ln\left[\frac{\delta\beta}{\gamma}\right] + \ln a.$$

Finally, we divide by βa and recall that a is an exponential function. Thereby, the optimal level of pollution at time t is

$$x^* = \frac{1}{\beta e^{gt}}\left(\ln\left[\frac{\delta\beta}{\gamma}\right] + gt\right) = \frac{1}{\beta e^{gt}}\ln\left[\frac{\delta\beta}{\gamma}\right] + \frac{gt}{\beta e^{gt}}. \tag{9.9}$$

Both terms of the final expression will approach zero when time goes to infinity.[3] In the long run, the representative household will thus find it optimal to choose a declining pollution level, which goes to zero. This is not surprising, since the marginal utility of consumption is falling rapidly, while the marginal disutility of pollution is constant. As it becomes possible to increase utility (due to the growth in a) the highest reward therefore comes from decreasing pollution.

Looking closer at the initial phase of development, we note that $x^*(0) > 0$ if and only if $\delta\beta/\gamma > 1$, because only then is the logarithmic term positive. We assume that this inequality holds. It implies that the marginal disutility of pollution is smaller than the marginal utility of consumption when $c = x = 0$. It is therefore urgent to raise consumption at this point, while a bit of (consequential) pollution is accepted.

The final question is: What is required to get an EKC? In other words, what makes pollution increase at low levels of t? To answer this question, we compute the derivative of x^* with respect to time:

$$\dot{x}^* = g\frac{1}{\beta}e^{-gt}\left(1 - gt - \ln\left[\frac{\delta\beta}{\gamma}\right]\right).$$

At $t = 0$ this derivative is positive if and only if $\ln(\delta\beta/\gamma) < 1$, that is $\delta\beta/\gamma < e$. If this equality is fulfilled, there is an EKC: pollution is growing during the initial period, before it starts to decline.[4]

---

[3] In the final term, the exponential function eventually grows faster than the linear function. This can be shown by computing the time derivative of this term:

$$\frac{d}{dt}\left(\frac{gt}{\beta e^{gt}}\right) = \frac{g\beta e^{gt} - gtg\beta e^{gt}}{(\beta e^{gt})^2} = \frac{g\beta e^{gt}(1 - gt)}{(\beta e^{gt})^2} = \frac{g(1 - gt)}{\beta e^{gt}}.$$

Although this expression is positive for small t, it turns negative when t reaches $1/g$.

[4] Alternatively, we can use $c = ax$ from (9.7), and $a = e^{gt}$ in (9.9) to get the optimal consumption level

$$c^* = \frac{1}{\beta}\left(\ln\left[\frac{\delta\beta}{\gamma}\right] + gt\right) = \frac{1}{\beta}\ln\left[\frac{\delta\beta}{\gamma}\right] + \frac{g}{\beta}\cdot t.$$

9.3 **The Stokey model**

The model above can be criticized for a certain property of its constraint, equation (9.2), namely that any country at any time can have as high an income as it wants, if it accepts a sufficiently large quantity of pollution. This clearly is unrealistic, since there must come a point where no more output can be obtained by caring less about the polluting consequences of economic activity. We will therefore assume that there is a highest possible level of production at every point of time (although it grows with a). More precisely, we follow Stokey (1998) and introduce an index of technology, with a highest possible level, which determines both income and the cleanliness of production.

9.3.1 CONSUMPTION AND POLLUTION

The index of technology is denoted by z and belongs to the unit interval, that is $z \in [0, 1]$. The consumption possibilities now become a function of z, instead of x, and they are expressed by the equation

$$c = az. \tag{9.10}$$

Choosing a technology with a higher index thus implies a higher consumption level. The highest level of consumption is obtained when $z = 1$, which means that $c = a$. The interpretation of a is therefore, in this section, that it captures the potential (maximum) output. We will continue to assume that a is an exogenously growing technology factor.

The downside of choosing a high z is that production becomes very polluting. This is seen in the equation

$$x = az^\phi, \quad \phi > 1. \tag{9.11}$$

With a given choice of technology, pollution increases when the production potential, a, (the scale) of the economy gets higher. If a dirtier technology is chosen, that is z gets higher (at given a), the level of pollution grows at an increasing rate, because z^ϕ is convex in z.

On the other hand, a decline in pollution will result if z falls rapidly enough when a grows. To see exactly what is required, we take logs of (9.11) and differentiate with respect to time, which gives $g_x = g_a + \phi g_z$. We thus have the following condition for declining pollution:

$$g_x < 0 \quad \Leftrightarrow \quad g_z < -g_a/\phi.$$

The optimal c is thus steadily increasing. At $t = 0$, $\beta c < 1$ if and only if $\ln(\delta\beta/\gamma) < 1$, which is equivalent to $\delta\beta/\gamma < e$. By (9.8) pollution is initially growing if this condition holds.

A central question in the subsequent analysis is under which assumptions about the parameters it is optimal to fulfill this condition.

In the following analysis we will devote considerable space to the possibility that the economy is at the corner solution, $z = 1$, over a period of time (when a is low). It is useful to note that (9.10) and (9.11) then imply that consumption and pollution are equal to potential output: $c = x = a$. Consequently, consumption and pollution will grow in step with the technology factor as long as the dirtiest possible technique is used.[5]

9.3.2 UTILITY MAXIMIZATION

The utility function of the representative household is now (for transparency of the analysis) chosen such that the elasticities are constant. Thus

$$U = u(c) - v(x) = \frac{c^{1-\sigma} - 1}{1 - \sigma} - \frac{x^{1+\kappa}}{1 + \kappa}, \tag{9.12}$$

where it is assumed that $\sigma \geq 0$ and $\kappa \geq 0$. (If $\sigma = 1$, then $u(c) = \ln c$.) The function $v(x)$ is convex in pollution, as in the general model above, and here $v''(x) \cdot x/v'(x) = \kappa$ is a constant. Similarly, we have that $-u'' \cdot c/u' = \sigma$ is a constant.

It is very important for the shape of the $u(c)$ function, and for the analytical results, whether σ is larger or smaller than unity. We have the following two possibilities:

- If $0 \leq \sigma < 1$ then $\lim_{c \to \infty} u(c) = \infty$.
- If $\sigma > 1$ then $\lim_{c \to \infty} u(c) = \frac{1}{\sigma - 1} > 0$.

These two cases are illustrated in Figures 9.3 and 9.4. If $\sigma > 1$ the utility of consumption thus goes to a satiation level, like in the example of the previous section. It could be expected to be more likely that pollution declines over time in this case, compared to a situation where $\sigma < 1$. In fact, σ will play a central role in the analysis below.

---

[5] It is also interesting to note that we can use (9.10) and (9.11) to eliminate z and get a relation between c and x that is similar to the constraint in (9.2). For example, solve (9.10) for $z = c/a$ and substitute into (9.11):

$$x = \frac{c^{\phi}}{a^{\phi-1}} \quad \text{or} \quad c = a^{\frac{\phi-1}{\phi}} x^{\frac{1}{\phi}}.$$

As in the general model (eq. (9.2)) pollution is higher if consumption increases, although it should be remembered that none of c and x can exceed a. As a grows, there is less pollution generated by a given level of consumption, since $\phi > 1$. Note also the similarity between the last equality and (9.2). For instance, in analogy with (9.2), $x^{1/\phi}$ is concave in x.

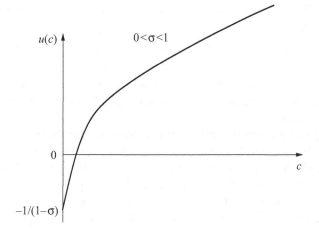

Figure 9.3. Utility of consumption 1

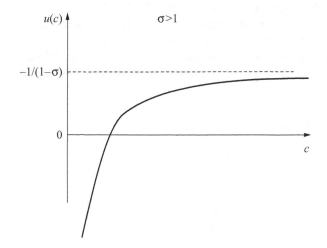

Figure 9.4. Utility of consumption 2

To solve the optimization problem, we could start by eliminating either c or x (using footnote 5) from the utility function and then maximizing with respect to the remaining variable. However, we will here perform the optimization in terms of the technology index z (which could be regarded as a policy variable). Thus, substituting (9.10) and (9.11) into (9.12), the function to be maximized is

$$U(z) = \frac{[az]^{1-\sigma}}{1-\sigma} - \frac{[az^\phi]^{1+\kappa}}{1+\kappa}. \tag{9.13}$$

As usual, the first-order derivative is important when we want to find the optimal z. It is

$$U'(z) = [az]^{-\sigma} \cdot a - [az^\phi]^\kappa \cdot \phi az^{\phi-1} = a^{1-\sigma} z^{-\sigma} - \phi a^{1+\kappa} z^{\phi(1+\kappa)-1}.$$
(9.14)

The first term represents the marginal benefit of increasing the technology index, while the second term captures the marginal cost (in disutility terms) of the same change.

A complication in the solution of this optimization problem is that z cannot be chosen higher than 1, although it could be desirable to do so. In particular, it is plausible that a very poor economy, that is a country with a low a, would prefer to choose a very high z, in spite of the high pollution that it implies, because it would mean a high income level. To see this, consider Figure 9.5, which depicts how $U'(z)$ in (9.14) varies with z.[6] The crossing point A implies that the desired technology level is $z_0 > 1$. This is not a feasible choice, so the actual choice will have to be $z = 1$.

We will now show that the $U'(z)$ curve shifts down as a increases. In Figure 9.5 this means that the ideal value of z declines over time, and eventually reaches the interval of feasible values, $[0, 1]$. This is illustrated by the leftward movements of the crossing points from A, through B, to C.

To establish this negative relation between a and the ideal (though not always feasible) z, we disregard for a moment the constraint that z must be in the

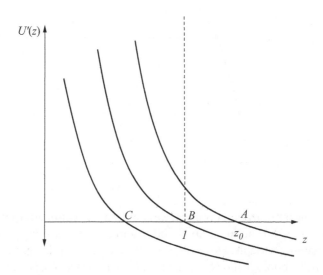

Figure 9.5. Marginal net benefit

[6] By differentiation of (9.14) it is easily confirmed that $U''(z) < 0$, so that the $U'(z)$ curve has a negative slope.

unit interval. We thus put $U'(z)$ in (9.14) equal to zero and move the negative term over to the other side of the equality sign, which gives $a^{1-\sigma} z^{-\sigma} = \phi a^{1+\kappa} z^{\phi(1+\kappa)-1}$. By collecting terms we then have

$$z^{-[\sigma+\phi(1+\kappa)-1]} = \phi a^{\sigma+\kappa}.$$

Since $\phi > 1$, the exponent over z is negative. Finally, we solve for the optimal (though unconstrained) z:

$$z = \phi^{\frac{-1}{[\sigma+\phi(1+\kappa)-1]}} a^{-\frac{\sigma+\kappa}{[\sigma+\phi(1+\kappa)-1]}} \equiv \psi a^{-\frac{\sigma+\kappa}{[\sigma+\phi(1+\kappa)-1]}}. \tag{9.15}$$

Because the exponent of a is negative, the optimal z declines as a grows. This confirms the movement through the points A, B, and C in Figure 9.5, which means that the $U'(z)$ curve must shift down as productivity grows. It is also clear, from (9.15), that the ideal z will exceed unity if a is small enough. But again, since $z > 1$ is not feasible, the best choice in such a situation will be $z = 1$. As a increases, the optimal z will decrease, and we eventually find the desired z in the unit interval.

9.3.3 SOLUTION

How high must a be, to make the desired z belong to the unit interval? To answer this question, we simply put $z = 1$ in (9.15) and solve for the critical a:

$$a = \psi^{\frac{[\sigma+\phi(1+\kappa)-1]}{\sigma+\kappa}} = \phi^{\frac{-1}{\sigma+\kappa}} \equiv \bar{a}.$$

We can now divide the optimal development of this economy into the following two phases:

Phase 1: $a < \bar{a}$, so $z^* = 1$. $(U'(z^*) > 0)$
Phase 2: $a \geq \bar{a}$, so $z^* = \psi a^{-\frac{\sigma+\kappa}{[\sigma+\phi(1+\kappa)-1]}}$. $(U'(z^*) = 0)$

These two phases are illustrated in Figure 9.6. During *Phase 1* the dirtiest possible technique is used. By (9.10) and (9.11), consumption and pollution equal a and consequently grow at the same rate as a. To understand what the driving forces are during this phase, note that $U'(z^*) > 0$ means that utility would increase if it were possible to raise z above 1. In other words, the marginal utility of increasing consumption is larger than the resulting marginal disutility of higher pollution. There is thus quite an urgent need for more consumption, and less serious harm from pollution at these low income and pollution levels. Therefore, when potential income increases, it is optimal to use it all to raise consumption and simply accept the additional pollution that comes along with this.

During *Phase 2* the optimal technique is declining as a increases. But is it falling rapidly enough to make pollution decrease? If so, is z declining so fast

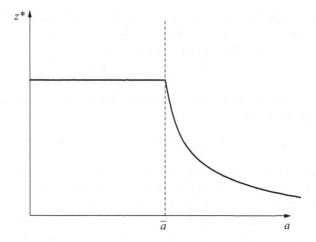

Figure 9.6. The two phases

that consumption declines over time? For both these questions, the answers depend on a race between the exogenous a and the endogenous z, which change in opposite directions. Starting with consumption, we use (9.10) and (9.15):[7]

$$c^* = az^* = \psi a^{\frac{(\phi-1)(1+\kappa)}{\sigma+\phi(1+\kappa)-1}}.$$

Because $\phi > 1$, the exponent of a is positive. Consumption will therefore increase over time, which is consistent with our findings in the earlier sections (see in particular Exercise 9.1)—consumption is a normal good.

Turning to the time path of pollution during *Phase 2*, we use (9.11) and (9.15) to obtain

$$x^* = a\left(z^*\right)^{\phi} = \psi^{\phi} a^{\frac{(\phi-1)(1-\sigma)}{\sigma+\phi(1+\kappa)-1}}.$$

We thus find that the slope of the time path for pollution depends crucially on σ. If $\sigma > 1$ the exponent over a is negative. Pollution then declines when a grows, and the economy is on the downward-sloping part of an EKC.[8] The explanation is that utility of consumption approaches a satiation level as c increases, when $\sigma > 1$. Consequently, a substantial part of the economy's increasing productivity is used to improve the environment. Given that $\sigma > 1$, the economy actually follows an environmental Kuznets curve, which is depicted in Figure 9.7.

---

[7] It is left as an exercise for the reader to confirm that this expression for $c*$ and the expression for $x*$ below are correct.

[8] Compare the result in Section 9.1.

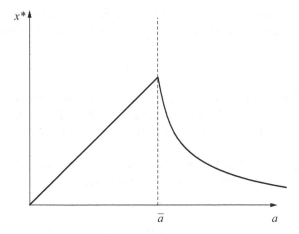

Figure 9.7. An environmental Kuznets curve

9.4 Increasing returns to abatement

In the previous examples the direction of change in pollution was explained by properties of the utility function. We now look at a case in which the assumptions about the abatement technology are crucial for the results.[9] By contrast, the utility function is here very simple:

$$U = u(c) - v(x) = c - x. \tag{9.16}$$

As in the previous examples, marginal utility of consumption is positive, whereas the the change in utility is negative when pollution increases. However, here these marginal changes are constant, that is $u' = v' = 1$ and thus $u'' = v'' = 0$. Hence, in terms of the utility function in (9.12) we here assume that $\sigma = \kappa = 0$. This can be regarded as making the utility function "neutral," leaving the centerstage to the abatement technology.

The representative consumer has an income equal to m, which grows at some exogenous rate. He uses some of this income for abatement—e—and the rest for consumption. The budget constraint is

$$c + e = m. \tag{9.17}$$

For simplicity of notation the price of abatement is assumed to be equal to the price of the consumption good, and they are both equal to unity. This could be achieved by appropriate choices of units.

The final component of the optimization problem is the expression for net pollution. It equals gross pollution minus abatement. Gross pollution is

---

[9] This section builds on Andreoni and Levinson (2001).

assumed to equal consumption (which is closely connected to production) and the result of abatement is a function of gross pollution and abatement expenses. This is represented by the function

$$x = c - c^\alpha e^\beta. \tag{9.18}$$

The idea with the final term of this equation is that the more pollution there is, the more you can catch with a given level of effort. For example, when you sweep a floor, you collect more dust from an hour's work if there is more dust on the floor.

The net pollution function in (9.18) can be substituted into (9.16), so that $U = c - (c - c^\alpha e^\beta)$. This is simplified to the function

$$U = c^\alpha e^\beta. \tag{9.19}$$

The resulting objective function of the representative consumer thus has the Cobb–Douglas form, increasing in consumption and in abatement. We will see below that the optimal evolution of net pollution over time will depend crucially on whether $\alpha + \beta$ is larger or smaller than 1.

It is now a straightforward exercise to maximize (9.19) subject to (9.17). The resulting demand functions are:[10]

$$c^* = \frac{\alpha}{\alpha + \beta} m \quad \text{and} \quad e^* = \frac{\beta}{\alpha + \beta} m. \tag{9.20}$$

These are the typical demand functions for a Cobb–Douglas objective function: demand is proportional to income (divided by the unitary prices) and the constants in front of m are the income shares.

More importantly, we are interested to see how pollution is related to income. To this end, we substitute the demand functions into (9.18):

$$x^* = \frac{\alpha}{\alpha + \beta} m - \left(\frac{\alpha}{\alpha + \beta}\right)^\alpha \left(\frac{\beta}{\alpha + \beta}\right)^\beta m^{\alpha + \beta}. \tag{9.21}$$

This equation directly relates pollution and income, the two central variables in the literature on the EKC. To see better how changes in income influence the optimal level of pollution, we differentiate (9.21) twice, to get

$$\frac{\partial x^*}{\partial m} = \frac{\alpha}{\alpha + \beta} - (\alpha + \beta) \left(\frac{\alpha}{\alpha + \beta}\right)^\alpha \left(\frac{\beta}{\alpha + \beta}\right)^\beta m^{\alpha + \beta - 1}$$

and

$$\frac{\partial^2 x^*}{\partial m^2} = -(\alpha + \beta - 1)(\alpha + \beta) \left(\frac{\alpha}{\alpha + \beta}\right)^\alpha \left(\frac{\beta}{\alpha + \beta}\right)^\beta m^{\alpha + \beta - 2}.$$

---

[10] It is left as an exercise for the reader to solve the optimization problem leading to the demand functions in (9.20).

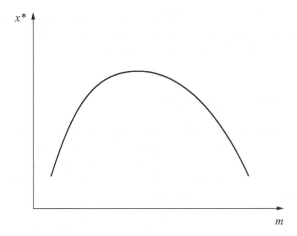

Figure 9.8. Another environmental Kuznets curve

In the case when $\alpha + \beta > 1$, that is when there are increasing returns to abatement, the second-order derivative is negative. The function is therefore concave and has a maximum at the point where the first-order derivative is equal to zero.[11] In this case we thus get an EKC, which is illustrated in Figure 9.8. At low levels of economic activity, including abatement, the returns to abatement effort is low. Abatement is therefore at a low level and does not grow fast enough to prevent net pollution from growing. However, e is like a normal good and so grows with m. At a sufficiently high income level, the returns to scale become so beneficial that abatement growth beats pollution growth; the economy enters the downward sloping part of the EKC.

9.5 **Empirics on the environmental Kuznets curve**

Recent years have witnessed the emergence of data on pollution in many places of the world, where either measured ambient concentrations or emissions are reported. This has led to intense activity among researchers, investigating the relations between various pollutants and per capita income. A seminal study was Grossman and Krueger (1995). The main question was whether pollution increased or decreased as income kept growing, or whether the relation was non-monotonous. In some cases an inverse-U relationship emerged, which

---

[11] The turning point is at the income level

$$m^T = \left(\frac{\alpha^{1-\alpha}\beta^{-\beta}}{(\alpha + \beta)^{2-(\alpha+\beta)}} \right)^{\frac{1}{\alpha+\beta-1}}.$$

was called an environmental Kuznets curve (EKC). This section describes the methods used in this research and some of the results. Finally, we present some of the problems with it that have been pointed out.

9.5.1 METHOD AND EARLY RESULTS

The empirical research on the EKC uses econometric methods to find out how per capita income "determines" pollution. The starting point is a regression equation, where the dependent variable, x_{it}, is the emission or concentration of the pollutant at site i in year t. The first independent variable, y_{it} is the per capita GDP in year t for the country where site i is located. In addition, these studies often include the variable $\bar{y}_{it}$, which is the average of y_{it} for a number of years, ending with year t. The motivation is that the pollution this year is likely to be influenced by the incomes of several previous years; the process by which a higher income changes the demand for a clean environment, which is then turned into political decisions and implementations, takes time.

There are many possible ways to specify the regression equation, but a fairly representative example is

$$x_{it} = \beta_1 y_{it} + \beta_2 y_{it}^2 + \beta_3 y_{it}^3 + \beta_4 \bar{y}_{it} + \beta_5 \bar{y}_{it}^2 + \beta_6 \bar{y}_{it}^3 + (\text{"Other Variables"}) + v_{it},$$

where v_{it} is a normally distributed error term, and the β_i's are parameters to be estimated. The terms with "Other Variables" (including their parameters) are added to the equation to control for effects from variables such as trade intensity and democracy.

Using the available data, the βs in this equation can be estimated by some econometric technique. After a statistical evaluation of such an estimation, the equation can be used to depict the relation between pollution and income. In doing this, it is not uncommon to lump the y_{it} and $\bar{y}_{it}$ terms together to $\widehat{\beta}_1 y$, where $\widehat{\beta}_1$ is the estimate of $\beta_1 + \beta_4$ and $y = y_{it} + \bar{y}_{it}$ and so on. By locking the "Other Variables" at their mean values (and using their estimated parameters), we get a constant, C_0. Thus, the equation

$$x = \widehat{\beta}_1 y + \widehat{\beta}_2 y^2 + \widehat{\beta}_3 y^3 + C_0$$

can be used to describe how pollution is related to income, under the assumption that the other variables are unchanged.

For simplicity, assume first that the results of the estimation are such that $\widehat{\beta}_3 = 0$ and that $\widehat{\beta}_1 > 0$ and $\widehat{\beta}_2 < 0$. For small values of y the positive $\widehat{\beta}_1$ term will dominate (in particular if $\widehat{\beta}_1 > |\widehat{\beta}_2|$) and make the curve rise. As y increases, however, the quadratic and negative $\widehat{\beta}_2$ term gets stronger and it eventually turns the curve into a negative slope. The relation between pollution and income is thus described by an inverse U curve, like in Figure 9.8. This is close to what Grossman and Krueger (1995) find for the variable "Smoke in Cities".

Allowing now for $\widehat{\beta}_3 \neq 0$, we may have the result that Grossman and Krueger (1995) obtain for "Sulfur Dioxide in Cities", namely that $\widehat{\beta}_1 > 0$, $\widehat{\beta}_2 < 0$, and $\widehat{\beta}_3 > 0$. For low ys, the curve is then quite similar to the previous case, that is an EKC. As income grows large, however, the cubic $\widehat{\beta}_3$ term has an increasing influence on the shape of the curve, and eventually turns the curve upward again. This result is greatly due to the high pollution levels of the USA and some other rich countries. It is perhaps a bit less worrying if one considers that only a small part of the upturn is within the sample of observations.

It is very difficult to try and summarize the early empirical results in this literature, not least because the robustness and representativeness have been questioned a lot. If we dare to do this anyway, it could look something like this:

- The EKC applies reasonably well for SO_2 and urban concentrations of particulate matters.
- For "Lack of Clean Water" and "Lack of Urban Sanitation" the curve is monotonously declining.
- For CO_2 per capita and municipal wastes per capita the curve is monotonously increasing.

As a seemingly common pattern one could say that the closer the effects of pollution are (in time and space) the more likely it is that emissions are reduced. But, again, be warned that this is merely an "impression" of the early results.

9.5.2 CRITICISM

There has subsequently been much discussion about the early results in the EKC literature. An important contribution was Harbaugh et al. (2002), which argued that the evidence were less robust than it appeared. They re-examined the earlier empirical results with an improved and extended data set, and also tried other specifications of the regression equation. Their conclusion is that these seemingly small changes generate very different shapes for the predicted pollution–income relationship. In particular pollutants that show an EKC in earlier works (e.g. SO_2) can (easily) display a totally different curve (for instance, U shaped instead of inverse U shaped) after the modifications.[12]

In another influential article, Dasgupta et al. (2002) start from the observation that the reaction to the early empirical EKC literature has been quite diverse, both optimistic and pessimistic. For example, while the decline of some pollutants is acknowledged, some authors emphasize the arrival of new

---

[12] For more about econometric issues, see Stern (2004).

and potentially toxic pollutants, so that the overall environmental risk is continuing to grow. In contrast, some optimistic views have also been expressed, according to which the curve is actually shifting down over time. A consequence would be that countries that develop late do not use as many polluting techniques as early developers. After a review of the literature, with some focus on developing countries, these authors side with the optimist, but not without reservations. Interestingly, they do not put much emphasis on technological progress, but instead stress the primary role of environmental regulation. (This does not, of course, exclude technological progress as a result of, or a useful precondition for, regulation.)

A more recent review article by Carson (2010) lifts the specification of the regression equation and the poor quality of data as important weaknesses with the previous literature. In addition to the questionable quality of the data that has been used, he also stresses the relative lack of observations for developing countries. As for the model specification, he argues that the regression equation should be more deeply rooted in microeconomic theory, so that more sophisticated behavioral mechanisms can be included. Thereby, one can get 'a more nuanced view of a relationship in which income works through other factors'.

It could finally be mentioned that the EKC literature has a closely related literature on the relation between pollution and international trade. International trade is expected to raise the income, and thereby we get back to the question of whether this higher income will spur a demand for a tighter environmental policy. Recent empirical research has found evidence for a pollution haven effect, meaning that environmental regulation has effects on plant location decisions and trade flows. It should be stressed that this is an effect on the margin. There is little convincing evidence that lower trade barriers cause very polluting industries to move from countries with stringent environmental policy to countries with weaker environmental policy. For further readings, see Copeland and Taylor (2003), Copeland and Taylor (2004) and Chapter 10 in Perman et al. (2011).

9.6 **Conclusion**

In this chapter, at last, a reason to avoid pollution is explicitly modeled: pollution decreases the utility of a representative consumer. To facilitate the exposition of how utility maximization drives the level of pollution over time, capital accumulation and endogenous technological change are taken out from the model. We find that a rapidly declining marginal utility of consumption (in a relative sense) is often crucial for the consumer to choose a declining time path of pollution. The conditions for falling emissions will clearly be more complicated in more elaborate models, but we have elements of them in this chapter.

Note that this analysis is carried out under the assumption that the political system works well, so that the actual pollution mirrors the preferences of the representative consumer. Obviously, this seldom happens, for instance because households/voters are heterogenous, and because there are (small) influential lobby groups. Thus, a large literature on the political economics of the environment has emerged; see e.g. Oates and Portney (2003) for a review.

▧ FURTHER READING

Chapter 3 in Copeland and Taylor (2003) contains further models on the environmental Kuznets curve, mostly based on a two-sector trade model. The analysis in Andreoni and Levinson (2001) is very accessible, as is the first model in Stokey (1998).

9.7 **Exercises**

9.1 Generalized basic model
Assume that the relation between consumption and pollution is described by the more general function

$$c = af(x),$$

where $f'(x) > 0$ and $f''(x) < 0$. The objective function can then be written as

$$U(x) = u(af(x)) - v(x).$$

1. State the necessary condition for utility maximization. Show also that $U''(x) < 0$.
2. Characterize the evolution of x over time, that is as a grows.

9.2 Consumption growth
In the general model, show that c^* increases when a increases. To do this, solve (9.2) for $x = (c/a)^{1/\alpha}$ and use this to eliminate x from (9.1). Then use the first-order condition for utility maximization to analyze the relationship between c and a.

■ BIBLIOGRAPHY

Acemoglu, D. (1998), 'Why do new technologies complement skills? Directed technical change and wage inequality', *Quarterly Journal of Economics* 113(4): 1055–1089.

—— (2002), 'Directed technical change', *Review of Economic Studies*, 69(4): 781–809.

—— (2003), 'Labor- and capital-augmenting technical change', *Journal of the European Economic Association*, 1(1): 1–37.

—— (2009), *Introduction to Modern Economic Growth*, Princeton University Press, Princeton, NJ.

——, P. Aghion, L. Bursztyn, and D. Hemous (2012), 'The environment and directed technical change', *American Economic Review*, 102(1): 131–166.

Aghion, P. and P. Howitt (1992), 'A model of growth through creative destruction', *Econometrica*, 60(2): 323–51.

—— —— (1998), *Endogenous Growth Theory*, MIT Press, Cambridge, MA.

—— —— (2009), *The Economics of Growth*, MIT Press, Cambridge, MA.

Andreoni, J. and A. Levinson (2001), 'The simple analytics of the environmental Kuznets curve', *Journal of Public Economics*, 80(2): 269–86.

Barrett, S. (2009), 'The coming global climate-technology revolution', *Journal of Economic Perspectives*, 23(2): 53–75.

Barro, R. J. and X. Sala-i-Martin (2004), *Economic Growth*, 2nd edition, MIT Press, Cambridge, MA.

Baumol, W. J. and W. E. Oates (1988), *The Theory of Environmental Policy*, 2nd edition, Cambridge University Press, Cambridge.

Bradford, T. (2006), *Solar Revolution: The Economic Transformation of the Global Energy Industry*, MIT Press, Cambridge, MA.

Brock, W. A. and M. S. Taylor (2005), 'Economic growth and the environment', in *Handbook of Economic Growth 1B*, edited by P. Aghion and S. N. Durlauf, Elsevier, Amsterdam: 1749–1821.

—— —— (2010), 'The green solow model', *Journal of Economic Growth*, 15(2): 127–153.

Carson, R. T. (2010), 'The environmental Kuznets curve: seeking empirical regularity and theoretical structure', *Review of Environmental Economics and Policy*, 4(1): 3–23.

Copeland, B. and S. Taylor (2003), *Trade and the Environment. Theory and Evidence*, Princeton University Press, Princeton NJ.

—— —— (2004), 'Trade, growth, and the environment', *Journal of Economic Literature*, XLII(March): 7–71.

Darmstadter, J. (1999), 'Innovation and productivity in U.S. coal mining', in *Productivity in Natural Resource Industries: Improvement through Innovation*, edited by R. D. Simpson, Resources for the Future, Washington DC: 35–72.

Dasgupta, P. (1993), 'Natural resources in an age of substitutability', in *Handbook of Natural Resource and Energy Economics*, volume III, chapter 23, edited by A. V. Kneese and J. L. Sweeney, Elsevier, Amsterdam: 1111–1130.

Dasgupta, P. and G. Heal (1974), 'The optimal depletion of exhaustible resources', *Review of Economic Studies, Symposium on the Economics of Exhaustible Resources*, 41(May): 3–28.

———— (1979), *Economic Theory and Exhaustible Resources*, Cambridge University Press, Cambridge.

Dasgupta, S., B. Laplante, H. Wang, and D. Wheeler (2002), 'Confronting the Environmetal Kuznets Curve', *Journal of Economic Perspectives*, 16(1): 147–168.

Diamond, J. (2005), *Collapse: How Societies Choose to Fail or Succeed*, Viking Press, New York NY.

Dixit, A. K. (1976), *The Theory of Equilibrium Growth*, Oxford University Press, Oxford.

Domar, E. (1946), 'Capital expansion, rate of growth and employment', *Econometrica*, 14(2): 137–147.

Eriksson, C. (2008), 'A knife-edge property of some pollution-and-growth models', Paper presented at the *SURED Conference*, 2008.

———— (2013), 'Phasing out a polluting input', *Technical report*, MDH.

Galor, O. (2005), 'From stagnation to growth: unified growth theory', in *Handbook of Economic Growth*, edited by P. Aghion and S. Durlauf, Elsevier, Amsterdam: 171–293.

Grimaud, A. and L. Rouge (2008), 'Environment, directed technical change and economic policy', *Environmental and Resource Economics*, 41(4): 439–463.

Grossman, G. M. and E. Helpman (1994), 'Endogenous innovation in the theory of growth', *Journal of Economic Perspectives*, 8(1): 23–44.

———— and A. Krueger (1995), 'Economic growth and the environment', *Quarterly Journal of Economics*, 110(2): 353–377.

Harbaugh, W., A. Levinson, and D. M. Wilson (2002), 'Reexamining the empirical evidence for an environmental Kuznets curve', *Review of Economics and Statistics*, 84(3): 541–551.

Harrod, R. (1939), 'An essay on dynamic theory', *The Economic Journal*, 49(June): 14–33.

Irz, X. and T. Roe (2005), 'Seeds of growth? Agricultural productivity and the transitional dynamics of the Ramsey model', *European Review of Agricultural Economics*, 32(2): 143–165.

Jackson, T. (2009), *Prosperity without Growth: Economics for a Finite Planet*, Earthscan, London.

Jevons, W. S. (1865), *The Coal Question: An Inquiry Concerning the Prospects of the Nation and the Probabale Exhaustion of Our Coal Mines*, Macmillan, London.

Jones, C. I. (1995), 'R&D-based models of economic growth', *Journal of Political Economy*, 103(4): 759–784.

———— (2002), *Introduction to Economic Growth*, 2nd edition, W. W. Norton, New York, NY.

———— (2005), 'Growth and ideas', in *Handbook of Economic Growth 1B*, edited by P. Aghion and S. N. Durlauf, Elsevier, Amsterdam: 1063–1111.

Jones, H. G. (1975), *An Introduction to Modern Theories of Economic Growth*, Nelson, London.

Kremer, M. (1993), 'Population growth and technological change: one million b:c to 1990', *The Quaterly Journal of Economics*, 108(3): 681–716.

La Grandville, O. (2009), *Economic Growth: A Unified Approach*, Cambridge University Press, Cambridge.

Layard, R. (2006), 'Happiness and public policy: a challenge to the profession', *The Economic Journal*, 116(3): C24–C33.

Meade, J. (1961), *A Neo-Classical Theory of Economic Growth*, Allen & Unwin, London.

Meadows, D. H., D. L. Meadows, J. Randers, and W. W. Behrens (1972), *The Limits to Growth: A report for the Club of Rome's Project on the Predicament of Mankind*, Earth Island, New York, NY.

—————— (1992), *Beyond the Limits: Global Collapse or Sustainable Future*, Earthscan, London.

—————— (2004), *Limits to Growth—The 30 Year Update*, Chelsea Green Publishing Company, White River Junction, Vermont.

Mundlak, Y. (2000), *Agriculture and Economic Growth: Theory and Measurement*, Harvard University Press, Cambridge, MA.

—— (2005), 'Economic growth: lessons from two centuries of american agriculture', *Journal of Economic Literature*, 43(4): 989–1024.

Neumayer, E. (2010), *Weak versus Strong Sustainability: Exploring the Limits of Two Opposing Paradigms*, Edward Elgar, Cheltenham.

Nordhaus, W. D. (1992), 'Lethal model 2: the limits to growth revisited', *Brookings Papers on Economic Activity*, 2: 1–59.

—— (2008), *A Question of Balance: Weighing the Options on Global Warming Policies*, Yale University Press, New Haven, Conn.

Oates, W. E. and P. R. Portney (2003), 'The political economy of environmental policy', in *Handbook of Environmental Economics 1*, edited by K.-G. Mäler and J. R. Vincent, Elsevier, Amsterdam: 325–354.

Perman, R., Y. Ma, M. Common, D. Maddison, and J. McGilvray (2011), *Natural Resource and Environmental Economics*, 4th edition, Addison Wesley, Harlow.

Ray, D. (1998), *Development Economics*, Princeton University Press, Princeton, NJ.

Romer, D. (2012), *Advanced Macroeconomics*, 4th edition, McGraw-Hill/Irwin, New York, NY.

Romer, P. M. (1990), 'Endogenous technological change', *Journal of Political Economy*, 98(5): S71–102.

—— (1993), 'Idea gaps and object gaps in economic development', *Journal of Monetary Economics*, 32(3): 543–73.

—— (1994), 'The origins of endogenous growth', *Journal of Economic Perspectives*, 8(1): 3–22.

Ruttan, V. (2002), 'Productivity growth in world agriculture', *Journal of Economic Perspectives*, 16(4): 161–184.

Schlicht, E. (2006), 'A variant of uzawas theorem', *Economics Bulletin*, 5(6): 1–5.

Smil, V. (2003), *Energy at the Crossroads: Global Perspectives and Uncertainties*, MIT Press, Cambridge, MA.

Snyder, C. M. and W. Nicholson (2008), *Microeconomic Theory: Basic Principles and Extensions*, 10th edition, Thomson Business and Economics, Belmont, CA.

Solow, R. M. (1956), 'A contribution to the theory of economic growth', *Quarterly Journal of Economics*, 70(1): 65–94.

—— (1957), 'Technical change and the aggregate production function', *Review of Economics and Statistics*, 39(3): 312–320.

—— (1967), 'Some recent developments in the theory of production', in *The Theory and Empirical Analysis of Production*, edited by M. Brown, Columbia University Press, New York, NY.

—— (1974), 'Intergenerational equity and exhaustible resources', *Review of Economic Studies, Symposium on the economics of exhaustible resources*, 41(May): 29–45.

—— (1994), 'Perspectives on growth theory', *Journal of Economic Perspectives*, 8(1): 45–54.

—— (2000), *Growth Theory: An Exposition*, Oxford University Press, Oxford.

Stern, D. (2004), 'The rise and fall of the environmental Kuznets curve', *World Development*, 32(8): 1419–1439.

Stern, N. (2007), *The Economics of Climate Change: The Stern Review*, Cambridge University Press, Cambridge.

Stiglitz, J. E. (1974), 'Growth with exhaustible natural resources: efficient and optimal growth paths', *Review of Economic Studies, Symposium on the Economics of Exhaustible Resources*, 41(May): 123–137.

Stokey, N. (1998), 'Are there limits to growth?', *International Economic Review*, 39(1): 1–31.

Tahvonen, O. and S. Salo (2001), 'Economic growth and transitions between renewable and nonrenewable energy resources', *European Economic Review*, 45(8): 1379–1398.

van der Ploeg, F. (2011), 'Natural resources: curse or blessing?', *Journal of Economic Literature*, 49(2): 366–420.

Warsh, D. (2006), *Knowledge and the Wealth of Nations—A Story of Economic Discovery*, Norton, New York, NY.

Weil, D. N. (2008), *Economic Growth*, 2nd edition, Pearson Addison-Wesley, Boston, MA.

World Commission on Environment and Development (1987), *Our Common Future*, Oxford University Press, Oxford.

Xepapadeas, A. (2005), 'Economic growth and the environment', in *Handbook of Environmental Economics 3*, edited by K.-G. Mäler and J. R. Vincent, Elsevier, Amsterdam: 1220–1266.

Yergin, D. (2011), *The Quest, Energy, Security, and the Remaking of the Modern World*, Penguin, London.

▪ AUTHOR INDEX

■ SUBJECT INDEX